DICTIONARY
OF
LANGUAGE GAMES,
PUZZLES,
AND
AMUSEMENTS

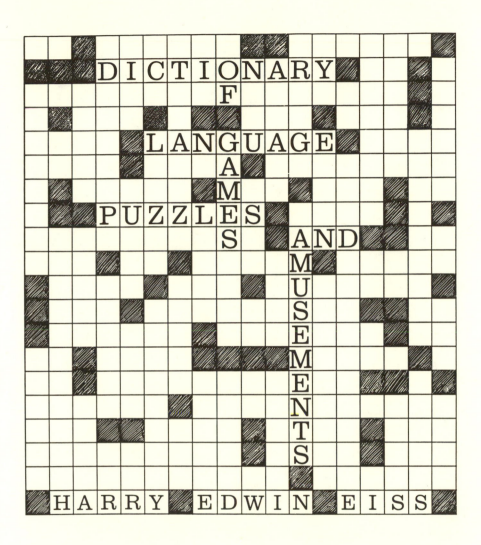

DICTIONARY OF LANGUAGE GAMES PUZZLES AND AMUSEMENTS

HARRY EDWIN EISS

GREENWOOD PRESS

New York • Westport, Connecticut • London

Library of Congress Cataloging-in-Publication Data

Eiss, Harry Edwin.
   Dictionary of language games, puzzles, and amusements.

   Bibliography: p.
   Includes index.
   1. Word games—Dictionaries.   2. Puzzles—Dictionaries.
3. Literary recreations—Dictionaries.   I. Title.
GV1507.W8E37   1986   793.73   85-27280
ISBN 0-313-24467-7 (lib. bdg. : alk. paper)

Library of Congress Catalog Card Number: 85-27280
ISBN: 0-313-24467-7

First published in 1986

Greenwood Press, Inc.
88 Post Road West, Westport, Connecticut 06881

Printed in the United States of America

The paper used in this book complies with the
Permanent Paper Standard issued by the National
Information Standards Organization (Z39.48-1984).

10 9 8 7 6 5 4 3 2 1

Copyright Acknowledgments

The author and the publisher are grateful to the following for granting use of their material:

Extract from C. C. Bombaugh, *Gleanings for the Curious,* 1890; reprinted in Martin Gardner, ed., *Oddities and Curiosities of Words and Literature,* 1961, reprinted courtesy of Dover Publications, Inc.

Extract from Roger D. Abrahams and Louis Rankin, eds., *Jump-Rope Rhymes: A Dictionary,* copyright © 1980 by the University of Texas Press, reprinted courtesy of the University of Texas Press.

Extracts from Iona and Peter Opie, eds., *The Lore and Language of School Children,* 1959; reprinted 1980, reprinted courtesy of Oxford University Press.

"Sir Christopher Wren," from *The Complete Clerihews of E. Clerihew Bentley,* 1981, reprinted courtesy of Oxford University Press.

Extract from Howard W. Bergerson, *Palindromes and Anagrams,* 1973, reprinted courtesy of Dover Publications, Inc.

Henry Ernest Dudeney, "The Abbey" from *300 Best Word Puzzles.* Copyright © 1968 Henry Ernest Dudeney. Reprinted with permission of Charles Scribner's Sons.

For my mother, Helen Eiss; my brother, John Eiss, and his wife, Bonnie; my unofficially adopted brothers, Jim and John Cagle; my father- and mother-in-law, Dave and Dorothy Palm; my children, Meghan, Israel, Angie, Jay, and Ryan; and most of all my wife, Betty.

CONTENTS

PREFACE

James Joyce took eighteen years to write *Finnegans Wake*, first published it in 1939, and then made additional corrections to it until his death in 1941. Literary critics remain divided. Did the genius who wrote *Ulysses, Dubliners,* and *A Portrait of the Artist as a Young Man* create another literary masterpiece (perhaps the ultimate work of literature), or, to take two phrases from the book itself, is *Finnegans Wake* a huge "Jabberwocky joke" of "pure chingchong idiotism with any way words all in one soluble?"[1]

Other twentieth-century writers and literary movements also balance dramatically on this same tightrope between literature of the highest seriousness and outrageous word play. The highly respected (and condemned) Dada movement, filled with madly imaginative humor, preaching the logic of illogic, and indulging in such things as free word-association poetry and nonsense lectures, resulted in such unclassifiable literature as Hugo Ball's *O Gadji Beri Bimba* (1916), a chant of syllables without meaning: "zimzim urallala zimzim zanzibar zimlalla zam."[2]

Such extreme stylistic practices overshadow the less extreme developments taking place in the works of other important writers of the time, such as Gertrude Stein and e. e. cummings, and in such contemporary poets as Lawrence Ferlinghetti. Nevertheless, the tension between serious literature and language play remains. And it is neither an isolated nor a new phenomenon.

William Shakespeare, generally considered the greatest of all English writers, consistently combined the highest expressions of drama with the highest (or lowest) forms of word play:

Falstaff: Welcome, Ancient Pistol. Here, Pistol, I charge you with a cup of sack. Do you discharge upon mine hostess.

Pistol: I will discharge upon her, Sir John, with two bullets.

Falstaff: She is pistol-proof, sir; you shall not hardily offend her.

Hostess: Come, I'll drink no proofs nor no bullets. I'll drink no more than will do me good; for no man's pleasure, I.

Pistol: Then to you, Mistress Dorothy; I will charge you.

Doll: Charge! I scorn you, scurvy companion. What! You poor, base, rascally, cheating, lack-linen mate! Away, you moldy rogue, away! I am meat for your master.''

(Henry IV, Part Two, act 2, sc. 4, lines 112–127)[3]

The obvious dual meanings of such terms as "pistol," "bullets," and "discharge" hardly need to be pointed out. Similar bouts of punning occur whenever Mercutio takes the stage:

Mercutio: Nay, if our wits run the wild-goose chase, I am done; for thou hast more of the wild goose in one of thy wits than, I am sure, I have in my whole five. Was I with you there for the goose?

Romeo: Thou wast never with me for anything when thou wast not there for the goose.

Mercutio: I will bite thee by the ear for that jest.

Romeo: Nay, good goose, bite not!

Mercutio: Thy wit is a very bitter sweeting; it is a most sharp sauce.

Romeo: And is it not, then, well served in to a sweet goose?

Mercutio: O, here's a wit of cheveril, that stretches from an inch narrow to an ell broad!

Romeo: I stretch it out for that word "broad," which, added to the goose, proves thee far and wide a broad goose.

(Romeo and Juliet, act 2, sc. 4, lines 72–89)

The Riddle of the Sphinx plays a central role in the Oedipus Rex trilogy. The Bible is filled with riddles (e.g., the Riddle of Samson) and puns (e.g., Jesus Christ's pun on Simon Peter's name). The Wellerism derives its name from a speech pattern of Sam Weller, a character in Charles Dickens's *Pickwick Papers.* Cryptography is central to Edgar Allen Poe's story "The Gold Bug." The riddle contest between Bilbo Baggins and Gollum in J. R. R. Tolkien's *The Hobbit* is an example of a literary tradition that goes back at least as far as the early English poetry of *Sir Gawain and the Green Knight.*

As the above examples suggest, if serious literature is filled with language play, then an interesting question arises, namely, what is the difference between language play and serious literature? It would be pretentious to offer an absolute answer, but perhaps a working distinction can be established. For the purposes of this book, serious literature might be considered that literature meant to express a reality beyond itself; it may contain a great deal of humorous word play, but the

word play in and of itself would not make the work important. Language play, on
the other hand, might be considered that body of writing and speaking respected
simply for its clever manipulation of the language, not because it expresses an
important reality beyond itself (though it may).

Even a working definition as general as this does not clearly distinguish the
two fields. For instance, how does one classify a Mother Goose rhyme? St.
Aldehelm's *Epistola ad Acircium de Metris?* Jonathan Swift's "We Are Little
Airy Creatures"? A clerihew? The limericks of Edward Lear? The poetry of
Ogden Nash? Lewis Carroll's *Through the Looking-Glass* and *Alice in Won-
derland?* Harry Mathews's *Tlooth?*

Dmitri A. Borgmann begins the introduction to his bibliography in *Beyond
Language: Adventures in Word and Thought* by pointing out that "strictly speaking, it is impossible to append a bibliography to *Beyond Language,* since no
work resembling it is known to exist." The same might be said about an attempt
to distinguish language games, puzzles, and amusements from serious literature.
(Nevertheless, Borgmann does include a bibliography.)

In spite of the commonalities and the fuzziness along the lines of division, the
two fields are separate. Such luminaries in the field of serious literature as
William Faulkner, Samuel Richardson, and Percy Bysshe Shelley, for example,
are relatively unimportant in the field of language play. On the other hand, such
key figures in language play as Henry Ernest Dudeney, Gyles Brandreth, and
Willard R. Espy receive no attention from scholars of literature.

It is the field of language play that this work addresses, and the need for a
beginning is evident. Indeed, Joseph T. Shipley laments in his bibliography for
"Word and Letter Games," in *Encyclopaedia Britannica: Macropaedia* (1979):
"There is no history of word and letter games."

What, then, is a game? a puzzle? an amusement? *Webster's New Twentieth
Century Dictionary* offers thirteen separate definitions of *game.* For the purposes
of this book, three of them are useful: 1. any contrivance, arrangement or contest
meant to furnish sport, recreation or amusement; 2. an amusement or sport
involving competition; and 3. something involving a number of points to win.
The same dictionary defines *puzzle* as "a toy or problem purposely arranged to
test mental ingenuity." And it defines *amusement* as "that which entertains."

The National Puzzlers' League, purposefully or not, simply by naming itself a
puzzlers' league classifies all of its word play as a form of puzzling. Henry
Ernest Dudeney does the same by titling his book *300 Best Word Puzzles.* Others
prefer to classify word play as games. Gyles Brandreth, for example, titles two
of his books *Indoor Games* and *The World's Best Indoor Games,* and David
Parlett uses the title *Botticelli and Beyond: Over 100 of the World's Best Word
Games.* Often the same forms of word play are referred to under separate categories. *Amusement* is generally used as a tag-along term to cover whatever might
not be considered either a game or a puzzle.

One of the criteria used in determining what to include in this book and what
terminology to use has been what the major creators, collectors, and players have

included and used. Therefore, the distinction between games and puzzles has been left blurred, though in general *puzzles* has been used to indicate forms of word play where one person attempts to solve some problem by and for himself, and *games* has been used to indicate forms of word play where more than one person competes to solve the problem, usually resulting in a winner and loser or losers. *Amusements* has been used to indicate forms of word play where no solution takes place (e.g., acting out rhymes).

The newness of serious scholarly study of language games, puzzles, and amusements is evident in the fact that no generally agreed upon term for the field has emerged. The term currently receiving the most promotion is *logology*. Dmitri A. Borgmann, *Language on Vacation: An Olio of Orthographical Oddities* (1965), suggested the term and used it to cover the recreational linguistics included in *Word Ways: The Journal of Recreational Linguistics,* which he founded and served as editor for its first year, 1968.

In its traditional English sense logology has generally been defined as "the science of words." It is true that, until Borgmann revived it, the term had fallen into disuse; nevertheless, the traditional meaning of the term ties it far more closely to serious linguistics than to word play. Furthermore, as Alexander and Nicholas Humez point out in *Alpha to Omega: The Life & Times of the Greek Alphabet, lógos,* the Greek term logology is based on, was not meant to refer to "word" in the strict grammatical sense. For this *épos* (hence the English "epic") or *rhêma* (hence the English "rhetoric") would have been used. *Lógos* was more accurately used to refer simultaneously to the outward expression of a concept (as opposed to its name) and the actual concept itself. This leads even more directly into serious linguistics and in the direction serious linguistics seems to be headed, the philosophy of thought itself.

Jeu d'esprit is the French term for a witticism, a literary work showing wit rather than profundity. The clerihew, the limerick, the cento, and other important categories of word play fit here, but word play also takes place outside of literature, in Botticelli, crossword puzzles, anagrams, and numerous other diversions.

A. Ross Eckler, the current editor of *Word Ways,* adopts Borgmann's term logology to designate the recreational linguistics published in that journal (the forms of word play and their designations in *Word Ways* are similar to, perhaps identical with, those pursued by the National Puzzlers' League and published in *The Enigma*) and offers a "brief taxonomy of logology's core." The taxonomy is valuable in the same sense that Borgmann's bibliography in *Beyond Language* or this book is valuable: they are beginning attempts to organize an important field of human endeavor. Eckler's taxonomy sets up very restricted categories for recreational language play (as does the National Puzzlers' League). For the purposes of this book, the categories are far too narrow. For instance, one of Eckler's major categories deals with the "relationship between sight and sound" in words. Although it is an important category, it nevertheless deals with only one form of pun. Failure to include the other types of pun would leave this book incomplete. The majority of the entries included here fall beyond the scope of Eckler's taxonomy.

It must be emphasized that this book is meant to be a collection of the language games, puzzles, and amusements that the major figures in the field have gathered, created, played, and published. Though an attempt has been made to produce the most complete volume possible, a fully comprehensive collection is not achievable. The National Puzzlers' League, for instance, creates new word play every month. The boundaries between language play and other fields of endeavor are not clear, and some somewhat arbitrary decisions have had to be made concerning those boundaries.

Linguistics, for instance, is an important area of language study that has an indefinite border with language play. As with the distinction between literature and language play, a working definition might separate the two in terms of their purpose. A brief survey of twentieth-century linguistics from Leonard Bloomfield's structural linguistics through the work of Zellig S. Harris and Charles Hocket and others to the "Transformational-Generative Syntax" of Noam Chomsky and beyond reveals a continual progression towards the equating of language and thought, as is evident in Chomsky's *Language and Mind.* Whether or not linguists eventually explain language and thought or discover Chomsky's universal language is not important to this comparison. What is important is that linguists are involved in something beyond the pleasure of dissecting and manipulating language (though experiencing that pleasure is undoubtedly part of the linguist's work). A person who plays language games does so only for the pleasure of playing the game. If the game should incidentally reveal some reality beyond itself, that is fine and good, but it is not the purpose of the activity.

Plato tells us that *rhetoric* can only be defined by its purpose, its use, its accomplishments. Thus, rhetoric can be of value only if it is used to reveal the "Ideal Reality." In other words, it can be of value only if it is used to bring about a greater knowledge of truth. Aristotle, on the other hand, does not judge rhetoric in ethical terms, but considers it merely a tool. For him, rhetoric is the effective use of language for persuasion. Cicero expands Aristotle's views and defines rhetoric as a means of instruction, delight, and persuasion. Quintilian gathers together all of these views and adds that only a good, honest, educated man can be a true rhetorician. Once again, though the techniques may be the same, the purpose is not. Language play is definitely concerned with delight (and delight is to be taken in its traditional meaning as an appreciation of the quality, the cleverness, of the endeavor), but the other classical requirements of rhetoric can be connected with language play only abstractly. Plato, Aristotle, Cicero, and Quintilian, very important to a study of rhetoric, are relatively unimportant to a study of language games, puzzles, and amusements.

Other boundaries are equally fuzzy and yet distinguish equally real fields of endeavor. Northrop Frye's *Anatomy of Criticism: four essays,* a landmark book in literary criticism, has little use in a study of language play. John Crowe Ransom and his brilliant students—Allen Tate, Robert Penn Warren, and Cleanth

Brooks—brought forth a new set of critical values, one that incorporated many of T. S. Eliot's views, promoted the view of literature as an organic tradition, and stressed a rigorous and analytical reading of the text. This "New Criticism" became the dominant critical system of the 1950s and, though less so today, is still very important in circles of literary criticism. It is relatively unimportant in circles of language play.

Works such as the *Encyclopedia of Poetry and Poetics,* edited by Alex Preminger et al., that are central to a study of serious literature are in some ways a valuable resource for a book such as this one (especially in dealing with entries, such as the one on parody, that straddle the two fields of study), but are more often parallel to this book (except that they deal with a field that has been far more researched, organized, and developed than has scholarship on language play). Works such as *Classical Rhetoric for the Modern Student* by Edward P. J. Corbett prove valuable in the same way, once again serving as a resource for numerous entries (e.g., pun), though the thrust of such books carries them far afield of language play.

Still another major area of study, *humor,* must be distinguished from language play. It is obviously central to many of the entries, especially those based on the pun, and the views of Max Eastman, Arthur Koestler, and Henri Bergson are important, if for no other reason than that they allow a clearer picture of where such things as puns fit into a larger context of human endeavor. Nevertheless, language play and humor involve activities far removed from each other. Humor is often connected with activities other than language (e.g., a man slipping on a banana). And language play may be connected with areas other than humor, perhaps partaking of delight or wit in an intellectual sense, but not dealing directly with humor (e.g., anagrams, palindromes, acrostics, crossword puzzles).

Mathematical play and language play often overlap (e.g., ABC words), yet these fields for the most part deal in two separate symbol systems. Perhaps it seems strange, but recreational mathematics and language play are nearly identical (perhaps completely identical) in all other aspects.

Codes and ciphers are language play if done for fun but fall into a separate category if done for a serious purpose beyond themselves.

Other similar areas of endeavor may border and even overlap language play; the reason for not including them here is that this is meant not to be the final definitive work on the subject but rather an important initial work. Thus, the decision to include or exclude various kinds of word play has been largely based on whether or not they have been included in major collections (or, at times, even minor collections) of word play by important names in the field. Only one entry has been included that was not found in a collection, "Telephone," and that was included because virtually everyone has played it at some time or other, and its general popularity made breaking the arbitrary rules a more sensible move than obeying them.

An attempt has been made to include origins and histories of the entries, but an echoing of Joseph T. Shipley's complaint, "There is no history of word and letter games," must be constantly borne in mind as the reader encounters entry after entry with no known origin or history. Once again, the lack of scholarship in this field makes anything approaching a book such as *Encyclopedia of Poetry and Poetics* an impossibility. This book must be viewed as an initial attempt at scholarship in a field where it is much overdue.

In an attempt to make cross-references more accessible, the first appearance of another entry in each main entry has been capitalized.

I thank Marilyn Brownstein, Acquisitions Editor at Greenwood Press, for seeing the value of the book and encouraging her company to publish it, Cynthia Harris, Reference Books Editor at Greenwood Press, for her continuous suggestions and for putting up with me throughout the process of getting the manuscript into final form, and Michelle Scott, the Production Editor at Greenwood Press, for seeing the work through its final form. The librarians at Northern Montana College under the direction of Terrence A. Thompson, in particular Vicki Gist and Ann Ritter, have been put to a great deal of what must have been annoying busywork as the result of my researches for this book, and I want them to know that I appreciate their efforts. Dr. Norton Kinghorn, Chairman of the English Department at the University of North Dakota, was the first person to show any interest in this pursuit; I want to thank him for that and for simply being the man he is. My wife and children have been forced to put up with my lack of time for them as a result of the many hours I have spent working on this project, and I appreciate their understanding and encouragement. Finally, I want to thank the many brilliant language game players and puzzlers, some dead for centuries, that I have come to know while sitting in my study late at night.

NOTES

1. Martin Gardner came up with this combination of phrases from *Finnegans Wake* and used it in his "Introduction" to *Oddities and Curiosities of Words and Literature*, the 1961 Dover reprint of C. C. Bombaugh's *Gleanings for the Curious* (1890), p. vi.

2. Quoted by H. H. Arnason in *A History of Modern Art* (Englewood Cliffs, N.J.: Prentice Hall, n.d.), p. 291.

3. The passages from William Shakespeare's play come from *The Complete Signet Classic Shakespeare*, edited by Sylvan Barnet (New York: Harcourt Brace Jovanovich, 1963).

DICTIONARY
OF
LANGUAGE GAMES,
PUZZLES,
AND
AMUSEMENTS

A

ABBREVIATIONS is a form of word play based on the common practice of substituting shorter forms for words or phrases.

The third definition of "abbreviation" in *Webster's New Twentieth Century Dictionary of the English Language* (Unabridged, 2d ed., 1971) is "a letter or letters used for a word or phrase; as, *Gen.* for Genesis; U.S.A. for United States of America. . . . Syn.—contraction, abridgement, curtailment."

An abbreviation is generally created by omitting some of the letters of the original word or phrase (ft. for feet, Minn. for Minnesota). If the abbreviation replaces a phrase or list of words, it often consists of the first letter of each word in the phrase or list (ABC warfare for atomic, biological, and chemical warfare). When this happens the abbreviation is an acronym, which in turn is a form of Acrostic. Sometimes the abbreviation is created by replacing part of the word or phrase with a symbol (Xmas for Christmas) in which case the abbreviation is a form of Rebus.

Willard R. Espy, *A Children's Almanac of Words at Play* (1982), uses abbreviations to create light verse similar to the following lines, which in turn contain the same "wrenched" rhythmic pattern as that of a Clerihew:

A Mr. married a Miss. and a Miss.
Who kept reading each other's mail;
"It's not our fault," each said with a kiss;
"The mailman can't tell us which Mrs. is Mrs."

Although some purists will cry out against any tampering with traditional Nursery Rhymes (even though traditional nursery rhymes have been tampered with for centuries, and many already have dozens of "standard" versions), an application of abbreviations to nursery rhymes can create fresh, often humorous versions of those rhymes. (The periods often used to designate abbreviations can be omitted as redundant, since the paradigm has already been established.)

Baby Bunting

B, Bb Bnt;
Ftr's gn a-hnt;
Gn to gt a rbt skn
To wrp the Bb Bnt n.

If done consistently for a lengthy passage or an entire book, a literary dialect (a dialect that does not exist outside of literature) results. No lengthy work in literary dialect is available at present; however, it is possible to apply abbreviations to great pieces of literature (to mutilate, some would say) and explore the results, both with the inner ear and with more scientific linguistic tools. Here is the first paragraph from Charles Dickens's *A Tale of Two Cities* properly mutilated:

T ws th bst f tms, t ws th wrt f tms, t ws th ag f wdm, t ws th ag f fls, t ws th eph f blf, t ws th eph f icdty, t ws th ssn f Lgt, t ws th ssn f Dks, t ws th spg f hp, t ws th wtr f dspr, w hd evythg bfr s, w hd nthg bfr s, w wr al gg drt t Hvn, w wr al gg drt th otr wy—n sht, th prd ws s fr lk th prst prd, tht sm f ts nsst athrts insstd n ts bng rcvd, fr gd r fr vl, n th sprltv dgr f dprsn oly.

As insulting as this passage may be to the original, a reader who rereads it several times, seriously attempting to pronounce the words as they are abbreviated, will find himself falling into a curious dialect. Why this is the case and what forms the dialect will take (though beyond the scope of this book) are possible questions for serious philosophical/linguistic study.

Though the differences are obvious, literary dialect and eye dialect (literary misspellings, phonetic respellings, of words meant to capture oral dialects of the language) both result in written communication other than that normally accepted as correct. The major difference between eye dialect and abbreviation is that eye dialect is an attempt to capture a form of speaking used in the real world, whereas abbreviation is a form of shorthand that forces the reader away from language used in the real world. An interesting contradiction inherent in this is that (as pointed out above) even when the abbreviations are very stilted, the reader will, if he approaches the passage seriously, likely create a dialect that either is or legitimately could be a real world dialect.

Here is an example of eye dialect from Stephen Crane's *Maggie: A Girl of the Streets:*

In front of the gruesome doorway he met a lurching figure. It was his father, swaying about on uncertain legs.

"Give me deh can. See?" said the man, threateningly.

"Ah, come off! I got dis can fer dat ol' woman an' it 'ud be dirt teh swipe it. See?'' cried Jimmie.

The father wrenched the pail from the urchin. He grasped it in both hands and lifted it to his mouth. He glued his lips to the under edge and tilted his head. His hairy throat swelled until it seemed to grow near his chin. There was a tremendous gulping movement and the beer was gone.

The man caught his breath and laughed. He hit his son on the head with the empty pail. As it rolled clanging into the street, Jimmie began to scream and kicked repeatedly at his father's shins.

"Look at deh dirt what yeh done me,'' he yelled. "Deh ol' woman 'ill be raisin' hell.''

He retreated to the middle of the street, but the man did not pursue. He staggered toward the door.

"I'll club hell outa yeh when I ketch yeh,'' he shouted, and disappeared.

(pp. 10–11)

Eye dialect is created by writers of fiction. The International Phonetic Association came up with a linguistic solution to the same problem approximately a hundred years ago. It is called the International Phonetic Alphabet (IPA). In an attempt to be more precise, the IPA includes symbols beyond those of a standard twenty-six-letter English alphabet, such as the following:

/ð/ /ʒ/ /ə/

Nevertheless, absolutely precise written transcription of human oral languages has not yet been reached, and linguists are in disagreement over whether such elements of oral communication as musical pitch, syllabic stress, and juncture are parts of phonemes (basic units of sound) or not, and thus disagree over whether or not the IPA should include indications of such elements. Such concerns go beyond the purposes of this book.

Here is an IPA transcription of the first line of Charlotte Brontë's *Jane Eyre*, originally published in 1847 under the pseudonym Currer Bell:

/ðer hwɔz nə pɔsəbiliti ɔf tækiŋ ə wək ðætdə/

Another form of writing closely associated with abbreviations is shorthand. Common shorthand abbreviations for America, England, and Canada are, in turn:

At this point it becomes evident that abbreviations are, or at least can be, a form of Code. Those who have not learned the meanings of the abbreviations used by a particular group, whether the group be linguists, shorthand experts, mathematicians, chemists, physicists, musicians, painters, or professional cryptologists, are lost, even though they may be very comfortable with standard written language. Furthermore, when abbreviations take the form of the rebus, it is evident that they are related to hieroglyphics (pictographic scripts—especially those of the ancient Egyptian civilization), some of which have yet to be decoded.

Abbreviations have permeated language since the beginning of recorded history. Ancient Hebrew poets used the Acrostic (a sophisticated form of abbreviation) as one of their major forms of poetry—evidenced by the original Hebrew form of the Psalms of the Old Testament. Psalm 119 in the King James Version still retains this structure, though no longer as a living part of the verse, since abbreviations are not amenable to translation. Roman numerals C and M are abbreviations for *centum* and *mille,* respectively. The symbol of the fish served as a pictorial acrostic (see Acrostic) for early Christians.

Abbreviations as light verse (such as that of Willard R. Espy) or as acrostic can be classified as a form of puzzle. For more examples of language puzzles based on or closely related to abbreviations, refer to ABC Language, Across-tic, Acrostic, Alphabet Poetry, Animal Alphabet, Code, Flat, Fractured Geography, Looks Like Poetry, Pictonym, Rebus, Spine Poetry, Square Poem, Triple Acrostic, Typitoons, and ZOO-LULU.

As a game, abbreviations can take the following form, or some variation of it.

Each player applies the rules of abbreviation to a number of passages of famous literature (poetry or fiction). The players in turn present their passages to the rest of the players, who compete to discover what the original passage was.

Whoever solves the passage first gets ten points and must choose one of his abbreviated passages for the others to solve. If a player guesses a wrong passage, he loses five points. If no one can solve one of the passages, it is simply discarded and another passage chosen.

The player with the most points at the end of the game wins.

For more examples of language games based on or closely related to abbreviations, refer to Acromania, Acrostic, Acrosticals, Category Puzzles, Guggenheim, Initial Answers, Initial Game, Initial Goals, and Sound Spelling.

BIBLIOGRAPHY

Brontë, Charlotte [Currer Bell, pseudo.]. *Jane Eyre.* London, 1847. Reprint. *The Complete Novels of Charlotte and Emily Brontë.* New York: Avenel Books, 1981.

Crane, Stephen. *Maggie: A Girl of the Streets (A Story of New York).* New York: Johnston Smith, 1893. Reprint. New York: W. W. Norton & Co., 1979.

Dickens, Charles. *A Tale of Two Cities.* London, 1859. Reprint. New York: International Collector's Library, n.d.

Espy, Willard R. *An Almanac of Words at Play.* New York: Clarkston N. Potter, Inc., 1975.

———. *A Children's Almanac of Words at Play.* New York: Clarkson N. Potter, Inc., 1982.

Jacobs, Roderick A., and Peter S. Rosenbaum. *Transformations, Style, and Meaning.* Waltham, Mass.: Xerox College Publishing, 1971.

King James Bible, 1611. Reprint. King James Version. Camden, N.J.: Thomas Nelson, Inc., 1970.

Leslie, Louis A.; Charles E. Zoubek; and Russell J. Hosler. *Gregg Shorthand for Colleges: Diamond Jubilee Series.* Vol. 1. New York: McGraw-Hill, 1965.

Liles, Bruce L. *A Basic Grammar of Modern English.* Englewood Cliffs, N.J.: Prentice-Hall, 1979.

McKechnie, Jean L., et al., eds. *Webster's New Twentieth Century Dictionary of the English Language: Unabridged.* 2d ed. New York: World Publishing Company, 1971.

Myers, L. A., and Richard L. Hoffman. *The Roots of Modern English.* 2d ed. Boston: Little, Brown and Co., 1979.

Opie, Peter, and Iona Opie. *The Oxford Dictionary of Nursery Rhymes.* Oxford, England: Clarendon Press, 1951.

Traupman, John C. *The New Collegiate Latin and English Dictionary.* New York: Grosset & Dunlap, 1966. Reprint. *The New College Latin and English Dictionary.* New York: Bantam Books, 1970.

Ullman, B. L., and Albert I. Suskin. *Latin for Americans: Third Book.* New York: Macmillan Company, 1965.

ABC LANGUAGE is a form of Rebus limited to the substitution of like-sounding letters or numerals for words or parts of words (morphemes); it is a form of paronomasia. As word play, it is closely related to Typitoons, though technically typitoons are able to include a slightly larger array of symbols.

As with any phonetically based system of spelling, comparisons can be made with standard systems of spelling (e.g., I and eye would be spelled the same phonetically). For example, the following verse has been written in ABC language:

Pigs
M R pigs!
L M R pigs!
O S M R pigs!

If the standard rules of spelling are applied to the verse, the following results:

Pigs
Them are pigs!
Hell them are pigs!
Oh yes, them are pigs!

Comparisons can also be made with other nonstandard forms of spelling. The International Phonetic Alphabet might represent the same passage in the following manner:

/ ðem ɑr piːgz!
Hæl ðem ɑr piːgz!
O jæz ðem ɑr piːgz! /

Eye dialect might represent the same verse in the following manner:

Pigs
'em are pigs!
'ell 'em are pigs!
Oh yeh, 'em are pigs!

Willard R. Espy employs ABC language to write light verse, sentences, and phrases for his readers to translate into standard language (*A Children's Almanac of Words at Play*). For other puzzles closely related to or based on ABC language, see Abbreviations, Code, Flat, Pun, Rebus, Spine Poetry, Typitoons, and ZOO-LULU.

BIBLIOGRAPHY

Baugh, Albert C., and Thomas Cable. *A History of the English Language.* 3d ed. Englewood Cliffs, N.J.: Prentice-Hall, 1978.

Bolton, W. F. *A Living Language: The History and Structure of English.* New York: Random House, 1982.

Espy, Willard R. *An Almanac of Words at Play.* New York: Clarkson N. Potter, Inc., 1975.

———. *A Children's Almanac of Words at Play.* New York: Clarkson N. Potter, 1982.

———. *The Game of Words.* New York: Grosset & Dunlap, 1972.

Myers, L. A., and Richard L. Hoffman. *The Roots of Modern English.* 2d ed. Boston: Little, Brown and Co., 1979.

ABC WORDS, <u>a</u>lphabetically <u>b</u>alanced <u>c</u>ombination words, is Dmitri Borgmann's term for words whose average numerical value is 13½.

The letters of the alphabet are given numerical values sequentially from 1 to 26, i.e., A = 1, B = 2, C = 3, and so on. Words are then translated into numbers. If the total value of all of the letters in the word divided by the number of letters equals 13½ (the exact mathematical center of the alphabet), then the word is balanced, an ABC word.

Borgmann's *Beyond Language* offers the coincidentally suitable word "love" as a perfectly balanced word (an ABC word): L = 12, O = 15, V = 22, and E = 5. All of the letters added together equal 54, which divided by 4 equals 13½.

Borgmann suggests the following concepts of mathematical balance that can be incorporated into the equation: those words where an equal number of letters come from both halves of the alphabet (even to the extent that the letters of the first half of the word come from the first half of the alphabet, and the letters of the second half of the word come from the second half of the alphabet, e.g., "bins"); those words where the letters are perfectly balanced (Emile Zola's surname fits this, i.e., Z = A, and O = L); those words which have no balanced letters, e.g., "rope"; those words which use no letter more than once, e.g., "smog"; those words which have an equal number of vowels and consonants, e.g., "tone"; and so on. In addition to the suggestions of Borgmann, ABC words can be combined with Anagrams to create ABC anagrams, e.g., "rope/pore" or "tone/note."

This is a form of mathematical play with the language and thus is related to the following entries: ACE Words, Centurion, Cipher, Code, Crypt-Arithmetic, Flat, Inflation, Numwords, and Oulipo Algorithms.

BIBLIOGRAPHY

Borgmann, Dmitri. *Beyond Language: Adventures in Word and Thought.* New York: Charles Scribner's Sons, 1967.
Brooke, Maxey. *150 Puzzles in Crypt-Arithmetic.* 2d rev. ed., New York: Dover Publ., 1963.
McKechnie, Jean L., et al., eds. *Webster's New Twentieth Century Dictionary of the English Language: Unabridged.* 2d ed. New York: World Publishing Co., 1971.
Stein, Jess, ed. *The Random House Dictionary of the English Language.* New York: Random House, 1983.

ACCIDENTAL LANGUAGE is a general term for the numerous forms of word play based on unintentional misconstruing, misspelling, miswriting, or mis-speaking of a word, phrase, or sentence resulting in humor:

A Slip of the Tongue:

Eager to win the cribbage game, but having just fallen behind, Betty said, "I'd better get my toes on!" instead of what she meant to say, "I'd better get on my toes!"

A Title More Accurate Than the Writer Realized:

Jerry, a student in a college business and technical writing class, typed boldly on the front page of his causal analysis paper: "A Casual Analysis."

Unintended Connotations:

At an English department get-together one of the members of the department began telling little known folk sayings. The following saying (freely interpreted) is filled with Freudian symbolism that he was totally unaware of: "Birds, only when wet, fly at night." The other members of the department were more than glad to fill him in.

For similar word play refer to Back Slang, Boner, Irish Bull, Malapropism, Pun, Spoonerism, and Wellerism.

BIBLIOGRAPHY

Espy, Willard R. *A Children's Almanac of Words at Play*. New York: Clarkson N. Potter,
    Inc., 1982.

ACE WORDS, alphabetically constant entity words, are a form of mathematical word play in which a word of seven or more letters is stabilized mathematically with a constant difference, and the first numeral, indicating the number
of letters in the original word, is less than one half of the second numeral, which
indicates the number of digits in the first constant difference level.

The letters of the alphabet are assigned numerical equivalents (A = 1, B = 2,
C = 3, etc.). A word is then chosen that has at least seven letters, and the
appropriate numerals are substituted for the letters. Dmitri Borgmann, the originator of the puzzle, *Beyond Language: Adventures in Word and Thought* (1967),
uses "inkling" as an example of an ACE 7-5 word:

INKLING

9-14-11-12-9-14-7

After the letters have been assigned their corresponding numerals, the difference
between successive letters can be determined mathematically by subtracting the
smallest from the largest:

$14 - 9 = 5$; $14 - 11 = 3$; $12 - 11 = 1$; $12 - 9 = 3$; $14 - 9 = 5$; $14 - 7 = 7$

This produces a mathematical difference at the 7-6 level of 5, 3, 1, 3, 5, 7. By
repeating the process the constant difference is achieved at the 7-5 level:

$5 - 3 = \underline{2}$; $3 - 1 = \underline{2}$; $3 - 1 = \underline{2}$; $5 - 3 = \underline{2}$; $7 - 5 = \underline{2}$

Mastery of the puzzle comes from the ability to memorize the numerical
equivalents of the letters of the alphabet and then add and subtract their differences at a twice-removed level:

HA-HA

H = 8; A = 1
$8 - 1 = 7$; $8 - 1 = 7$; $8 - 1 = 7$
$7 - 7 = 0$; $7 - 7 = 0$

This would be a 4-2 word, not acceptable as an ACE word, but useful to indicate
the type of mental process necessary.

Borgmann divides ACE words into three orders of reduplication. The first
order is exact reduplication (e.g., "ring-ring"). The second order consists of
words in which only one letter is changed, and is divided into three subdivisions.
The first of these subdivisions contains all of the words where the reduplication is

done on purpose (e.g., "flip-flop"). The second subdivision consists of all the words where the reduplication is accidental but occurs at the exact center (Borgmann offers "shoeshop" as an example). The third subdivision consists of words where the accidental reduplication does not fall along well-defined syllable or word divisions (Borgmann offers "jingling" as an example). The third order of reduplication contains the words that have more than one letter changed (Borgmann offers "postpone" as an example).

As Borgmann indicates, there are ACE words that contain no reduplication (he offers "America" as an example).

For additional word puzzles based on mathematics, refer to ABC Words, Centurion, Cipher, Code, Crypt-Arithmetic, Flat, Numwords, and Oulipo Algorithms.

BIBLIOGRAPHY

Borgmann, Dmitri A. *Beyond Language: Adventures in Word and Thought*. New York: Charles Scribner's Sons, 1967.
McKechnie, Jean L., et al., eds. *Webster's New Twentieth Century Dictionary of the English Language: Unabridged*. 2d ed. New York: World Publishing Co., 1971.
Stein, Jess, ed. *The Random House Dictionary of the English Language*. New York: Random House, 1983.

ACROMANIA, also known as initial sentences, is a game based on a combination of Ghosts and acronyms.

An acronym is a word formed from the initial letters of a name, as in WAC for Women's Army Corps, or by the combination of parts of a series of words, as in RADAR for Radio Detecting and Ranging; it is a form of Acrostic.

Various puzzles and games have been developed based on acronyms. Elliott Espy, Willard R. Espy's son, turned the first lines of Nursery Rhymes into acronyms and challenged others to guess the nursery rhyme. Here are some examples:

TTTPS

(Answer: Tom, Tom, the piper's son)

PPPE

(Answer: Peter, Peter, pumpkin eater)

PPPAPOPP

(Answer: Peter Piper picked a peck of pickled peppers)

Dmitri Borgmann, *Beyond Language: Adventures in Word and Thought* (1967), challenged his readers to find common English words which are also acronyms (i.e., SHAZAM).

In acromania, one of the players starts a sentence by announcing the subject of it, e.g., Jim. The next player adds a word to the sentence in such a way that the first letters of each word lead to the spelling out of another word:

Sally chooses "Jim."
Bill chooses "is."
Sally chooses "good."
The sentence is "Jim is good." The word is "Jig."

When the rules of ghost are added, the player who completes a word of four or more letters loses. Players may challenge each added word, but if the first letter of the word continues an as of yet uncompleted word, the challenger loses.

Play continues until a player cannot add a word. The player before him is the winner:

Jeff chooses "Bob."
Marge chooses "eats."
Janet chooses "four."
Marge challenges "four," but Janet indicates that it could lead to a spelling of
    "befall." Marge is out of the game.
Jeff chooses "olives."
Janet chooses "regularly."
Jeff cannot think of a word.
Janet wins.

For puzzles similar to Acromania, refer to Across-tic, Acrostic, Crossword Puzzle, Flat, Forms, Magic Word Squares, Square Poem, and Triple Acrostic.

For games similar to Acromania, refer to Acrostic, Acrosticals, Alphacross, Arrow of Letters, Black Squares, Ghost and Superghost, Lynx, SCRABBLE, SCRABBLEGRAM, Scramble, and Ultraghost.

BIBLIOGRAPHY

Borgmann, Dmitri A. *Beyond Language: Adventures in Word and Thought.* New York:
    Charles Scribner's Sons, 1967.
Espy, Willard R. *A Children's Almanac of Words at Play.* New York: Clarkson N. Potter,
    Inc., 1982.
_____. *The Game of Words.* New York: Grosset & Dunlap, 1972.
Parlett, David. *Botticelli and Beyond: Over 100 of the World's Best Word Games.* New
    York: Pantheon Books, 1981.

ACROSS-TIC is a combination of Acrostics and Crossword Puzzles.

First of all, the grid, though it looks like a crossword puzzle grid, does not consist of "crossing" words. The words read only from left to right, book fashion.

The black spaces do indicate ends of words. However, a white square at the end of a line may or may not indicate the end of a word.

The across-tic is built from a passage of prose or poetry, and the words on the grid are that passage.

A list of definitions comes with each across-tic. Next to each definition the correct number of blanks for the word being defined is included, and beneath each blank is designated the space on the grid where that letter fits.

The first letters of the defined words spell out the author and title of the work from which the quotation is taken.

Here is an example:

1 O	2 F	3 Q	4 B	5 D	■	6 R	7 B	■	8 G	9 A
10 O	■	11 D	12 S	13 S	14 C	15 S	16 L	17 L	18 N	19 N
■	20 M	21 M	22 R	23 H	24 N	■	25 L	26 B	27 J	28 J
29 P	30 P	31 P	32 H	■	33 S	34 G	35 P	36 D	37 M	38 F
■	39 F	40 M	41 M	■	42 F	43 I	■	44 H	45 I	46 G
■	47 O	48 A	49 S	50 S	■	51 J	52 L	53 C	54 S	■
55 G	56 I	57 R	58 K	59 E	60 C	■	61 Q	62 C	63 L	64 E
65 Q	66 J	■	67 P	68 P	69 G	■	70 J	71 N	72 K	73 N
74 M	75 B	■	76 N	77 A	78 H	79 L	80 J	81 E	82 A	83 P
■	84 A	85 A	86 J	87 D	■	88 C	89 Q	90 B	91 G	92 B
■	93 K	94 C	95 E	96 H	■	97 M	98 K	99 E	100 I	101 C
102 O	■	103 R	104 Q	105 D	106 B	■	■	■	■	■

Definitions:

A. A loud, resounding noise

$\overline{77}$ $\overline{9}$ $\overline{85}$ $\overline{82}$ $\overline{84}$ $\overline{48}$ $\overline{103}$

B. Students in their final year

$\overline{92}$ $\overline{75}$ $\overline{106}$ $\overline{4}$ $\overline{90}$ $\overline{26}$ $\overline{7}$

C. Coming into

$\overline{14}$ $\overline{101}$ $\overline{8}$ $\overline{62}$ $\overline{88}$ $\overline{94}$ $\overline{53}$ $\overline{60}$

D. The state flower of New Hampshire

$\overline{87}$ $\overline{105}$ $\overline{5}$ $\overline{36}$ $\overline{11}$

E. Shortened form of introduction

$\overline{81}$ $\overline{59}$ $\overline{95}$ $\overline{99}$ $\overline{64}$

F.   An interjection to express chagrin

<u> 42 </u> <u> 39 </u> <u> 2 </u> <u> 38 </u>

G.   Measured chronologically

<u> 91 </u> <u> 34 </u> <u> 55 </u> <u> 46 </u> <u> 69 </u>

H.   Secure

<u> 44 </u> <u> 78 </u> <u> 32 </u> <u> 96 </u> <u> 23 </u>

I.   High fidelity (compound word)

<u> 45 </u> <u> 56 </u> <u> 43 </u> <u> 100 </u>

J.   Older

<u> 28 </u> <u> 51 </u> <u> 70 </u> <u> 27 </u> <u> 80 </u> <u> 86 </u> <u> 66 </u>

K.   Small, light, delicate

<u> 93 </u> <u> 58 </u> <u> 72 </u> <u> 98 </u>

L.   A person who walks slowly

<u> 52 </u> <u> 63 </u> <u> 25 </u> <u> 16 </u> <u> 17 </u> <u> 79 </u>

M.   Pouch of skin that contains the testes

<u> 97 </u> <u> 37 </u> <u> 74 </u> <u> 21 </u> <u> 41 </u> <u> 40 </u> <u> 20 </u>

N.   Proposition

<u> 19 </u> <u> 24 </u> <u> 71 </u> <u> 76 </u> <u> 73 </u> <u> 18 </u>

O.   A mild oath

<u> 10 </u> <u> 102 </u> <u> 1 </u> <u> 47 </u>

P.   Place where goods are loaded

<u> 35 </u> <u> 67 </u> <u> 68 </u> <u> 29 </u> <u> 30 </u> <u> 31 </u> <u> 83 </u>

Q.   Shield against weapons

<u> 104 </u> <u> 3 </u> <u> 61 </u> <u> 89 </u> <u> 65 </u>

R.   Nothing

<u> 22 </u> <u> 6 </u> <u> 57 </u>

S.   A stupid person

<u> 54 </u> <u> 13 </u> <u> 15 </u> <u> 33 </u> <u> 49 </u> <u> 12 </u> <u> 50 </u>

Answers:
A. <u>T</u>hunder
B. <u>S</u>eniors
C. <u>E</u>ntering
D. <u>L</u>ilac
E. <u>I</u>ntro
F. <u>O</u>ops
G. <u>T</u>imed
H. <u>T</u>ight
I. <u>H</u>i-fi
J. <u>E</u>lderly
K. <u>W</u>isp
L. <u>A</u>mbler
M. <u>S</u>crotum
N. <u>T</u>hesis
O. <u>E</u>gad
P. <u>L</u>anding
Q. <u>A</u>rmor
R. <u>N</u>ix
S. <u>D</u>ullard

For similar puzzles refer to Acrostic, Crossword Puzzle, Flat, Forms, Magic Word Squares, Square Poem, and Triple Acrostic.

For similar games refer to Acromania, Acrosticals, Alphacross, Arrow of Letters, Black Squares, Lynx, SCRABBLE, SCRABBLEGRAM, and Scramble.

BIBLIOGRAPHY

Eliot, T. S. *The Waste Land and Other Poems.* 1933. Reprint. New York: Harcourt, Brace & World, Inc., 1962.

Hart, Harold H. *Grab a Pencil.* New York: Hart Publ. Co., 1958.

McKechnie, Jean L., et al. *Webster's New Twentieth Century Dictionary of the English Language: Unabridged.* 2d ed. New York: World Publishing Co., 1971.

Stein, Jess, ed., *The Random House Dictionary of the English Language.* New York: Random House, 1983.

ACROSTIC, also called category columns, is derived from the ancient Greek word *akrostich* (''first letter verse''); today it designates a composition, usually in verse, in which one or more sets of letters, generally the initial letters of the lines, sometimes the medial letters of the lines (a mesostich), and sometimes the final letters of the lines (a telestich), taken in order form a word or phrase.

A telestich is also used to designate an acrostic where the initial and final letters form words of opposite meanings. C. C. Bombaugh, *Gleanings for the Curious* (1890), includes the following example:

Unite and untie are the same—so say you.
Not in wedlock, I ween, has this unity been.
In the drama of marriage each wandering gout
To a new face would fly—all except you and I—
Each seeking to alter the spell in their scene.

According to Henry Ernest Dudeney, *300 Best Word Puzzles* (1968), acrostic was first applied to the verses of the Erythraean sibyls, women of antiquity who were reputed to possess powers of prophecy and who generally gave their prophecies in obscure riddles.

Cicero, ''De Divinatione,'' includes the following passage (translated by Bombaugh):

The verses of the Sybils are distinguished by that arrangement which the Greeks call Acrostic; where, from the first letters of each verse in order, words are formed which express some particular meaning; as is the case with some of Ennius's verses, the initial letters of which make ''which Ennius wrote.''

Ancient bards and oral singers, the same men who passed on the epics of Homer, made use of acrostic forms as an aid in memorizing their songs and poems. The early Hebrew poets, prophets, and writers of the Old Testament established the acrostic as one of their major verse forms, beginning each twenty-two-line verse or stanza with a successive letter of the alphabet. This form is not retained in translations, but is indicated in standard versions of Psalm 119. The Greek word for "fish" served as a secret acrostic for early Christians:

Ιnθοus = Jesus

ΧρLθΤοs = Christ

Θεθu = Of God

ΥLοs = Son

Σωτηρ = Saviour

The symbol of a fish was then used to stand for this acrostic; it was a pictorial acrostic.

The acrostic form continued through the Dark Ages and into the Renaissance. According to Bombaugh, Giovanni Boccaccio (1313–1375) wrote a poem of fifty cantos based on it. The best known of the early English practitioners is Sir John Davies (1570–1626).

Dmitri Borgmann, *Beyond Language: Adventures in Word and Thought,* suggests that Shakespeare deliberately formed an acrostic of Titania in the following passage from *A Midsummer Night's Dream,* act 3, scene 1:

Thou shalt remain here whether thou wilt or no.
I am a spirit of no common rate.
The summer still doth tend upon my state;
And I do love thee. Therefore, go with me.
I'll give thee fairies to attend on thee;
And they shall fetch thee jewels from the deep. . . .

Lewis Carroll is perhaps the most famous of the nineteenth-century writers who employed the acrostic. The following sample is quoted by Martin Gardner in his "Notes" to the 1961 Dover reprint of Bombaugh's *Gleanings for the Curious:*

INSCRIBED TO A DEAR CHILD:

In Memory of Golden Summer Hours
  and Whispers of a Summer Sea

Girt with a boyish garb for boyish task,
  Eager she wields her spade: yet loves as well
Rest on a friendly knee, intent to ask
  The tale he loves to tell.

Rude spirits of the seething outer strife,
  Unmeet to read her pure and simple spright,
Deem, if you list, such hours a waste of life,
  Empty of all delight!

Chat on, sweet Maid, and rescue from annoy
  Hearts that by wiser talk are unbeguiled,
Ah, happy he who owns that tenderest joy,
  The heart-love of a child!

Away, fond thoughts, and view my soul no more!
  Work claims my wakeful nights, my busy days—
Albeit bright memories of that sunlit shore
  Yet haunt my dreaming gaze!

The first letter of each line has been underlined to emphasize the acrostic spine: Gertrude Chataway.

The first known double acrostic (where the final letters as well as the first letters spell a word) has been attributed to Cuthbert Bede; it appeared in the *Illustrated London News,* August 30, 1856. It must have been immediately popular, for within five years royalty were writing double acrostics. According to Bombaugh, even Queen Victoria wrote one. Bombaugh quotes the following double acrostic (one in which the letters are doubled) written on the death of Lord Hatherton (1863):

Hard was his final fight with ghastly Death,
He bravely yielded his expiring breath.
As in the Senate fighting freedom's plea,
And boundless in his wisdom as the sea.
The public welfare seeking to direct,
The weak and undefended to protect.
His steady course in noble life from birth,
Has shown his public and his private worth.
Evincing mind both lofty and sedate,
Endowments great and fitted for the State,
Receiving high and low with open door,
Rich in his bounty to the rude and poor.
The crown reposed in him the highest trust,
To show the world that he was wise and just.
On his ancestral banners long ago,
Ours willingly relied, and will do so.
Nor yet extinct is noble Hatherton,
Now still he lives in gracious Littleton.

Gyles Brandreth, *The World's Best Indoor Games* (1981), includes the following game based on the acrostic.

First, a word of six or seven letters is chosen, and each player writes the word down the left side of his paper:

S
I
C
K
N
E
S
S

Then each player writes the word in reverse down the right side of his paper:

S		S
I		S
C		E
K		N
N		K
E		C
S		I
S		S

Then the players are given five minutes to write the longest word they can think of that begins and ends with the letters for each row:

S	OMETIME	S	9 pts.
I	SOMEROU	S	9 pts.
C	ORRESPONDENC	E	14 pts.
K	ITCHE	N	7 pts.
N	AMSOO	K	7 pts.
E	CLIPTI	C	8 pts.
S	AMURA	I	7 pts.
S	TATISTIC	S	10 pts.
			71 pts.

The players score a point for each letter used, and the player with the most points wins.

For similar games refer to Acromania, Acrosticals, Alphacross, Arrow of Letters, Black Squares, Lynx, SCRABBLE, SCRABBLEGRAM, Scramble, and Send a Wire.

For similar puzzles refer to Across-tic, Combinations, Crossword Puzzle, Flat, Forms, Magic Word Squares, Square Poem, and Triple Acrostic.

BIBLIOGRAPHY

Bombaugh, C. C. *Gleanings for the Curious.* 1890. Reprint. *Oddities and Curiosities of Words and Literature,* ed. Martin Gardner. New York: Dover, 1961.

Borgmann, Dmitri A. *Beyond Language: Adventures in Word and Thought.* New York: Charles Scribner's Sons, 1967.

————. *Language on Vacation: An Olio of Orthographical Oddities.* New York: Charles Scribner's Sons, 1965.

Brandreth, Gyles. *The World's Best Indoor Games.* New York: Pantheon Books, 1981.

Dudeney, Henry Ernest. *300 Best Word Puzzles.* New York: Charles Scribner's Sons, 1968.

Eckler, A. Ross. *Word Recreations: Games and Diversions from "Word Ways."* New York: Dover, 1979.

Espy, Willard R. *An Almanac of Words at Play.* New York: Clarkson N. Potter, Inc., 1975.

————. *The Game of Words.* New York: Grosset & Dunlap, 1972.

ACROSTICAL ENIGMA. See FLAT.

ACROSTICALS, also called dictionary, is a word game variation on Word Hunt.

One person selects a word of ten letters with as few letter repetitions as possible. Each player then writes the word vertically down the left-hand side of his paper. The players are given a designated amount of time (ten minutes) to complete a word for each letter of the chosen word by using only the letters in the chosen word:

<u>S</u>	at	3 pts.
<u>A</u>	ctors	6 pts.
<u>C</u>	arnal	6 pts.
<u>R</u>	ats	4 pts.
<u>O</u>	ats	4 pts.
<u>S</u>	ons	4 pts.
<u>A</u>	rt	3 pts.
<u>N</u>	ot	3 pts.
<u>C</u>	ans	4 pts.
<u>T</u>	urns	<u>5 pts.</u>
		42 pts.

The first letter of the first word must begin with the first letter of the chosen word, and so on (grammatical relatives of the chosen word are not allowed). The object is to create as long a word for each letter as possible, since one point is awarded for each letter used. The player scoring the most points wins.

Gyles Brandreth, *Indoor Games* (1977), discusses a narrower form of acrosticals called dictionary. In this version, "dictionary" is always the chosen word.

Players are given five minutes to write ten words, one each beginning with each letter of "dictionary" and containing only the letters from "dictionary" in them. Once again, players score one point for each letter used. Brandreth suggests the possibility of using other words, thus making dictionary identical to acrosticals.

All of the various word hunt activities can be played as either a game or a puzzle. For additional entries on this type of word play, see Word Hunt.

Acrosticals employs the word play activities of two of the more important forms of word play, Acrostic and Anagram. Refer to those entries for detailed discussions.

BIBLIOGRAPHY

Brandreth, Gyles. *Indoor Games*. London: Hodder & Stoughton, Ltd., 1977.
Parlett, David. *Botticelli and Beyond: Over 100 of the World's Best Word Games*. New York: Pantheon Books, 1981.

ACTING OUT RHYMES is a form of word play that consists of the reciting of verses while performing some other activity.

Though it is possible to create games and puzzles incorporating these rhymes, in their common use and purest form they are neither a game nor a puzzle. They are more closely related to the songs people sing to work by and those that soldiers sing or chant to march by, and to the Nursery Rhymes children enjoy hearing over and over, and in a sense include all of these. Acting out rhymes also overlap Mnemonics.

Here are two popular acting out rhymes often included among nursery rhymes:

The incey wincey spider climbed up the water spout;
Down came the rain and washed the spider out;
Out came the sunshine and dried up all the rain;
The incey wincey spider climbed up the spout again.
(Recited while acting out the actions, i.e., walking two fingers up a child's arm.)

This little pig went to market,
This little pig stayed home,
This little pig had roast beef,
This little pig had none,
And this little pig cried "Wee-wee-wee" all the way home.
(Said while squeezing each of the child's toes in turn, often tickling the child on the final line.)

Acting out rhymes have a long and obscure history. "This Little Pig Went to Market," for instance, has been traced back by Iona and Peter Opie, *The Oxford Dictionary of Nursery Rhymes* (1951), to a line quoted in "The Nurse's Song," written about 1728 and included in the fourth volume of Ramsey's *The Tea-Table Miscellany* (1740).

For similar entries see Ball Bouncing Rhymes, Charms, Counting Rhymes,

Game Rhymes, Hand Clapping Rhymes, Incantations, Jump Rope Rhymes, Mnemonics, Nursery Rhymes, Skipping Rhymes, and Tongue Twister.

BIBLIOGRAPHY

Abrahams, Roger D. *Jump-Rope Rhymes: A Dictionary*. Austin: University of Texas, 1969.

Abrahams, Roger D., and Lois Rankin. *Counting-Out Rhymes: A Dictionary*. Austin: University of Texas, 1980.

Carpenter, Humphrey, and Mari Prichard. *The Oxford Companion to Children's Literature*. New York: Oxford University Press, 1984.

Laubach, David C. *Introduction to Folklore*. Rochelle Park, N.J.: Hayden Book Co., 1980.

Opie, Peter, and Iona Opie. *Children's Games in Street and Playground*. 1969. Reprint. New York: Oxford University Press, 1979.

———. *The Lore and Language of Schoolchildren*. 1959. Reprint. New York: Oxford University Press, 1980.

———. *The Oxford Dictionary of Nursery Rhymes*. 1951. Reprint. New York: Oxford University Press, 1983.

———. *The Oxford Nursery Rhyme Book*. 1955. Reprint. New York: Oxford University Press, 1984.

Shipley, Joseph T. *Playing with Words*. Englewood Cliffs, N.J.: Prentice-Hall, 1960.

Sutton-Smith, Brian. *The Folkgames of Children*. Austin: University of Texas Press, 1972.

Volland, P. F. *Mother Goose*. Chicago: P. F. Volland & Co., 1915. Reprint. New York: Rand McNally & Co., 1982.

ACTION SPELLING is a word game variation of Spelling Bee where selected letters must be acted out rather than spelled.

For example, instead of saying "c" when spelling the word "cat" the player must point to his eyes. Sounds might also be substituted, e.g., a whistle for the letter "v."

Players are eliminated either for misspelling a word or for saying a letter meant to be acted out.

Refer to Spelling Bee for the standard game from which this variation is derived.

BIBLIOGRAPHY

Brandreth, Gyles. *The World's Best Indoor Games*. New York: Pantheon Books, 1981.

ADDITIVES. See ADD-ON.

ADD-ON, also called additives, is a game or puzzle where words are formed by adding on letters to the beginning and/or the end of other words.

For example, "m" can be added on to "eat" to form "meat." As a game, this can be played as follows. One player chooses a short word (one that begins with a vowel will probably work best) and has the other players attempt to create as many new words as they can by adding one, two, or more letters to the original word. The players may specify that letters may be added only to the beginning or end of the word—or to both.

Add-on is closely related to Ghost and Superghost and to Progressive Anagram. Refer to these entries for more detailed discussions and other similar puzzles and games.

BIBLIOGRAPHY

Borgmann, Dmitri A. *Language on Vacation: An Olio of Orthographical Oddities.* New York: Charles Scribner's Sons, 1981.
Espy, Willard R. *The Game of Words.* New York: Grosset & Dunlap, 1972.

AD LIB, also called he who hesitates, just a minute, and what nonsense?, is a game involving the ability to think and talk fast.

One player is selected as umpire. It is up to him to choose a subject and keep time.

The other players in turn must talk about the subject selected for thirty seconds each (for one minute in the case of just a minute). No interruptions or hesitations are allowed. The talk will inevitably drift away from the selected subject, but it cannot jump too illogically off the track. If it does, whoever is talking is out of the game. Anyone who hesitates is also out of the game.

The game continues until only one player is left. He is the winner and becomes the umpire for the next round.

Refer to Hobby Horse, Monosyllables, Railroad Carriage Game, and Word Associations for other games involving the ability to think and talk fast.

BIBLIOGRAPHY

Brandreth, Gyles. *Indoor Games.* London: Hodder & Stoughton, Ltd., 1977.
————. *The World's Best Indoor Games.* New York: Pantheon Books, 1981.
Parlett, David. *Botticelli and Beyond: Over 100 of the World's Best Word Games.* New York: Pantheon Books, 1981.

ADVERBS is a game involving the ability to guess adverbs.

One player leaves the room. The other players choose an adverb for him to guess.

The player returns. He has three opportunities to ask questions of three different players, each of whom must reply to the best of his ability in the manner of the adverb concerned.

After each guess the player may guess the adverb (three points for guessing it on the first try, two points on the second, one point on the third).

It is the manner in which the answer is delivered that counts—whether it be brutishly, enthusiastically, lovingly, elegantly, carefully, laughingly, or whatever the adverb is.

The player giving the winning clue may also be awarded points.

Refer to Aesop's Mission, Botticelli, and Password for similar games.

BIBLIOGRAPHY

Brandreth, Gyles. *Indoor Games*. London: Hodder & Stoughton, Ltd., 1977.
Fuller, John G. *Games for Insomniacs; or, A Lifetime Supply of Insufferable Brain Twisters*. New York: Doubleday, 1966.
Parlett, David. *Botticelli and Beyond: Over 100 of the World's Best Word Games*. New York: Pantheon Books, 1981.

ADVERTISING WORDS, also called word advertisements, is word play that involves creating puns from common advertising slogans.

Dmitri Borgmann describes this form of word play in *Beyond Language: Adventures in Word and Thought* (1967). The object is to take common advertising slogans and replace the product advertised with "word" or "words," e.g., the "word generation" for the "Pepsi generation," in an attempt to come up with clever Puns.

As a game, it can be played as a challenge between individuals or teams to come up with the cleverest phrases, or to discover the original slogan from ones already changed.

Refer to Pun for similar word play.

BIBLIOGRAPHY

Borgmann, Dmitri A. *Beyond Language: Adventures in Word and Thought*. New York: Charles Scribner's Sons, 1967.

AESOP'S MISSION is a Victorian parlor game involving the avoidance of taboo letters.

In Victorian times, one person was selected to play Aesop, and he even dressed the part, complete with a hump under his coat, an eye patch, a false nose, and a crutch—though, as David Parlett comments in *Botticelli and Beyond: Over 100 of the World's Best Word Games,* the costumed person looked more like Long John Silver than Aesop.

Aesop's mission was to discover which of the animals had displeased the gods by choice of menu. Having previously picked a letter of the alphabet as taboo, Aesop then asked each player in turn a question requiring a one-word answer. If the player responded with a word containing the taboo letter, Aesop expressed disapproval, and the player lost his life (a player could lose his life only three times).

The object of the game was to guess the taboo letter before losing one's life three times.

Refer to Adverbs for a similar game and to Charades for a more lengthy discussion of a common Victorian parlor game.

BIBLIOGRAPHY

Parlett, David. *Botticelli and Beyond: Over 100 of the World's Best Word Games*. New York: Pantheon Books, 1981.

AGILE ANTONYMS, a game created by William and Mary Morris, *The Word Game Book* (1959), involves the ability to come up with Antonyms quickly.

One player is chosen master of ceremonies. He names a word. The first player to name an antonym gets a point. When a player reaches five points, he wins the game, becomes master of ceremonies, and starts a new game.

Dmitri Borgmann, *Language on Vacation: An Olio of Orthographical Oddities* (1965), has come up with two forms of sophisticated word puzzles involving antonyms. The first he calls antonymic reversals, words which, when read backwards, have very different or opposite meanings (e.g., God-dog). The second he calls antonymic transdeletion, the deleting of a letter from a word and changing the order of the other letters to form words of opposite meanings.

For similar word play refer to Flat and Improbable Opposites.

BIBLIOGRAPHY

Borgmann, Dmitri A. *Language on Vacation: An Olio of Orthographical Oddities.* New York: Charles Scribner's Sons, 1965.
Morris, William, and Mary Morris. *The Word Game Book.* New York: Harper & Brothers, 1959.

ALFABITS is a puzzle or game involving the forming of as many words of an established length as possible from a larger word.

Here is an example:

Chosen Word: Paratrooper
Established Length of Words: Five Letters
Some Possible Responses: Troop, Paper, Trope, Porte, Pater, Apart, Rater, Taper

Refer to Anagram for a more detailed discussion of this type of word play and for similar games and puzzles.

BIBLIOGRAPHY

Hart, Harold H. *Grab a Pencil.* New York: Hart Publ. Co., 1958.

ALLITERATION is the repetition of initial or medial consonants in two or more adjacent words; it is one of the major schemes of rhetoric. (It is closely related to another scheme, assonance, the repetition of similar vowel sounds, preceded and followed by different consonants, in the stressed syllables of adjacent words.)

In Anglo-Saxon versification (seventh to twelfth centuries) alliteration, rather than rhyme, was used to hold the verses together. Though *Sir Gawain and the Green Knight* was written some 200 years after the end of the Anglo-Saxon period, it now ranks as an ideal example of this form of poetry. The following lines are from Marie Borroff's translation, which is included in *The Norton Anthology of World Masterpieces*, volume 1, fourth edition:

Since the siege and the assault was ceased at Troy,
The walls breached and burnt down to brands and ashes,
The knight that had knotted the nets of deceit
Was impeached for his perfidy, proven most true, . . .

Alliteration is such an obvious mannerism, however, that it is rarely used today, except as a mnemonic device, a form of word play, or as light or humorous verse, such as the following:

The Sterile Serpent

The sterile serpent sadly sighed
And slipped into a cave;
No fire flowed, no flame came forth
To sooth the sickly snake;
He hung his head between his legs
And softly slouched asleep.

At least two important forms of word play employ alliteration. The first, alliterative acrostics, flirts with serious poetry, though it is seldom used as such, and really is closer to the light, humorous verse of "The Sterile Serpent." What it does is to combine alliteration with the form of the Acrostic, as in the following:

Sandy's Death

She sits so still
All activities are at adjournment
Needing no new news
Death, denouement, doings done
Young, yet a yearling

The second, alphabetic alliteration, is used in numerous alphabet games and puzzles. The object is to go through all or most of the letters of the alphabet, finding one or more words that begin with each letter.

If alphabetic alliteration is played as a game, the object is to find more words, find the words faster, or find longer words than the other players.

The game or puzzle can be made more sophisticated. In one version the players must write a sentence for each letter of the alphabet (the sentence can be no more than five words long, and there must be at least three occurrences of alliteration):

Adam ate an apple.
Bob built a boat.
Carol caught a cold.
and so on.

For similar word play refer to Acrostic, Alpha, and Alphabet Poetry.

BIBLIOGRAPHY

Baugh, Albert C., and Thomas Cable. *A History of the English Language*. 3d ed., 1957. Reprint. Englewood Cliffs, N.J.: Prentice-Hall, 1978.
Bolton, W. F. *A Living Language: The History and Structure of English*. New York: Random House, 1982.
Corbett, Edward P. J. *Classical Rhetoric for the Modern Student*. 2d ed. New York: Oxford University Press, 1971.
Daiches, David; Malcolm Bradbury; and Eric Mottram, eds. *The Avenel Companion to English and American Literature*. New York: Avenel Books, 1981.
Espy, Willard R. *A Children's Almanac of Words at Play*. New York: Clarkson N. Potter, Inc., 1982.
————. *The Game of Words*. New York: Grosset & Dunlap, 1972.
Holman, C. Hugh. *A Handbook to Literature*. 4th ed. Indianapolis: Bobbs-Merrill Educational Publishing, 1980.
Mack, Maynard, et al., eds. *The Norton Anthology of World Masterpieces*. 4th ed., 1956. Reprint. New York: W. W. Norton & Co., 1979.
Myers, L. A., and Richard Hoffman. *Companion to "The Roots of Modern English."* 2d ed. Boston: Little, Brown and Co., 1979.
————. *The Roots of Modern English*. 2d ed. Boston: Little, Brown and Co., 1979.

ALLITERATIVE ACROSTIC. See ALLITERATION.

ALPHA is a puzzle or game involving the finding of as many words as possible beginning and ending with the same letter, e.g., a̲lph̲a̲, b̲omb̲, O̲hio̲.

If played as a game, a time limit is established (five to ten minutes) and players are scored according to the total number of letters used or words formed.

Refer to Alliteration, Alphabet Word Chain, and Stepladders for similar word play.

BIBLIOGRAPHY

Brandreth, Gyles. *Indoor Games*. London: Hodder & Stoughton, Ltd., 1977.
————. *The World's Best Indoor Games*. New York: Pantheon Books, 1981.

ALPHABENT, also called alphabetter, is a puzzle involving the creation of a sentence, a paragraph, or even a story beginning each successive word with a successive letter of the alphabet.

Here is an example:

A̲ b̲oy c̲an d̲ie e̲ven f̲rom g̲reat h̲elp i̲n j̲ust k̲aleidoscopic, l̲ittle m̲oments; n̲ow o̲nly p̲ersonal q̲uiet, r̲est, s̲leep, t̲enderness, u̲tmost v̲irtue w̲ill x̲in y̲our Z̲achariah.

Oral alphabent can be played by having players call out words beginning with successive letters of the alphabet that also fit grammatically together.

Similar word play is discussed under the following entries: Acrostic, Alphabetical Adjectives, Alphabet Word Chain, A to Z Banquet, First Letters, Hypo-chondriac, I Gave My Love, I Love My Love, I Packed My Bag, I Went to Market, Nymphabet, Pangram, Sequences, Single-Rhymed Alphabet, Sliding Alphabet, and Travelling Alphabet.

BIBLIOGRAPHY

Parlett, David. *Botticelli and Beyond: Over 100 of the World's Best Word Games*. New York: Pantheon Books, 1981.

ALPHABET CODE. See CODE.

ALPHABETICAL ADJECTIVES is a game that involves finding adjectives for successive letters of the alphabet and combining them with nouns beginning with the same letter of the alphabet as the original adjectives chosen.

The first contestant gives an adjective/noun combination, the adjective begin-ning with the letter A. The next contestant chooses an adjective beginning with the letter B and combines it with a noun beginning with the same letter as that of the original noun (e.g., alphabet soup; blue sock; cold sink; and so on). Adjec-tives beginning with X and Z may be eliminated.

Numerous variations are possible. For example, the nouns chosen may also begin with successive letters of the alphabet (e.g., animal airplane; blue ball; cute cat; and so on). Or the adjective may continue to begin with the same letter as the original adjective while the noun works its way through the alphabet (e.g., cold apple; clean boy; cold cuts, and so on). In a slightly more complex version, the adjective may work its way from the end of the alphabet while the noun works its way from the beginning (e.g., zoo animal; young boy; xanthochroid characteristics; and so on).

For similar word play refer to Alliteration, Alphabent, Alphabet Poetry, Al-phabet Word Chain, I Gave My Love, I Love My Love, I Packed My Bag, and I Went to Market.

BIBLIOGRAPHY

Espy, Willard R. *The Game of Words*. New York: Grosset & Dunlap, 1972.

ALPHABETIC ALLITERATION. See ALLITERATION.

ALPHABET POETRY, also called alphabet rhymes, is a word puzzle where each line of a poem (though this would seldom be considered serious poetry) begins with a successive letter of the alphabet (e.g., apple, ball, cat, dog, and so on).

In more sophisticated versions, the length of the lines of verse is longer than one word, and often other rules are added. For some of these versions refer to Alliteration, Alphabent, Alphabetical Adjectives, Alphabet Pyramids, Alphabet Word Chain, Animal Alphabet, I Gave My Love, I Love My Love, Initial

Answers, I Packed My Bag, I Went to Market, Looks Like Poetry, Single-Rhymed Alphabet, Sliding Alphabet, and Spine Poetry.

BIBLIOGRAPHY

Gensler, Kinereth, and Nina Nyhart. *The Poetry Connection: An Anthology of Contemporary Poems with Ideas to Stimulate Children's Writing.* New York: Teachers & Writers, 1978.

Shipley, Joseph T. *Playing with Words.* Englewood Cliffs, N.J.: Prentice-Hall, 1960.

ALPHABET PYRAMIDS are puzzles involving the building of an ever increasing line of words by adding different parts of speech, each new word beginning with the same letter.

The pattern is as follows (though other patterns can easily be established):

Line 1: noun
Line 2: adjective and noun
Line 3: adjective and noun and verb
Line 4: adjective and noun and verb and adverb

Here is an example:

Bob
Bad Bob
Bad Bob bawls
Bad Bob bawls boldly

For similar word play refer to Alliteration, Alphabent, Alphabetical Adjectives, Alphabet Poetry, Alphabet Word Chain, Animal Alphabet, Diamantes, Dictionary Digest, Lanterne, and Single-Rhymed Alphabet.

BIBLIOGRAPHY

Carlson, Ruth Kearney. *Sparkling Words.* Geneva, Ill.: Paladin House Publ., 1979.

ALPHABET RACE. See ALPHACROSS.

ALPHABETTER. See ALPHABENT.

ALPHABET WORD CHAIN is a puzzle requiring the tying together of letters of the alphabet.

The first word must begin with one letter of the alphabet and end with the next letter of the alphabet. The second word must begin with the letter that ended the first word and must end with the next letter of the alphabet, e.g., aplombicodinelfogrithi.

For similar word play refer to Alliteration, Alpha, Alphabent, Alphabetical Adjectives, Alphabet Poetry, Alphabet Pyramids, Heads and Tails, I Gave My

Love, I Love My Love, I Packed My Bag, I Went to Market, Life Sentence, Stepladders, and Word Chains.

BIBLIOGRAPHY

Dudeney, Henry Ernest. *300 Best Word Puzzles*. New York: Charles Scribner's Sons, 1968.

Espy, Willard R. *The Game of Words*. New York: Grosset & Dunlap, 1972.

Morris, William, and Mary Morris. *The Word Game Book*. New York: Harper & Brothers, 1959.

Parlett, David. *Botticelli and Beyond: Over 100 of the World's Best Word Games*. New York: Pantheon Books, 1981.

ALPHACROSS, also called alphabet race, is a game that uses the techniques of Crossword Puzzles in an effort to eliminate letters of the alphabet.

Each player begins with a pencil and a piece of paper. A third sheet of paper is used as the board. Each player lists the twenty-six letters of the alphabet on his paper.

The first player writes a word on the board and crosses off from his alphabet the letters used in the word.

The second player then adds a word crossword fashion and crosses off from his alphabet the letters he has used in the word:

The first player writes "stone" on the board and crosses off "s," "t," "o," "n," "e," from his alphabet.

```
S
T
O
N
E
```

The second player writes "running" on the board and crosses off "r," "u," "n," "i," "g," from his list (he would not have been allowed to cross off "n" if he had not used an "n" of his own.

```
        S
        T
        O
R U N N I N G
        E
```

Play continues until one player uses all of his letters and wins, or until neither player can play, in which case the player with the fewest letters remaining wins.

For additional games of this type refer to Arrow of Letters, Black Squares, Crossword Puzzle, Flat, Forms, Last Word, Lynx, Magic Word Squares, Puzzling Squares, Quizl, Ragaman, SCRABBLE, SCRABBLEGRAM, and Scramblegram.

BIBLIOGRAPHY

Brandreth, Gyles. *Indoor Games*. London: Hodder & Stoughton, Ltd., 1977.
Parlett, David. *Botticelli and Beyond: Over 100 of the World's Best Word Games*. New York: Pantheon Books, 1981.

ALPHAMETIC. See CRYPT-ARITHMETIC.

ALPHAWORDS is a puzzle or poem requiring the use of all the letters of the alphabet to create what amounts to a free-floating Crossword Puzzle or Acrostic.

The better examples use words that are all related to the same subject, as in the following:

```
                                    P
                                    L
                           A        U   Z O D I A C
                           S        T   E W
                           T    M O O N   A
                           R    A      I   R
                           O    R      T   F
                     V E N U S        H
               Q         O
               U         M
         G A L A X Y
               S
         C     A
     B O H R
         P
         E
 J U P I T E R
         N           K
     E I N S T E I N
         C           P
         U           L
         S           E
                     R
```

The above example does not attempt to form a word picture to correspond to the subject matter, nor does it restrict itself to using each letter as few times as possible (ultimately using each letter only once). Both result in more sophisticated challenges.

For similar word play refer to Across-tic, Acrostic, Alphabent, Alphabet Poetry, Crossword Puzzle, and Pangram.

BIBLIOGRAPHY

Shipley, Joseph T. *Playing with Words*. Englewood Cliffs, N.J.: Prentice-Hall, 1960.

ALTERNADE. See FLAT.

ANABLANK is a game based on Anagrams.

One player chooses a word, finds other words within the chosen word, and makes sentences using those words (attempting to base the content of the sentences around one theme or idea). Then he tells the other players what his base word is and gives them the sentences he has created; blanks are substituted for the words taken from his base word.

The first player to fill in all of the blanks wins. Here is an example:

The base word is "substitute."
Some words found within "substitute": it, sit, bite, bus, bit, set, tut, tub, but, sub, stub, bust.
Sentences created:
1. He _____ on the _____. (sat, bus)
2. The lady next to him was taking a bath in a _____. (tub)
3. _____ the _____ jerked, causing the snake in the _____ to _____ the lady in the _____. (But, bus, tub, bite, bust)
4. She screamed, _____ the man merely said _____ _____ and continued to _____ on the _____. (but, tut, tut, sit, bus)

For similar word play refer to Anagame, Anagram, Crossword Puzzle, Espygram, Flat, Last Word, Reversible Anagram, and Scramblegram.

BIBLIOGRAPHY

Shipley, Joseph T. *Playing with Words*. Englewood Cliffs, N.J.: Prentice-Hall, 1960.

ANAGAME is a game based on Anagrams.

One player chooses a fairly long word, breaks it into a number of other words, devises a clue for each word (clues are generally based on Synonyms or definitions), and gives the other players the base word. The players must solve the words taken from the base word by answering the clues.

Here is an example:

The base word is "eliminate."
Some words found within "eliminate": lime, ate, eat, time, mine, ten.

The clues:
1. Something you do with a fork. (eat)
2. Something a clock tells you. (time)
3. Either a fruit or something mixed with cement. (lime)
4. A homonym for "eight." (ate)
5. Where you dig for gold. (mine)
6. What you become after nine. (ten)

For similar word play refer to Anablank, Anagram, and Espygram.

BIBLIOGRAPHY

Shipley, Joseph T. *Playing with Words*. Englewood Cliffs, N.J.: Prentice-Hall, 1960.

ANAGHOST. See GHOST AND SUPERGHOST.

ANAGRAB is a variation of SCRABBLE.

It is usually played with SCRABBLE tiles, but need not be. Any number of persons can play, but more than seven or eight makes for a confusing game.

Turn all the letters (tiles) face down and mix. Then, one at a time, turn them over. Once the fourth tile has been revealed, and for each subsequent tile, any player may call out a word. The following rules apply:

1. Each word must be at least four letters long.
2. Each word must use at least one letter from those turned up.
3. Words may include the exact same letters as a previous word, so long as they are mixed up anagram style (changing the root of the word, not simply the grammatical form of it, e.g., no simple plurals are allowed).
4. Words must be able to be located in an accepted authority, i.e., a dictionary.

When "capturing" an opponent's word (rule 3) *all* of the letters of that word must be used in the new word, though new letters from the pool may also be included in the new word.

The game ends when all players agree that no new words can be formed. If SCRABBLE tiles are used, the points on the tiles each player has finished with are added to determine the winner.

Two additional rules:

1. If two players call out a word at the same time, the player calling out the longest word gets it. If the words are the same length, or if the same word is called out, neither gets it, and the word is banned from the game.
2. If a player calls out an unacceptable or incorrect word he is punished by not being allowed to call out a word for the next two turns.

For similar word play refer to Anagram, SCRABBLE, and SCRABBLE-GRAM.

BIBLIOGRAPHY

Sharp, Richard, and John Piggott. *The Book of Games*. New York: Galahad Books, 1977.

ANAGRAM is a word or phrase formed by the reordering of the letters of another word or phrase (e.g., opts, pots, tops, stop, spot, post).

In Greek, *ana* means "up, back, again" and *gra* means to "graft or write" (from the Greek word *graphein*, "to write"). This then passes into Low German as *anagramma*, which means "reversal of letters." *Anagramma* becomes *ana-*

gramme in Early to Modern French, and *anagramme* becomes *anagram* in English.

According to Howard W. Bergerson, *Palindromes and Anagrams* (1973), anagrams were invented by the Greek poet Lycophron in 260 B.C. C. C. Bombaugh, *Gleanings for the Curious* (1890), includes two anagrams from Lycophron's poem, "Cassandra": The first is an anagram of Ptolemy Philadelphus. The anagram means "made of honey." The second is an anagram of Ptolemy's queen, Arsinoë. The anagram means "Juno's violet."

Ι Ι Τ Ο ΠΕ ΜΑ Ι ۶

Α Ι Ι Ο ΜΕ Λ Ι Τ Ο ۶

Ε ΡΑ ۶Ι Ο Ν

Α Ρ ۶ Ι Ν Ο ۶

During the Renaissance, anagrammatizing was so popular that King Louis XIII of France even appointed a royal anagrammatist, Thomas Billon. Cotton Mather (1663–1728), the New England minister, historian, and scholar, is described in a quote in Bombaugh's book as distinguished for "care to guide his flock and feed his lambs / By words, works, prayers, psalms, alms, and anagrams."

Martin Gardner, "Notes," includes two anagrams Lewis Carroll wrote on William Ewart Gladstone (1809–1898), English prime minister: "Wilt tear down all images!" and "Wild agitator! Means well."

Presently, anagrams form one of the National Puzzlers' League's major categories of word play. They define "anagram" as a word or phrase rearranged to create an "apposite" clue (other forms of anagram they label "mutations"). Furthermore, they define "antigram" (see Flat) as an anagram opposite in meaning to the original or key word.

A. Ross Eckler, *Word Recreations: Games and Diversions from "Word Ways,"* establishes a strong distinction between anagram and Transposal. According to him, an anagram must have the same meaning as the word it is an anagram of; a transposal, on the other hand, rearranges the letters of a word into a new word (see Transposal).

Gyles Brandreth, *The World's Best Indoor Games,* includes the following game titled anagram. A question master chooses a category (e.g., dogs, cars, food) and prepares a list of words belonging to that category. If he chooses "dogs," he might come up with fleas, bark, growl, animal, hair, hunting, bone, and so on. He then mixes up the letters of the words belonging to the category and gives this list (e.g., saelf, krab, wolrg, imanal, riah, tunghni, oneb) to the other players, who must then solve the scrambled words in a given time period.

For additional word play involving anagrams refer to Acrosticals, Add-on, Alfabits, Anablank, Anagame, Cap Me, Category Puzzles, Circular Reversals, Crossword Puzzle, Doublets, Espygram, Flat, Jumbles, Last Word, Marsupials, Middleput, Middletake, Missing Words, Name in Vain, Palindrome, Progressive Anagram, Put and Take, Quaternade, Quinade, Removers, Reversible Anagram, Scaffold, Scramblegram, Word Knock-downs, and Word Ping-Pong.

BIBLIOGRAPHY

Bergerson, Howard W. *Palindromes and Anagrams*. New York: Dover, 1973.

Bombaugh, C. C. *Gleanings for the Curious*. 1890. Reprint. *Oddities and Curiosities of Words and Literature*, ed. Martin Gardner. New York: Dover, 1981.

Borgmann, Dmitri A. *Beyond Language: Adventures in Word and Thought*. New York: Charles Scribner's Sons, 1967.

————. *Language on Vacation: An Olio of Orthographical Oddities*. New York: Charles Scribner's Sons, 1965.

Brandreth, Gyles. *The World's Best Indoor Games*. New York: Pantheon Books, 1981.

Eckler, A. Ross. *Word Recreations: Games and Diversions from "Word Ways."* New York: Dover, 1979.

Espy, Willard R. *A Children's Almanac of Words at Play*. New York: Clarkson N. Potter, Inc., 1982.

————. *The Game of Words*. New York: Grosset & Dunlap, 1972.

Gardner, Martin. "Notes." In *Oddities and Curiosities of Words and Literature*. New York: Dover, 1981.

————. *Perplexing Puzzles and Tantalizing Teasers*. New York: Simon & Schuster, 1969.

McKechnie, Jean L., et al., eds. *Webster's New Twentieth Century Dictionary of the English Language: Unabridged*. 2d ed. New York: World Publishing Co., 1971.

Morris, William, and Mary Morris. *Dictionary of Contemporary Usage*. New York: Harper & Row, 1985.

Parlett, David. *Botticelli and Beyond: Over 100 of the World's Best Word Games*. New York: Pantheon Books, 1981.

Partridge, Eric. *Origins: A Short Etymological Dictionary of Modern English*. New York: Greenwich House, 1983.

Shipley, Joseph T. *Dictionary of Word Origins*. New York: Philosophical Library, 1945.

————. *Playing with Words*. Englewood Cliffs, N.J.: Prentice-Hall, 1960.

Spenser, Dwight. *Word Games in English*. New York: Regents Publishing Co., 1976.

Stein, Jess, ed. *The Random House Dictionary of the English Language*. New York: Random House, 1983.

ANAGRAM CHARADES. See CROSSWORD PUZZLE.

ANAGRAM CROSSWORD. See CROSSWORD PUZZLE.

ANAQUOTE. See EXTRAS.

ANGUISH LANGUISH. See PUN.

ANIMAL ALPHABET is a form of Alphabet Poetry, i.e., the first letter of each line must begin with a subsequent letter of the alphabet. The lines may be as long as wished and may rhyme, but only animal names may be used.

Here is an example:

Ape, monkey, turtle, rat,
Badger, beaver, elephant, bat,
Cat, canary, crocodile, rail,
Duck, panther, ostrich, whale,
Elephant, gannet, skua, baboon,
Finch, jay, pelican, loon,
Giraffe, reindeer, katydid, gull,
Horse, hummingbird, pickerel, owl,
Iguana, lion, buffalo, bear,
Jacana, beetle, pheasant, hare,
Kangaroo, chicken, bumblebee, frog,
Lynx, polliwog, scorpion, dog,
Monkey, nautilus, ostrich, ox,
Nuthatch, nightingale, butterfly, moth,
Owl, camel, muskrat, sloth,
Parakeet, panda, anteater, moose,
Quail, mule, alligator, sole,
Rat, rattlesnake, märmose, mole,
Squirrel, squid, salamander, shark,
Toad, tiger, angleworm, lark,
Umbrina, robin, sparrow, hawk,
Vulture, viper, ermine, auk,
Worm, whippoorwill, cuttlefish, mouse,
Xeme, dragonfly, scorpion, grouse,
Yak, eagle, wasp, swan,
Zebra, cockatoo, leopard, fawn.

For similar word play refer to Alliteration, Alphabent, Alphabetical Adjectives, Alphabet Poetry, Alphabet Pyramids, Alphabet Word Chain, I Gave My Love, I Love My Love, I Packed My Bag, I Went to Market, Looks Like Poetry, Single-Rhymed Alphabet, and Spine Poetry.

BIBLIOGRAPHY

Espy, Willard R. *A Children's Almanac of Words at Play*. New York: Clarkson N. Potter, Inc., 1982.

Gensler, Kinereth, and Nina Nyhart. *The Poetry Connection: An Anthology of Contemporary Poems with Ideas to Stimulate Children's Writing*. New York: Teachers & Writers, 1978.

McKechnie, Jean L., et al. *Webster's New Twentieth Century Dictionary of the English Language: Unabridged*. 2d ed. New York: World Publishing Co., 1971.

ANIMAL CRACKERS. See PUN.

ANIMALISTICS is word play involving the creation of new names for musical instruments by using animal names, e.g., snakinet, elephantuba, lionophone, hippodrum.

For similar word play refer to Confusing and Confounding Cats, Conundrum, Invent-a-Name, Portmanteau, Pun, and Vulture Up To?

BIBLIOGRAPHY

Morris, William, and Mary Morris. *The Word Game Book.* New York: Harper & Brothers, 1959.

ANIMATED WORDS. See PICTONYM.

ANSWER VERSE is a word guessing game involving the writing of short verses.

Each player is given two sheets of paper. On the first he writes a question, on the second a word or short phrase.

The question sheets and the answer sheets are collected and shuffled separately.

Each player picks one of each.

In a four-line stanza, each player must answer the question he has chosen, including in his answer the word or phrase chosen.

The object is to disguise the word or phrase used so that the other players cannot guess it.

Each player in turn gets a chance to guess the word or phrase used.

For similar word play refer to Bouts Rimés, Bouts Rimés Retournés, and Pass it On.

BIBLIOGRAPHY

Dudeney, Henry Ernest. *300 Best Word Puzzles.* New York: Charles Scribner's Sons, 1968.

Loyd, Samuel. *Sam Loyd's Cyclopeaia of 5000 Puzzles, Tricks and Conundrums with Answers.* New York: Pinnacle Books, 1976.

ANTANACLASIS. See PUN.

ANTANACLASIS CONUNDRUM. See CONUNDRUM.

ANTIGRAM. See ANAGRAM; FLAT.

ANTONYM is a word having the opposite or nearly the opposite meaning of another word.

Here are some antonyms for the word ''proof'': disproof, disproval, confutation, rebuttal, refutation, refutal, invalidation, retort, contradiction, negation.

Antonyms can be combined with other forms of word play, such as beheadments, to create slightly more sophisticated versions. For example, antonymic beheadments are beheadments in which the original word and the beheaded word are antonyms, e.g., bridge: to connect; abridge: to cut off.

Dmitri Borgmann, *Beyond Language: Adventures in Word and Thought,* discusses a form of word play based on finding Synonyms which are also antonyms, e.g. with/for (with can be either for or against; for can be either in favor of or against).

For numerous forms of word play with which antonyms can be combined, refer to Flat. See also Synonym.

BIBLIOGRAPHY

Borgmann, Dmitri A. *Beyond Language: Adventures in Word and Thought.* New York: Charles Scribner's Sons, 1967.

Lewis, Norman, ed. *The New Roget's Thesaurus of the English Language in Dictionary Form.* Lib. ed. New York: G. P. Putnam's Sons, 1978.

McKechnie, Jean L., et al. *Webster's New Twentieth Century Dictionary of the English Language: Unabridged.* 2d ed. New York: World Publishing Co., 1971.

Morris, William, and Mary Morris. *Dictionary of Contemporary Usage.* New York: Harper & Row, 1985.

APHORISM. See PROVERB.

APPROPRIATE NAMES. See PUN.

ARENA is a game of alternating vowels and consonants.

Players have ten minutes to come up with as many words as they can which have five letters and consist of alternating vowels and consonants, as is the case with the game's title. The words must begin with a vowel, e.g., emery, elide, image, elite, irony.

BIBLIOGRAPHY

Brandreth, Gyles. *The World's Best Indoor Games.* New York: Pantheon Books, 1981.

ARITHMETICAL RESTORATION. See CRYPT-ARITHMETIC.

ARROW OF LETTERS, also called verbal sprouts, is a game involving the building up of words.

It was thought up by Michael Grendon and first published in *Games and Puzzles.*

On a plain piece of paper, each player in turn writes a letter within a circle in a straight line, until a four-letter word has been made. The four letters must be different and must form a word:

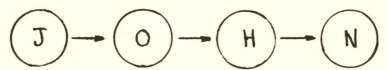

Then each player in turn adds a new letter (letters may not be repeated) and draws arrows to form his new word:

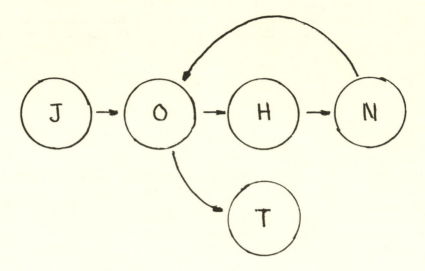

Each player scores one point for each letter he uses in each word formed by the addition of his letters.
Additional rules:

1. Words may only be made by following the direction of the arrows.

2. Arrows may not cross one another.

3. No encircled letters may be attached to more than four arrows.

4. No given pair of letters may be connected by more than one arrow (one direction only).

5. A shorter word may not be counted if it is contained within a longer word.

   For similar word play refer to Add-on, Ghost and Superghost, and Progressive Anagram.

BIBLIOGRAPHY

Eckler, A. Ross. *Word Recreations: Games and Diversions from "Word Ways."* New York: Dover, 1979.

Parlett, David. *Botticelli and Beyond: Over 100 of the World's Best Word Games.* New York: Pantheon Books, 1981.

A TO Z BANQUET is a memory game.
   The first player begins with "I went to a banquet and ate some (a)nchovies" (a word beginning with A).
   The next player continues, "I went to a banquet and ate some (a)nchovies and some (b)eets" (a word beginning with A and a word beginning with B).

This continues through the alphabet.

For similar games refer to Alphabent, Alphabetical Adjectives, Alphabet Poetry, Alphabetter, Alphabet Word Chain, I Gave My Love, I Love My Love, I Packed My Bag, I Went to Market, and Travelling Alphabet.

BIBLIOGRAPHY

Parlett, David. *Botticelli and Beyond: Over 100 of the World's Best Word Games.* New York: Pantheon Books, 1981.

AUTANTONYMS are games and puzzles employing words with multiple meanings, one of which, through some strange turn in the growth of the language, is the opposite of another meaning.

Here are some examples of autantonyms:

```
Let = to allow
    = to hinder
Cleave = to cut apart
       = to cling together
Fast = quick
     = to hold still or solid
Weather = to last
        = to wear out
Bad = not good
    = extra good
```

As a game autantonyms can be played as follows. Each player makes a list of autantonyms. Then each player in turn reads the two definitions for each of his autantonyms and allows the other players to try and guess the word that both definitions fit. The player who guesses the most words wins.

For similar word play refer to Anagram, Antonym, Flat, and Synonym.

BIBLIOGRAPHY

Shipley, Joseph T. *Playing with Words.* Englewood Cliffs, N.J.: Prentice-Hall, 1960.

A WAS AN APPLE PIE is a traditional children's game based on finding verbs for successive letters of the alphabet.

The idea is to supply verbs beginning with each letter of the alphabet in turn and having something to do with the first sentence: "A was an apple pie."

Here is an example:

B baked it; C created it; D donated it; E eats it; F found it; G grew the apples; H heated it in the oven; I ignored it; J joked about it; K kneaded the dough; L loved the smell of it; M mooched it; N named it Pie Deluxe; O opened the oven door to smell it; P prepared the apples; Q quaked at the thought of eating it; R relished the taste of it; T took it to the table; U uncovered it; V valued it; W welcomed it; X x-rayed it; Y yearned for it; Z zigzagged to the table for a piece.

As in most alphabet games, the letters X and Z may be omitted.

For similar word play refer to Alphabent, Alphabetical Adjectives, Alphabet Poetry, Alphabet Word Chain, A to Z Banquet, I Love My Love, I Went to Market, and Travelling Alphabet.

BIBLIOGRAPHY

Brandreth, Gyles. *The World's Best Indoor Games.* New York: Pantheon Books, 1981.

B

BACKENFORTH is a game involving the ability to guess words when they are spelled backwards.

One player reads a word backwards. The first player to call it out forward gets a point and the caller gets a point. Only the caller is allowed to write the word down. Whoever guesses the word becomes the next caller.

For additional word play of this type refer to Accidental Language, Anagram, Back Slang, Boner, Irish Bull, Malapropism, Spoonerism, and Wellerism.

BIBLIOGRAPHY

Parlett, David. *Botticelli and Beyond: Over 100 of the World's Best Word Games*. New York: Pantheon Books, 1981.

BACK SLANG, also called bacronym, is writing or saying words backwards.

The object is generally to come up with amusing phrases, expressions, or sounds by writing or saying words backwards.

Here is an example of a poem employing back slang:

A nam of htlaew and emaf
Fell in evol with a princess erup,
But he looked like a gip
And dellems like a god;
So ehs said ehs dah to throw-up.

Back slang forces the reader to create an artificial dialect similar to but slightly different from the artificial dialects discussed in the entry on Abbreviations.

Back slang also reveals some interesting Puns (as in "god/dog" above) by offering fresh juxtapositions of seemingly unrelated words (graphic or phonic metaphors).

For similar word play and more detailed discussions, refer to Abbreviations, Accidental Language, Anagram, Backenforth, Boner, Irish Bull, Malapropism, Pun, Spoonerism, and Wellerism.

BIBLIOGRAPHY

Borgmann, Dmitri A. *Beyond Language: Adventures in Word and Thought*. New York: Charles Scribner's Sons, 1967.
————. *Language on Vacation: An Olio of Orthographical Oddities*. New York: Charles Scribner's Sons, 1965.
Brandreth, Gyles. *The World's Best Indoor Games*. New York: Pantheon Books, 1981.
Corbett, Edward P. J. *Classical Rhetoric for the Modern Student*. 2d ed. New York: Oxford University Press, 1971.
Espy, Willard R. *A Children's Almanac of Words at Play*. New York: Clarkson N. Potter, Inc., 1982.
McKechnie, Jean L., et al. *Webster's New Twentieth Century Dictionary of the English Language: Unabridged*. 2d ed. New York: World Publishing Co., 1971.
Parlett, David. *Botticelli and Beyond: Over 100 of the World's Best Word Games*. New York: Pantheon Books, 1981.

BACKSWITCH. See FLAT.

BACKWARD SPELLING. See BACK SLANG.

BACRONYM. See BACK SLANG.

BALL BOUNCING RHYMES are verses said to the bouncing of a ball.

Roger D. Abrahams quotes the following example in his book *Jump-Rope Rhymes: A Dictionary,* noting that it is commonly used for ball-bouncing:

One, two, three, O'lary (O'Leary)
My first name is Mary,
Don't you think that I look cute,
In my papa's bathing suit?

For similar word play refer to Acting Out Rhymes, Counting Rhymes, Dialogue Games, Hand Clapping Rhymes, and Jump Rope Rhymes.

BIBLIOGRAPHY

Abrahams, Roger D., ed. *Jump-Rope Rhymes: A Dictionary*. Austin: University of Texas, 1969.
Abrahams, Roger D., and Lois Rankin, eds. *Counting-Out Rhymes: A Dictionary*. Austin: University of Texas, 1980.
Carpenter, Humphrey, and Mari Prichard. *The Oxford Companion to Children's Literature*. New York: Oxford University Press, 1984.

Opie, Peter, and Iona Opie. *Children's Games in Street and Playground.* 1969. Reprint. New York: Oxford University Press, 1979.
_____. *The Lore and Language of Schoolchildren.* 1959. Reprint. New York: Oxford University Press, 1980.
_____. *The Oxford Dictionary of Nursery Rhymes.* 1951. Reprint. New York: Oxford University Press, 1983.
_____. *The Oxford Nursery Rhyme Book.* 1955. Reprint. New York: Oxford University Press, 1984.

BANANAS. See TEAPOT.

BAXTERISM. See PUN.

BEHEADING, also called decapitation, is the removal of the first letter(s) of a word to form another (generally amusing) word, e.g., date/ate.

The National Puzzlers' League includes this (under the title beheadment) as one of the standard Flats.

The National Puzzlers' League has also come up with a game based on beheading. The object is to list twenty-six words, starting with the successive letters of the alphabet, which, when beheaded, form other words. One point is given for each letter of the word after the beheading takes place. According to David Parlett, if the main entries in the *Merriam-Webster Pocket Dictionary* are established as the possible word list, the highest possible score is 199 points.

Refer to Flat and Teetotaler for additional word play of this type.

BIBLIOGRAPHY

Borgmann, Dmitri A. *Beyond Language: Adventures in Word and Thought.* New York: Charles Scribner's Sons, 1967.
_____. *Language on Vacation: An Olio of Orthographical Oddities.* New York: Charles Scribner's Sons, 1965.
Gardner, Martin. "Mathematical Games: The flip strip sonnet, the lipogram, and other mad modes of word play," *Scientific American* (February 1977):121–125.
Parlett, David. *Botticelli and Beyond: Over 100 of the World's Best Word Games.* New York: Pantheon Books, 1981.

BINADE. See FLAT.

BLACK SQUARES is an extremely sophisticated form of Crossword Puzzle.

It was first developed by Harry Woolerton and later refined by David Parlett.

Players each obtain a sheet of squared grid (inked or printed, not penciled). David Parlett suggests a grid of about eleven by eleven squares for a quick game of about two hours.

The game is based on crossword puzzle rules that demand that adjacent letters form words in both directions and that all words must connect up with the puzzle.

Proper nouns and phrases are usually outlawed, and all words must be found in a nearby dictionary.

The object is not to form words, but to identify black squares or prove that an opponent's claim of a black square can actually be filled with a letter.

A black square is one where a letter cannot be added to form part of a genuine crossword. For example, if "fruity" were entered it would be possible to claim a black square on both sides, since (as far as I can tell) no words can be formed by adding letters in either direction. A black square could not be claimed either before or after "eat," however, because words can be formed in either direction, e.g., "meat," "eaten."

The object, then, is to avoid completing a word such as "fruity," unless it is next to the edge of the grid or a black square already formed. Otherwise, the other player will pencil in the black squares.

Pencils should be used for the original markings, as successfully challenged letters or black squares will need to be erased. Accepted letters and black squares can be inked in.

Each player always starts his turn by either challenging letters or black squares, and ends it by penciling in.

The play proceeds as follows:

The first player enters any letter in the center square:

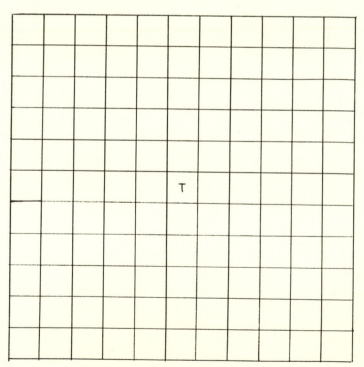

First player places a T in the center square.

Thereafter, each player in turn either challenges the previous move or inks it in, and then either claims one or more black squares or pencils in one or more letters. (He cannot both claim black squares and enter new letters in the same turn.)

Entering letters: Letters entered on the grid may either extend an existing word, form a complete word, or form a sequence leading to another word. A player may enter as many letters as he wishes anywhere on the board, as long as they line up with another letter already accepted, either directly or through other letters placed on the grid. The letters must be capable of being turned into a word.

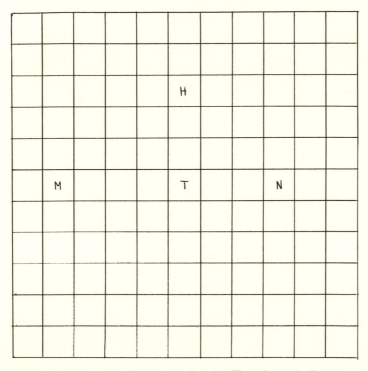

Second player adds an H, an N, and an M. First player challenges M.

Challenging: Letters may be challenged on two grounds: 1) they do not form a valid word; 2) they cannot be properly connected to already existing words. If a challenge is successful, the player challenged must simply remove the wrong letters and enter different letters (the only penalty is that he can enter only letters at this time, not black squares). If the challenged player successfully defends his letters, then he may ink in all of the necessary connections and claim any resulting black squares.

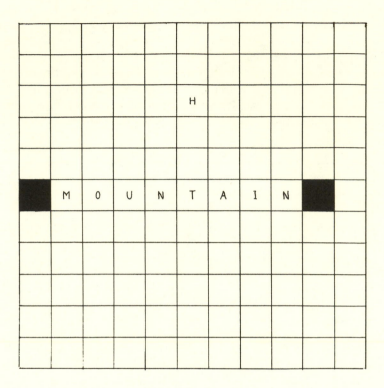

Second player pencils in "Mountain" and fills in black squares. First player accepts the square next to M and inks it in (thus giving the second player one point), but challenges the black square next to N successfully by adding an S (first player receives one point).

Claiming black squares: To claim a black square a player simply pencils a line through it. If the claim is successful, then the square is inked in. A player may claim more than one black square in a turn. Players receive one point for each successfully claimed black square.

Challenging black squares: If an opponent accepts the penciled-in black squares, he simply inks them in. If the opponent does not accept the black squares, then he must pencil in the letters necessary to indicate why the black squares are incorrect. After this, the opponent continues as if he were just starting his turn. (He receives one point for each disproved black square.)

First player continues his turn by adding H, T, and L.

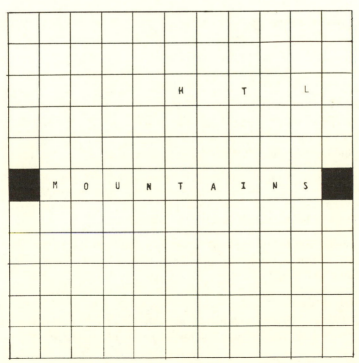

Second player claims a black square after S.

Additional rules:

1. A black square cannot be successfully claimed unless it must be a black square. If one of two squares must be black, then that does not yet indicate which must be black.
2. The game ends when both players pass. This may and most likely will be before all of the possible words or black squares have been filled in. There may come a time when neither player wishes to move, because a move will only give the opponent a black square.
3. If a player accepts the letters of his opponent and inks them in, then the opponent successfully challenges the inked in letters, simply white out the inked-in letters.
4. If an accepted misspelled word is inked in, the misspelling must then be accepted.

For similar word play refer to Across-tic, Acrostic, Crossword Puzzle, Forms, Lynx, Magic Word Squares, Pi, and SCRABBLE.

BIBLIOGRAPHY

Parlett, David. *Botticelli and Beyond: Over 100 of the World's Best Word Games.* New York: Pantheon Books, 1981.

BLANKIE. See PROGRESSIVE ANAGRAM.

BLANK VERSE. See BOUTS RIMÉS.

BLOT AND CARRY. See MEANDER.

BONER is an accidental or sometimes intentional exchange of one word for a similar sounding word resulting in a humorous statement; it is a Pun of paronomasia.

Joseph T. Shipley, *Playing with Words,* quotes the following example from Sir Walter Scott's *Ivanhoe* (1819): "The schoolboy said, 'Brian asked Rebecca to be his mistress, and she *reclined* to do so.' "

As Shipley states in "Word and Letter Games":

The presenting of amusingly irrelevant images, as in Wellerisms; and the humorous perverting of a thought by the misapplication of words, as in malapropisms, boners, and bulls, may have analogues in actual blunders but are for the most part deliberate, a source of fun in books and plays, and stimulants to word games.

For similar sources of word play refer to Accidental Language, Back Slang, Burlesque, Cliché, Conundrum, Irish Bull, Malapropism, Parody, Pun, Spoonerism, and Wellerism.

BIBLIOGRAPHY

Shipley, Joseph T. *Playing with Words.* Englewood Cliffs, N.J.: Prentice-Hall, 1960.
————. "Word and Letter Games." In *Encyclopaedia Britannica: Macropaedia.* 1979.

BOOK CONVERSATION is punning on the titles of books and authors' names.

John G. Fuller, *Games for Insomniacs,* states that John Porter, a sports car racer, gave him this game. The idea is to take the name of a book or an author and unite it with a Cliché that plays on the title or name (e.g., "Have you read *The Scarlet Letter?* Yes, it turned me <u>red</u> with embarrassment").

For similar word play refer to Captions Courageous, Fractured Book-Reviews, Fractured Geography, Fractured Industry, Pun, and Subject Matter.

BIBLIOGRAPHY

Fuller, John G. *Games for Insomniacs; or, A Lifetime Supply of Insufferable Brain Twisters.* New York: Doubleday, 1966.

BOSS. See RATE YOUR MIND PAL.

BOTTICELLI, also called "Who am I?," is a guessing game.

The quizzer assumes an identity and gives the initial of the identity's major name.

The questioners then ask specific questions of the quizzer. The quizzer must name the person the question refers to or submit to a general yes/no question.

This continues until the questioners guess the identity's name.

Here is an example:

The quizzer gives the clue "D."
Q: Are you a baseball player?
A: No, I am not Joe DiMaggio.
Q: Are you good with a slingshot?
A: No, I am not the David who killed Goliath.
Q: Did you sing with Tony Orlando?
A: The quizzer does not know the answer (Dawn) and so must submit to a general question.
Q: Are you male?
A: Yes.
Eventually someone asks if the quizzer is a famous Kentucky frontiersman and the quizzer must admit that he is Daniel Boone.

For similar word play refer to Adverbs, Aesop's Mission, Alphabetical Adjectives, Charades, First Letters, Initial Answers, Initial Game, Initial Goals, Leading Lights, Password, Quick Thinking, Shouting Proverbs, Taboo, Teapot, and Twenty Questions.

BIBLIOGRAPHY

Brandreth, Gyles. *Indoor Games.* London: Hodder & Stoughton, Ltd., 1977.
_____. *The World's Best Indoor Games.* New York: Pantheon Books, 1981.

Parlett, David. *Botticelli and Beyond: Over 100 of the World's Best Word Games*. New
    York: Pantheon Books, 1981.
Sharp, Richard, and John Piggott. *The Book of Games*. New York: Galahad Books, 1977.

BOUTS RIMÉS, also called rhyming ends, is a game involving end rhymes.
Its origin is uncertain. However, according to C. C. Bombaugh, *Gleanings for
the Curious* (1890), Goujet claims that it was invented by Dulot, a French poet.
    At least four rhyming words are distributed, and each player is asked to write a
verse using those words as end rhymes. Bombaugh offers the following example:

The words chosen for end rhymes are: nettle, pains, mettle, remains, natures, rebel,
graters, and well. The resulting verse is:

Tender-handed stroke a nettle,
    And it stings you for your pains;
Grasp it like a man of mettle,
    And it soft as silk remains.
'Tis the same with common natures,
    Use them kindly, they rebel;
But be rough as nutmeg-graters,
    And the rogues obey you well.

Willard R. Espy, *The Game of Words*, points out that William Cole came
across the following variation in a Victorian volume, *Evening Amusements:
Mirthful Games, Shadow Plays, Chemical Surprises, Fireworks, Forfeit, Etc.*:
One person reads a line of poetry to which another must supply a line corresponding to the first line's measure, rhyme, and sense.
    Another variation, sometimes called blank verse (only vaguely related to the
important form of dramatic and epic poetry employed by Shakespeare and
Milton), requires that each player write down a line of verse, fold his paper so
that only the final word is visible, and pass his paper to the right. The process is
repeated until four lines of verse have been written on each piece of paper (the
fourth ending in a word that rhymes with one of the previous lines). The papers
are then unfolded and the resulting verses read out loud.
    For similar word play refer to Answer Verse, Bouts Rimés Retournés, Cento,
Charades, Clerihew, Constructapo, Crambo, Homosyntaxism, Pass It On, Pass
Rhyme, and Renga.

BIBLIOGRAPHY

Bombaugh, C. C. *Gleanings for the Curious*. 1890. Reprint. *Oddities and Curiosities of
    Words and Literature*, ed. Martin Gardner. New York: Dover, 1961.
Espy, Willard R. *The Game of Words*. New York: Grosset & Dunlap, 1972.
Holman, C. Hugh. *A Handbook to Literature*. 4th ed. Indianapolis: Bobbs-Merrill Educa-
    tional Publishing, 1980.
Shipley, Joseph T. *Playing with Words*. Englewood Cliffs, N.J.: Prentice-Hall, 1960.
———. "Word and Letter Games." In *Encyclopaedia Britannica: Macropaedia*. 1979.

BOUTS RIMÉS RETOURNÉS is a variation on Bouts Rimés where the end rhymes from a poem are reversed and the challenge is to write another poem from the reversed end rhymes, the final word of the final line becoming the final word of the first line, and so on.

For more detailed discussion and additional word play, refer to Answer Verse, Bouts Rimés, Clerihew, and Pass It On.

BIBLIOGRAPHY

Bombaugh, C. C. *Gleanings for the Curious.* 1890. Reprint. *Oddities and Curiosities of Words and Literature,* ed. Martin Gardner. New York: Dover, 1961.

BUILDING BLOCKS is a name given by Joseph T. Shipley to various games and puzzles involving building words from common word stems.

One such game is to pick a common word stem (Latin and Greek stems work well) and have players attempt to come up with as many words containing that stem as they can in a set amount of time. Here are two examples:

Soph (wise): phil<u>osoph</u>y, <u>soph</u>omore, <u>soph</u>istry
Log (talk): dia<u>log</u>ue, eu<u>log</u>y, bio<u>log</u>y

For similar word play refer to Acrosticals, Add-on, Alfabits, Anablank, Anagame, Build-ups, Crossword Puzzle, Flat, Last Word, Name in Vain, Palindrome, Reversible Anagram, Scramblegram, Word Knock-downs, and Word Ping-Pong.

BIBLIOGRAPHY

Shipley, Joseph T. *Playing with Words.* Englewood Cliffs, N.J.: Prentice-Hall, 1960.

BUILD-UPS are series of words built on a given letter.

In each step a letter is added to form a new word that fits a given definition. Here is an example:

Letter chosen:	E	
Given question:	What I call myself. Answer:	ME
Given question:	Opposite of women. Answer:	MEN
Given question:	Not nice. Answer:	MEAN
Given question:	Intended. Answer:	MEANT

For similar word play refer to Acrosticals, Add-on, Alfabits, Anablank, Anagame, Anagram, Antigram, Building Blocks, Crossword Puzzle, Flat, Last Word, Name in Vain, Palindrome, Reversible Anagram, Scramblegram, Word Knock-downs, and Word Ping-Pong.

BIBLIOGRAPHY

Shipley, Joseph T. *Playing with Words.* Englewood Cliffs, N.J.: Prentice-Hall, 1960.

BULL. See IRISH BULL.

BURIED WORDS are words hidden in sentences.
Here is an example:

My brother is a moron. Who is my brother? (answer: Sam)

As a game, players can make up sentences with buried words and challenge other players to come up with the words in a certain time period, scoring one point for each word or letter.

For similar word play refer to Charades, Cipher, Code, Flat, and Hidden Names.

BIBLIOGRAPHY

Dudeney, Henry Ernest. *300 Best Word Puzzles.* New York: Charles Scribner's Sons, 1968.
Espy, Willard R. *A Children's Almanac of Words at Play.* New York: Clarkson N. Potter, Inc., 1982.
Shipley, Joseph T. *Playing with Words.* Englewood Cliffs, N.J.: Prentice-Hall, 1960.

BURLESQUE is a particularly indecorous form of Parody (a comic imitation of a serious poem).

Lewis Carroll wrote a number of burlesques. The following is a burlesque of Jane Taylor's "The Star":

Twinkle, twinkle little bat!
How I wonder what you're at!
Up above the world you fly,
Like a teatray in the sky.

For similar word play refer to Accidental Language, Back Slang, Conundrum, Irish Bull, Malapropism, Parody, Pun, Spoonerism, and Wellerism.

BIBLIOGRAPHY

Espy, Willard R. *An Almanac of Words at Play.* New York: Clarkson N. Potter, Inc., 1975.
_____. *The Game of Words.* New York: Grosset & Dunlap, 1972.
Gardner, Martin. "Notes." In *Oddities and Curiosities of Words and Literature.* New York: Dover, 1961.

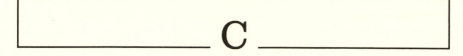

C

CALENDAR VERSE is a form of Acrostic where each line begins with a successive day of the week or month of the year.

Recent recordings by the Beatles, *Lady Madonna,* and Neil Sedaka, *Calendar Girl,* are examples of this, as are a number of Nursery Rhymes. Perhaps the best known is "Monday's Child":

Monday's child is fair of face,
Tuesday's child is full of grace,
Wednesday's child is full of woe,
Thursday's child has far to go,
Friday's child is loving and giving,
Saturday's child works hard for a living,
And the child that is born on the Sabbath day
Is bonny and blithe, and good and gay.
("Sunday's child is full of grace" is often substituted for the final day.)

A more sophisticated form allows for each line to start with the first syllable of a day or month, e.g., money for Monday.

For similar word play refer to Acromania, Across-tic, Acrostic, Acrosticals, Alliteration, Alphabent, Alphabetical Adjectives, Alphabet Pyramids, Alphabet Word Chain, Animal Alphabet, I Gave My Love, I Love My Love, I Packed My Bag, I Went to Market, Looks Like Poetry, Single-Rhymed Alphabet, and Spine Poetry.

BIBLIOGRAPHY

Espy, Willard R. *An Almanac of Words at Play.* New York: Clarkson N. Potter, Inc., 1975.

Gensler, Kinereth, and Nina Nyhart. *The Poetry Connection: An Anthology of Contemporary Poems with Ideas to Stimulate Children's Writing.* New York: Teachers & Writers, 1978.

Opie, Peter, and Iona Opie. *Children's Games in Street and Playground.* 1969. Reprint. New York: Oxford University Press, 1979.

———. *The Lore and Language of Schoolchildren.* 1959. Reprint. New York: Oxford University Press, 1980.

———. *The Oxford Dictionary of Nursery Rhymes.* 1951. Reprint. New York: Oxford University Press, 1983.

———. *The Oxford Nursery Rhyme Book.* 1955. Reprint. New York: Oxford University Press, 1984.

CAP ME is a round robin game involving the building of words.

Each player is given a number for identification. He writes his number and next to it a one-syllable word.

The papers are passed to the right, and each player must add onto the word, creating a new word. (Players place their number next to the new word they have added.) If a player cannot think of a new word he leaves the line blank.

Before passing the sheets to the right again, each player adds an additional one-syllable word to the sheet, meaning that now there are two sets of words being passed. This continues, each player attempting to add new syllables to each set of words as it is passed to him (and initialing his additions) until the papers have reached their original owners.

If a one-syllable word goes around without anyone adding to it, the originator of the word gets ten points if he can add to it, but loses ten points if he cannot. Players receive two points for each syllable they add and lose five points for wrong words.

For similar word play refer to Acrosticals, Add-on, Alfabits, Anablank, Anagame, Anagram, Crossword Puzzle, Flat, Last Word, Name in Vain, Palindrome, Progressive Anagram, SCRABBLE, Scramblegram, Word Knockdowns, and Word Ping-Pong.

BIBLIOGRAPHY

Shipley, Joseph T. *Playing with Words.* Englewood Cliffs, N.J.: Prentice-Hall, 1960.

CAPTIONS COURAGEOUS is a game in which captions are created for illustrations.

David Parlett developed this game from two books of the same name by Bob Reisner. Reisner's books consisted of famous paintings with humorous captions appended, e.g., for Jean Millet's *The Gleaners:* "On your mark, get set, go."

In Parlett's game, each player provides several sheets of paper upon which he has placed a cut-out illustration from a magazine or newspaper. The best illustrations are those which have a legitimate caption. (Such captions should be separated from the illustrations and listed on a separate sheet of paper.)

A player is chosen as the "quizzer." The player who brought each illustration in turn submits the real caption to the quizzer. The illustration is passed around, and each of the other players makes up a caption for it. These are also turned in to the quizzer.

The illustration (captionless) is passed around again, and each of the suggested captions (including the real caption) is read. The players vote on the correct caption.

Each player is awarded one point for voting on the correct caption, plus one point for each vote on the caption he created. The person who brought the illustration gets one point per person if no one guesses his caption.

The game continues in this manner, each player in turn submitting an illustration, each player in turn serving as the quizzer.

For similar word play refer to Book Conversation, Conundrum, Defective Detective, Fractured Book-Reviews, Fractured Geography, Fractured Industry, MADvertisements, Pun, and Subject Matter.

BIBLIOGRAPHY

Parlett, David. *Botticelli and Beyond: Over 100 of the World's Best Word Games.* New York: Pantheon Books, 1981.

CAR GAME is a traditional travelling game involving the creation of words from license plates.

The object is to take the letters of a license plate and create words which use those letters in the order of their appearance on the license plate.

Here is an example:

The license plate has: FNH 307
A possible solution is: Funhouse

When played as a game, each contestant seeks to come up with a solution first. The winner is the contestant who reaches an established number of first solutions before the rest of the players.

A more common, though less demanding, license plate game requires simply that the players work their way through the alphabet finding the letters sequentially on passing license plates (often other sources of letters are allowed, e.g., road signs).

Refer to Ultraghost for a similar word game and to Alphabet Poetry for other puzzles and games based on the alphabet.

BIBLIOGRAPHY

Fixx, James. *Solve It! A Perplexing Profusion of Puzzles.* New York: Doubleday, 1978.
Parlett, David. *Botticelli and Beyond: Over 100 of the World's Best Word Games.* New York: Pantheon Books, 1981.

CATCH is a Riddle in which the question or clue is definitely intended to mislead, often based on a Pun.

Here is an example:

"If you think you're such a good speller that you can even spell Mississippi, then tell me how many ss's are in <u>it</u>?"
"Four."
"Wrong. <u>It</u> has no s's."

For similar word play refer to Boner, Burlesque, Conundrum, Irish Bull, Malapropism, Parody, Pun, Riddle, Spoonerism, and Wellerism.

BIBLIOGRAPHY

Shipley, Joseph T. *Playing with Words.* Englewood Cliffs, N.J.: Prentice-Hall, 1960.

CATEGORIES. See CATEGORY PUZZLES.

CATEGORY COLUMNS. See ACROSTIC.

CATEGORY COUNTERTYPES is a game requiring classification.

It was created by William and Mary Morris, *The Word Game Book* (1959).

Each player starts with a pencil and a piece of paper. Five categories of persons, places, and things are agreed on. A time limit is set.

Either one category is selected at a time, and the players list as many names as they can think of in the set time, or all categories are done at the same time.

The winner is the person who lists the most names.

For similar word play refer to Category Puzzles and Guggenheim.

BIBLIOGRAPHY

Morris, William, and Mary Morris. *The Word Game Book.* New York: Harper & Brothers, 1959.

CATEGORY PUZZLES, also called categories and initialettes, is a form of word play involving definitions, classification, Anagrams, and Beheading.

In the standard category puzzle, a number of definitions are given, one for each of a list of words that contain other words within them (Progressive Anagrams in reverse) that fit into a chosen category:

The category chosen is baseball.
The definitions are as follows:
humble, degrade:
wash, clean:
an inflatable rubber bag:

The first step, then, is to figure out the words being defined:

humble, degrade: abase
wash, clean: bath
an inflatable rubber bag: balloon

The next step is to find the word contained within each of the defined words that fits the chosen category:

<u>aba</u>se
<u>bath</u>
<u>ball</u>oon

Similar word play known as categories or initialettes involves finding words that fit selected classifications and start with a certain letter of the alphabet.

According to Gyles Brandreth, the following version was a popular Victorian parlor game. A set of category headings (twenty is a suitable number) is agreed upon. Each player lists the categories down the left side of his paper. A letter of the alphabet is selected at random (though it would be best to avoid q, x, z, j, k, u, v, and y).

Each player then tries to find an example for each category that begins with the letter chosen. Players score one point for each category filled. Scoring may be varied by offering fewer points for duplicated answers.

For similar word play refer to Acrosticals, Add-on, Alfabits, Anablank, Anagame, Cap Me, Crossword Puzzle, Flat, Guggenheim, Last and First, Last Word, Name in Vain, Palindrome, Progressive Anagram, Reversible Anagram, SCRABBLE, Scramblegram, Word Knock-downs, and Word Ping-Pong.

BIBLIOGRAPHY

Brandreth, Gyles. *Indoor Games*. London: Hodder & Stoughton, Ltd., 1977.
————. *The World's Best Indoor Games*. New York: Pantheon Books, 1981.
Espy, Willard R. *The Game of Words*. New York: Grosset & Dunlap, 1972.
Hart, Harold H. *Grab a Pencil*. New York: Hart Publ. Co., 1958.
Morris, William, and Mary Morris. *The Word Game Book*. New York: Harper & Brothers, 1959.
Parlett, David. *Botticelli and Beyond: Over 100 of the World's Best Word Games*. New York: Pantheon Books, 1981.
Sharp, Richard, and John Piggott. *The Book of Games*. New York: Galahad Books, 1977.

CENTO, also called mosaic verse and Patchwork Poetry, is the taking of verses or phrases from different authors and patching them together; literally, a cloak of many patches.

According to C. C. Bombaugh, *Gleanings for the Curious* (1890), Ausonius, the author of the *Nuptial Cento,* first set down the rules as follows: the pieces may be taken from the same poet or from several; and the verses may be taken entire or divided into two, one half to be connected with another half taken from another place; but the two halves are never to be taken together.

The Empress Eudoxia, according to Bombaugh, wrote the life of Jesus Christ in centos taken from Homer, as did Proba Falconia and Alexander Ross with centos from Virgil.

Mark Twain's *The Adventures of Huckleberry Finn* contains an excellent example:

To be, or not to be; that is the bare bodkin
That makes calamity of so long life;
For who would fardels bear, till Birnam Wood do come to Dunsinane,
But that the fear of something after death
Murders the innocent sleep,
Great nature's second course,
And makes us rather sling the arrows of outrageous fortune
Than fly to others that we know not of.
There's the respect must give us pause:
Wake Duncan with thy knocking! I would thou couldst;
For who would bear the whips and scorns of time,
The oppressor's wrong, the proud man's contumely,
The law's delay, and the quietus which his pangs might take,
In the dead waste and middle of the night, when churchyards yawn
In customary suits of solemn black,
But that the undiscovered country from whose bourne no traveler returns,
Breathes forth contagion on the world,
And thus the native hue of resolution, like the poor cat i' the adage,
Is sicklied o'er with care,
And all the clouds that lowered o'er our housetops,
With this regard their currents turn awry,
And lose the name of action.
'Tis a consummation devoutly to be wished. But soft you, the fair Ophelia:
Ope not thy ponderous and marble jaws,
But get thee to a nunnery—go!

The following is one of a number of centos Bombaugh includes in *Gleanings for the Curious:*

LIFE

    1.—Why all this toil for triumphs of an hour?
    2.—Life's a short summer, man a flower.
    3.—By turns we catch the vital breath and die—
    4.—The cradle and the tomb, alas! so nigh.
    5.—To be is better far than not to be,
    6.—Though all man's life may seem a tragedy.
    7.—But light cares speak when mighty griefs are dumb;
    8.—The bottom is but shallow whence they come.
    9.—Your fate is but the common fate of all,
   10.—Unmingled joys, here, to no man befall.
   11.—Nature to each allots his proper sphere,
   12.—Fortune makes folly her peculiar care.
   13.—Custom does not often reason overrule
   14.—And throw a cruel sunshine on a fool.
   15.—Live well, how long or short permit, to heaven;
   16.—They who forgive most, shall be most forgiven.
   17.—Sin may be clasped so close we cannot see its face—

18.—Vile intercourse where virtue has not place.
19.—Then keep each passion down, however dear,
20.—Thou pendulum, betwixt a smile and tear;
21.—Her sensual snares let faithless pleasure lay,
22.—With craft and skill, to ruin and betray.
23.—Soar not too high to fall, but stop to rise;
24.—We masters grow of all that we despise.
25.—Oh then renounce that impious self-esteem;
26.—Riches have wings and grandeur is a dream.
27.—Think not ambition wise, because 'tis brave,
28.—The paths of glory lead but to the grave.
29.—What is ambition? 'Tis a glorious cheat,
30.—Only destructive to the brave and great.
31.—What's all the gaudy glitter of a crown?
32.—The way to bliss lies not on beds of down.
33.—How long we live, not years but actions tell;
34.—That man lives twice who lives the first life well.
35.—Make then, while yet ye may, your God your friend,
36.—Whom Christians worship, yet not comprehend.
37.—The trust that's given guard, and to yourself be just;
38.—For, live we how we can, yet die we must.

1. Young, 2. Dr. Johnson, 3. Pope, 4, Prior, 5. Sewell, 6. Spenser, 7. Daniel, 8. Sir Walter Raleigh, 9. Longfellow, 10. Southwell, 11. Congreve, 12. Churchill, 13. Rochester, 14. Armstrong, 15. Milton, 16. Baily, 17. Trench, 18. Somerville, 19. Thompson, 20. Byron, 21. Smollet, 22. Crabbe, 23. Massinger, 24. Crowley, 25. Beattie, 26. Cowper, 27. Sir Walter Davenant, 28. Gray, 29. Willis, 30. Addison, 31. Dryden, 32. Francis Quarles, 33. Watkins, 34. Herrick, 35. William Mason, 36. Hill, 37. Dana, 38. Shakespeare.

For similar word play refer to Constructapo, Homosyntaxism, Möbius Strip, Oulipo Algorithms, Perverb, and Slygram.

BIBLIOGRAPHY

Bombaugh, C. C. *Gleanings for the Curious.* 1890. Reprint. *Oddities and Curiosities of Words and Literature,* ed. Martin Gardner. New York: Dover, 1961.
Espy, Willard R. *The Game of Words.* New York: Grosset & Dunlap, 1972.
Shipley, Joseph T. *Playing with Words.* Englewood Cliffs, N.J.: Prentice-Hall, 1960.
Twain, Mark. *The Adventures of Huckleberry Finn (Tom Sawyer's Comrade).* New York: Charles L. Webster & Co., 1891.

CENTURION is a game combining language and mathematics.

The letters of the alphabet are assigned numerical value successively (A = 1, B = 2, C = 3, and so on).

The first player writes down a word whose combined numerical value is ten or less: ACE = 1 + 3 + 5 = 9.

The second player writes another three-letter word beginning with the final

letter of the first word, and indicates the total of all of the letters so far: EAT =
26 (5 + 1 + 20) + 9 = 35.

This continues until a three-digit total (100 or more) is reached. The player
who reaches it "bursts" and loses.

Double centurion can be played by three or more players with the burst score
upped to at least 200 points.

For other mathematical word play refer to ABC Words, ACE Words, Cipher,
Code, Crypt-Arithmetic, Flat, Inflation, Numwords, and Oulipo Algorithms.

BIBLIOGRAPHY

Parlett, David. *Botticelli and Beyond: Over 100 of the World's Best Word Games*. New
     York: Pantheon Books, 1981.

CHAINS, also called chain verse and concatenation, is a form of verse which
requires the repetition of the final word of each line at the beginning of the next
line.

According to C. C. Bombaugh, *Gleanings for the Curious* (1890), Lasphrise,
a French poet, claims to have invented it. Here are two examples Bombaugh
includes in his book and apparently wrote himself:

Truth

Nerve thy soul with doctrines noble,
    Noble in the walks of Time,
Time that leads to an eternal,
    An eternal life sublime;
Life sublime in moral beauty,
    Beauty that shall ever be,
Ever be to lure thee onward,
    Onward to the fountain free;
Free to every earnest seeker,
    Seeker at the Fount of Youth,
Youth exultant in its beauty,
    Beauty found in the quest of Truth.

Trying Skying

Long I looked into the sky,
    Sky aglow with gleaming stars,
Stars that stream their courses high,
    High and grand, those golden cars,
Cars that ever keep their track,
    Track untraced by human ray,
Ray that zones the zodiac,
    Zodiac with milky-way,
Milky-way where worlds are sown,
    Sown like sands along the sea,
Sea whose tide and tone e'er own,
    Own a feeling to be free,

Free to leave its lowly place,
  Place to prove with yonder spheres,
Spheres that trace all through all space,
  Space and years—unspoken years.

According to S. L. Mooney, the repeated sound must carry a different meaning.

For similar word play refer to Echoes, Heads and Tails, Last and First, Overlaps, and Tell-A-Tall-Tale.

BIBLIOGRAPHY

Bombaugh, C. C. *Gleanings for the Curious*. 1890. Reprint. *Oddities and Curiosities of Words and Literature*, ed. Martin Gardner. New York: Dover, 1961.
Eckler, A. Ross. *Word Recreations: Games and Diversions from "Word Ways."* New York: Dover, 1979.
Espy, Willard R. *The Game of Words*. New York: Grosset & Dunlap, 1972.
Mooney, S. L. "Chain Rhyme." In *Encyclopedia of Poetry and Poetics*. Princeton: Princeton University Press, 1965.

CHAIN VERSE. See CHAINS.

CHARADES is a game involving the solving of syllables of a word or phrase; also, a form of word play involving the division of words, phrases, or sentences to create different meanings.

The word "charade" comes either from the Italian word *schiarare*, which means to unravel or clear up, or, according to Gyles Brandreth, Eric Partridge, and Joseph T. Shipley, from the Spanish word *charrade*, which means the chatter of clowns.

The term is used to designate a number of forms of word play which fall into two general categories: written, and acted out.

The standard written form, also called punctuation puzzles and shifty sentences, goes as follows: A clue is given for the first syllable of a word; a clue is given for the second syllable of the word; and a clue is given for the entire word:

Airplane = the word.
1. My first syllable is something you breathe. (air)
2. My second syllable is a flat space. (plane)
3. My whole is a flying machine. (airplane)

Another form of written charades involves the breaking up of words, phrases, or sentences at different points to produce different meanings:

1. I ran over; John and Bill wished I hadn't.
2. I ran over John, and Bill wished I hadn't.

The standard acting-out form of the game involves dividing players into two teams. One player from each team is given a word or phrase to act out; the object is to get his team to guess the word or phrase. The winning team is the one that guesses the phrase in the shortest amount of time.

According to Gyles Brandreth, this form of charades came to England in 1776 and had been transformed into its modern form by Victorian times. Charlotte Brontë includes a scene in *Jane Eyre* where members of the English upper class entertain themselves by playing charades. A description is also included in *Cassell's Book of In-Door Amusements, Card Games, and Fireside Fun* (1881).

In the mid-nineteenth century charades was a much more elaborate game than it is today. Players were divided up into two teams. One team chose a word or phrase which the other team had to guess. The team that knew the word or phrase then staged full-blown scenes (sometimes with dialogue, sometimes without) for each syllable of the word or phrase, thus incorporating drama into the game to a far greater extent than is the case today.

A sophisticated version of Crossword Puzzle combines the crossword puzzle with charades. Refer to Crossword Puzzle for a discussion of that form of word play.

BIBLIOGRAPHY

Adler, Irving, and Peggy Adler. *The Adler Book of Puzzles and Riddles, or Sam Loyd Up to Date.* New York: John Day Co., 1962.
Borgmann, Dmitri A. *Beyond Language: Adventures in Word and Thought.* New York: Charles Scribner's Sons, 1967.
_____. *Language on Vacation: An Olio of Orthographical Oddities.* New York: Charles Scribner's Sons, 1965.
Brandreth, Gyles. *Indoor Games.* London: Hodder & Stoughton, Ltd., 1977.
_____. *The World's Best Indoor Games.* New York: Pantheon Books, 1981.
Brontë, Charlotte [Currer Bell, pseud.]. *Jane Eyre.* London, 1847. Reprint. *The Complete Novels of Charlotte and Emily Brontë.* New York: Avenel Books, 1981.
Eckler, A. Ross. *Word Recreations: Games and Diversions from "Word Ways."* New York: Dover, 1979.
Espy, Willard R. *The Game of Words.* New York: Grosset & Dunlap, 1972.
Parlett, David. *Botticelli and Beyond: Over 100 of the World's Best Word Games.* New York: Pantheon Books, 1981.
Partridge, Eric. *Origins: A Short Etymological Dictionary of Modern English.* New York: Greenwich House, 1983.
Sharp, Richard, and John Piggott. *The Book of Games.* New York: Galahad Press, 1977.
Shipley, Joseph T. *Dictionary of Word Origins.* New York: Philosophical Library, 1945.
_____. *Playing with Words.* Englewood Cliffs, N.J.: Prentice-Hall, 1960.

CHARMS are verses or formulas credited with magical power; incantations or spells; or words, phrases, or songs spoken, chanted, or sung to invite supernatural powers.

Charms are among the earliest examples of recorded literature and accompany the magical rites of nearly all preliterate peoples. Though some people continue to consider charms seriously, charms are also central to a number of games and may be used to turn people into statues, to make them kiss, to make them perform silly stunts, or simply to make them be "it" for the next round of play.

Peter and Iona Opie quote a number of charms they have collected from all over the world in *The Lore and Language of Schoolchildren*. Here are two connected with games:

In the first one, a girl will say to regain her luck while skipping rope: "Touch wood, no good; / Touch iron, rely on."

In the second one, marble players in East Orange, New Jersey, say: "Roll, roll, tootsie roll, / Roll marble, in the hole."

For similar word play refer to Acting Out Rhymes, Ball Bouncing Rhymes, Counting Rhymes, Dialogue Games, Game Rhymes, Hand Clapping Rhymes, Incantations, Jump Rope Rhymes, Nursery Rhymes, Proverb, and Tongue Twister.

BIBLIOGRAPHY

Hoffman, Daniel G. "Charm." In *Encyclopedia of Poetry and Poetics*, ed. Alex Preminger. Princeton: Princeton University Press, 1965.
Leland, Charles Godfrey. *Gypsy Sorcery and Fortune Telling*. New York: University Books, 1963.
Norris, David, and Jacquemine Charrott-Lodwidge. *Book of Spells*. New York: Simon & Schuster, 1974.
Opie, Peter, and Iona Opie. *The Lore and Language of Schoolchilren*. 1959. Reprint. New York: Oxford University Press, 1980.
Sutton-Smith, Brian. *The Folkgames of Children*. Austin: University of Texas Press, 1972.

CHRONOGRAMS are Puns on the sounds of roman numerals, e.g., XL = excel (by sound); XL = forty (by number). They are puns of paronomasia.

Here is an example from William Shakespeare, *Love's Labour's Lost:*

If sore be sore, then L to sore makes fifty sores;
  o'sorel.
Of one sore I an hundred make, by adding but one more L.

According to C. C. Bombaugh, *Gleanings for the Curious* (1890), the title page of *Hugo Grotius His Sophompaneas* includes the publication date, 1652, in the author's name: Franci s Gold smith.

Refer to Pun for similar word play.

BIBLIOGRAPHY

Bombaugh, C. C. *Gleanings for the Curious*. 1890. Reprint. *Oddities and Curiosities of Words and Literature*, ed. Martin Gardner. New York: Dover, 1961.
Espy, Willard R. *The Game of Words*. New York: Grosset & Dunlap, 1972.
Shakespeare, William. *Love's Labour's Lost*. In *The Complete Signet Classic Shakespeare*, ed. S. Bennet. New York: Harcourt Brace Jovanovich, Inc., 1963.

CIPHER is a coded message, generally one in which each letter of the alphabet is represented by a different letter or symbol.

Ciphers generally fall into three categories: concealment ciphers, transposition ciphers, and substitution ciphers.

In a concealment cipher the true letters are hidden or disguised and are meant to pass unnoticed, as in written Charades.

In a transposition cipher the true letters are rearranged by some key or pattern, as in an Anagram.

In a substitution cipher the original letters are replaced with substitutes, as in a Rebus or various kinds of word play based on mathematics.

A cipher differs from a Code in that a code requires a code book or dictionary to decode and can only be successful if the symbols are applied in a purely haphazard manner.

For word play employing ciphers or similar to ciphers, refer to ABC Language, ABC Words, ACE Words, Anagram, Centurion, Charades, Code, Crypt-Arithmetic, Cryptic Quotes, Cryptogram, Flat, Numwords, Oulipo Algorithms, and Rebus.

BIBLIOGRAPHY

Borgmann, Dmitri A. *Language on Vacation: An Olio of Orthographical Oddities*. New York: Charles Scribner's Sons, 1965.

Gaines, Helen Fouché. *Cryptanalysis: A Study of Ciphers and Their Solution*. New York: Dover, 1939.

CIRCULAR REVERSALS are words which when written clockwise in a circle may be read counterclockwise, starting at a suitable point, to yield another word, phrase, or sentence; they are pictorial Palindromes.

Here is an example:

```
              p
      n               u
      o               t
            t i
```

Clockwise: put it on
Counterclockwise: not it up

For other word play employing palindromes refer to Acrosticals, Add-on, Alfabits, Anablank, Anagame, Anagram, Cap Me, Category Puzzles, Flat, Last Word, Name in Vain, Progressive Anagram, Reversible Anagram, Scramble-gram, Word Knock-downs, and Word Ping-Pong.

For other word play employing word pictures refer to Looks Like Poetry and Rebus.

BIBLIOGRAPHY

Bergerson, Howard W. *Palindromes and Anagrams*. New York: Dover, 1973.

Borgmann, Dmitri A. *Language on Vacation: An Olio of Orthographical Oddities*. New York: Charles Scribner's Sons, 1965.

CLERIHEW is a form of nonsense verse that offers a purposefully wrong-footed caricature of some person. It consists of four lines forming two rhyming couplets. The first couplet introduces the subject's name and ends with a rhyme for it. The rhymes are as awkward as possible. The number of accents in each line is irregular, and one line is often extended to tease the ear.

The clerihew was invented by Edmund Clerihew Bentley (1875–1956), a British journalist and writer of detective fiction and humorous poetry. He was born in London and educated at St. Paul's School and Merton College, Oxford (where he became friends with G. K. Chesterton, who later illustrated Bentley's first book of clerihews, *Biography for Beginners,* 1905). This book was followed by two additional books of clerihews, *More Biography* (1929) and *Baseless Biography* (1939), and by a collection of all his clerihews, *Clerihews Complete* (1951). Though devoting most of his time to journalism, in addition to his nonsense verse Bentley wrote *Trent's Last Case* (1913)—a landmark in detective fiction, bridging the romantic detective fiction of Sir Arthur Conan Doyle's Sherlock Holmes with the realistic detective fiction of the twentieth century—as well as a number of other Trent books and an autobiography, *Those Days* (1940).

Here is his first clerihew; he is said to have written it while being bored in a chemistry class:

Sir Christopher Wren
Said, "I am going to dine with some men.
If anybody calls
Say I am designing St. Paul's."

A number of twentieth-century writers and satirists have employed the clerihew. Some of the best examples are to be found in the works of W. H. Auden, Clifton Fadiman, and Sir Francis Meynell.

Here are some examples of my own:

"You've got it all wrong!" shouted Humpty.
"The Queen came along and she bumped me.
The King had no horses; the King had no men.
The Queen simply sewed me together again."

There once was a man named Roy Rogers,
Who never played ball with the Dodgers;
The only thing he could hit
Was a musical pitch.

President Nixon had plans
For all Americans,
But after the break-in at Watergate
Americans said, "Your plans can wait!"

For similar word play refer to Bouts Rimés, Double-Dactyl, Impossible Rhymes, and Limerick.

BIBLIOGRAPHY

Espy, Willard R. *An Almanac of Words at Play*. New York: Clarkson N. Potter, Inc., 1975.
————. *A Children's Almanac of Words at Play*. New York: Clarkson N. Potter, Inc., 1982.
————. *The Game of Words*. New York: Grosset & Dunlap, 1972.
Gardner, Martin. "Notes." In *Oddities and Curiosities of Words and Literature*. New York: Dover, 1961.
Hunt, Cecil. *Word Origins*. New York: Philosophical Library, 1949.
Shipley, Joseph T. *Playing with Words*. Englewood Cliffs, N.J.: Prentice-Hall, 1960.
————. "Word and Letter Games." In *Encyclopaedia Britannica: Macropaedia*. 1979.
Smith, A. J. M. "Clerihew." In *Encyclopedia of Poetry and Poetics*, ed. Alex Preminger. Princeton: Princeton University Press, 1966.

CLICHÉ is a trite, overused saying.

Joseph T. Shipley, *Dictionary of Word Origins*, offers the following etymology:

Cliché.
Used in Eng. to mean *stereotyped* (cp. *stern*), this word has a round-about story. The three words used in English were first French. *Claque* imitates the sound of flat hands striking; then it was used of a group hired to applaud, in the theatre. The shorter sound, *clique*, was similarly later applied to a group of intriguers. (*Click* and *clack*, in Eng., are used only for the sounds.) But Fr. *cliquer*, to strike, had a doublet *clicher;* then this was applied, as though a print were made with the flat of the hand, to the process of printing from a metal plate, of stereotyping. And the past participle, *cliché*, developed in Fr. and was thus borrowed in Eng., the sense of repeated time and again, hence trite.

Since clichés are meant to capture a large truth in a short, clever saying, when the saying has become overused and is no longer clever, it becomes just the opposite, a comment on just how unclever the person using the cliché is and, unless he is doing it purposely for humor or satire, how unaware the person is of his own dullness.

This property (a form of Pun on the connotative meanings of a saying) serves as the basis for a good deal of sophisticated word play. Two examples follow: In the first each player lists as many clichés as possible on a sheet of paper (one game might be simply to see who can list the most), then, on a separate sheet of paper, mixes the first half of each cliché with the second half of another cliché. The papers are exchanged and the players are asked to sort out the clichés: e.g., "strong as an ox" gets mixed with "a stitch in time saves nine." The result: "a stitch in an ox" and "strong as time saves nine."

When twenty such clichés have been mixed at random, sorting them out is not as easy as it might at first appear. The resulting sayings are also often amusing.

The second form of word play involves creating hypothetical origins for clichés, e.g., "better safe than sorry" might have originated at a national hypochondriacs' convention.

For similar word play refer to Accidental Language, Back Slang, Boner, Burlesque, Conundrum, Fancy Fairy Tales, Hackneyed Images, Irish Bull, Malapropism, Möbius Strip, Number Associations, Parody, Perverb, Pun, Silly Similes, Spoonerism, and Wellerism.

BIBLIOGRAPHY

Espy, Willard R. *An Almanac of Words at Play*. New York: Clarkson N. Potter, Inc., 1975.
_____. *The Game of Words*. New York: Grosset & Dunlap, 1972.
Morris, William, and Mary Morris. *The Word Game Book*. New York: Harper & Brothers, 1959.
Perrine, Laurence. "Cliché." In *Encyclopedia of Poetry and Poetics*, ed. Alex Preminger. Princeton: Princeton University Press, 1965.
Shipley, Joseph T. *Dictionary of Word Origins*. New York: Philosophical Library, 1945.

CLUE WORDS is a word guessing game. According to David Parlett, it was invented by Gyles Brandreth.

One player thinks of a word of eight different letters as the target word and offers three clues to its identity.

The first clue is a word of three (different) letters, each of which occurs in the target word. Each player in turn may guess the target word. If successful, the player guessing it receives three points and sets the next word.

If no one guesses the target word, a second clue is given of four letters from the clue word. This time a successful guess is worth two points.

Failure elicits a third clue of five letters from the target word. Success here equals one point.

If the target word is not guessed, the setter scores a point and the next in turn takes over.

For similar word play refer to Aesop's Mission, Anagram, and Charades.

BIBLIOGRAPHY

Brandreth, Gyles. *Indoor Games*. London: Hodder & Stoughton, Ltd., 1977.
Parlett, David. *Botticelli and Beyond: Over 100 of the World's Best Word Games*. New York: Pantheon Books, 1981.

CODE is a system of arbitrarily assigned symbols, often secret, for letters, words, or phrases.

According to Helen Fouché Gaines, *Cryptanalysis: A Study of Ciphers and Their Solution*, a code differs from a Cipher in that a code requires a code book or dictionary to decode and can only be successful if the symbols are applied in a purely haphazard manner. This distinction is ignored in most word play.

For instance, an alphabet code is one in which one letter in the code stands for another letter of the alphabet; the order of the letters remains consistent (e.g., A = B, B = C, C = D, and so on).

The distinction between code and cipher is also ignored in *The Random House Dictionary of the English Language* and *Webster's New Twentieth Century Dictionary,* both of which indicate that a cipher may be used to refer to the solution of a code rather than to the code itself; otherwise, in terms of word play, the two terms are interchangeable.

Dmitri Borgmann, *Beyond Language: Adventures in Word and Thought* (1967), humorously describes a code, which he admits is really a play on the letter rebus (see Flat), where each letter is connected to a phrase to create words:

a L = Al
a N = an
Sing in G = singing

For similar word play refer to Cipher, Cryptic Quotes, Cryptoglyphics, Cryptograms, Flat, Hidden Word Search, Musical Messages, Pun, Rebus, Reflected Writing, and Scramble Code.

BIBLIOGRAPHY

Borgmann, Dmitri A. *Beyond Language: Adventures in Word and Thought.* New York: Charles Scribner's Sons, 1967.
————. *Language on Vacation: An Olio of Orthographical Oddities.* New York: Charles Scribner's Sons, 1965.
Gaines, Helen Fouché. *Cryptanalysis: A Study of Ciphers and Their Solution.* New York: Dover, 1939.
McKechnie, Jean L., et al. *Webster's New Twentieth Century Dictionary of the English Language: Unabridged.* 2d ed. New York: World Publishing Co., 1971.
Stein, Jess, ed. *The Random House Dictionary of the English Language.* New York: Random House, 1983.

COFFEE POT is a game based on Puns.

One player thinks of a word with dual meanings (a pun of syllepsis) or a pair of words with different meanings but the same sound (a pun of paronomasia). He then says out loud a sentence using both meanings, but substitutes the phrase "coffee pot" for both of them, for example:

The pair of words = sense, cents.
The sentence: It took little coffee pot to see we only had enough coffee pot for two candy canes.

Each of the other players may then ask one question. The first player's answer must include one of his words disguised as "coffee pot":

Question: How much money did it take to buy two candy canes?
Answer: Twenty coffee pot.

If one of the guessers identifies the word he scores a point. If no one does, the "coffee-potter" scores a point.

Each player in turn plays the coffee-potter. The winner is the player with the most points at the end of the game.

For a further discussion of paronomasia, syllepsis, and other puns, refer to Pun. A list of word play based on puns is also included under that entry.

BIBLIOGRAPHY

Brandreth, Gyles. *The World's Best Indoor Games*. New York: Pantheon Books, 1981.

COMBINATIONS is a word-building game.

Each player is given the same list of two- or three-letter combinations:

> th
> ent
> gh
> un
> aft

The players then have five minutes to think of words in which the combinations appear (one for each combination). They score one point for each letter in each word; thus, the longer the words the higher the score:

th	thunder	7 points
ent	different	9 points
gh	through	7 points
un	unusual	7 points
aft	aftertaste	10 points
		40 points

For similar word play refer to Acrostic, Acrosticals, Add-on, Ghost and Superghost, and Progressive Anagram.

BIBLIOGRAPHY

Brandreth, Gyles. *Indoor Games*. London: Hodder & Stoughton, Ltd., 1977.

CONCATENATION. See CHAINS.

CONCRETE POETRY, also called Emblematic Poetry, Looks Like Poetry, Rebus poetry, and picture poetry, is poetry in which the words or symbols on the page look like the subject matter. Refer to Emblematic Poetry for examples.

CONFUSING AND CONFOUNDING CATS is word play based on Puns.

This game was created by William and Mary Morris, *The Word Game Book* (1959). The object is to write clues to words beginning with ''cat'':

What ''cat'' digs dirt?
(Answer: a caterpillar)

What ''cat'' is well organized?
(Answer: category)

What ''cat'' was a Roman statesman, soldier and writer?
(Answer: Cato)

What ''cat'' is very religious?
(Answer: a Catholic)

For similar word play refer to Animalistics, Cross-breed, Form-a-Word, Galaxy of Gals, Hidden Names, Hidden Words, Pun, Quiz That Man, Shifting, Spare the Prefix, and Vulture Up To?

BIBLIOGRAPHY

Morris, William, and Mary Morris. *The Word Game Book.* New York: Harper & Brothers, 1959.

CONSEQUENCES is a form of word play involving the group writing of a story.

The game goes back prior to 1881, when *Cassell's Book of In-door Amusements, Card Games, and Fireside Fun* described it as ''old-fashioned.''

Each player is given a sheet of paper and starts by writing at the top an adjective or adjectival phrase descriptive of a male person, e.g., boring, funny, sickly. The top of the paper is then folded over to hide the phrase, and the paper is passed to the next player.

On the second line the next player writes the name of a male person (real or fictional). This is then concealed and the paper passed again.

The entire listing is as follows:

1. adjective describing man

2. man's name (followed by ''met'')

3. adjective describing woman

4. woman's name

5. place where they met (followed by ''he gave her'')

6. what he gave her (followed by ''and said'')

7. what he said to her (followed by ''she said to him'')

8. what she said to him (followed by ''the consequence was'')

9. the consequence(s) (followed by "and the world said")

10. what the world said about it

The finished papers are then read aloud with the transitional phrases included.

Gyles Brandreth's description of the same game in *The World's Best Indoor Games* suggests that the standard list may vary from the one above. He offers the following:

1. a female character

2. met a male character

3. where they met

4. what he did

5. what she did

6. what he said

7. what she said

8. what the consequence was

9. what the world said

For similar word play refer to Bouts Rimés, Bouts Rimés Retournés, Headlines, and Pass It On.

BIBLIOGRAPHY

Brandreth, Gyles. *The World's Best Indoor Games.* New York: Pantheon Books, 1981.

Parlett, David. *Botticelli and Beyond: Over 100 of the World's Best Word Games.* New York: Pantheon Books, 1981.

Sharp, Richard, and John Piggott. *The Book of Games.* New York: Galahad Books, 1977.

CONSTRUCTAPO, also called vocabularyclept poetry, involves the reconstruction of a poem.

All of the words of a well-known poem are mixed up or put in alphabetical order. Then either the person who mixed up the words or the other players must put the words back in the original order (or into another order that makes sense):

The first verse of Edgar Allan Poe's "The Raven" mixed randomly:

Once Over While As 'Tis upon many I of some some a a nodded visitor' midnight quaint nearly one I muttered dreary and napping rapping gently 'tapping while I curious suddenly rapping at my at my there came volume pondered of weak forgotten and weary lore chamber chamber door door a tapping more' nothing and this only.

The solution:

Once upon a midnight dreary, while I pondered, weak and weary,
Over many a quaint and curious volume of forgotten lore—
While I nodded, nearly napping, suddenly there came a tapping,

As of some one gently rapping, rapping at my chamber door.
'Tis some visitor,' I muttered, 'tapping at my chamber door—
Only this and nothing more.'

For similar word play refer to Answer Verse, Bouts Rimés, Bouts Rimés Retournés, Homosyntaxism, Möbius Strip, Pass It On, and Renga.

BIBLIOGRAPHY

Eckler, A. Ross. *Word Recreations: Games and Diversions from "Word Ways."* New York: Dover, 1979.
Gardner, Martin. "Mathematical Games: The flip strip sonnet, the lipogram, and other mad modes of word play." *Scientific American* (February 1977): 121–125.
Parlett, David. *Botticelli and Beyond: Over 100 of the World's Best Word Games.* New York: Pantheon Books, 1981.
Poe, Edgar Allan. "The Raven." 1845. Reprint. London: Octopus Books, 1981.

CONUNDRUM is a Riddle solved with a Pun.

Though Henry Ernest Dudeney states that, as late as 1824, such word play was commonly called "queries," satirist Thomas Nashe is credited with using "conundrum" as early as 1596, when he swore he'd make Gabriel Harvey "confess himself a conundrum."

The conundrum is closely related to the major fields of word play that surround both puns and riddles, which can be found in such divergent literature as the Bible, the plays of Shakespeare, the novels of James Joyce, and the Nursery Rhymes of Mother Goose. (See Pun and Riddle for more in-depth discussion.)

Mike Thaler, author of over eighty children's books and acclaimed by many to be America's riddle king, offers a workable means of creating conundrums in his article "Reading, Writing and Riddling." The following is a brief restatement of his explanation:

First, pick a general subject (airplanes, sports, food, rockets, television, and so on).

Next, make a list of words associated with the subject. As an example, take the general subject "chickens." The list will consist of such words as cluck, hen, fowl, egg, bird, peck, shell, chick, rooster, cock, feathers, yoke, barnyard, fried, wings, farm, gravy, and so on.

Next, pick a proper noun, e.g., Davy Crockett, and divide it into its syllables (Dav-y Crock-ett).

Next, pick words from the list that *sound* like the syllables in the chosen proper noun and substitute them (Davy Clucket, Gravy Crockett, Davy Chickett, and so on). These new creations are puns of paronomasia and will serve as the answers to paronomasia conundrums.

Next, refer to an encyclopedia, almanac, dictionary, or other reference for facts about the proper noun (Davy Crockett). For example, Davy Crockett was a United States frontiersman, politician, and folklore hero who died at the Alamo in 1836, during the Texas war for independence.

Next, turn the facts into questions, substituting the general category (chicken) for the general category of Davy Crockett (man) and the puns of paronomasia for Davy Crockett.

Here are a few examples:

What famous American chicken died at the Alamo?
(Answer: Davy Cluckett)

What famous American chicken politician represented Tennessee in Congress?
(Answer: Davy Peckett)

What famous American chicken killed him a bar when he was only three?
(Answer: Gravy Chickett)

Since there are three forms of pun (Edward P. J. Corbett, *Classical Rhetoric for the Modern Day Student*), it follows that there are three basic forms of conundrum: the antanaclasis conundrum, the paronomasia conundrum, and the syllepsis conundrum.

The antanaclasis conundrum is based on the pun of antanaclasis (the repetition of a word in two different senses).

Examples:

What was the first <u>rock</u> music played in America?
(Answer: Plymouth <u>Rock</u>)

When did someone first say "God Bless <u>America</u>"?
(Answer: When <u>America</u> first sneezed)

Why did the moron throw <u>butter</u> out the window?
(Answer: He wanted to see a <u>butterfly</u>)

The paronomasia conundrum is based on the pun of paronomasia (the use of words alike in sound but different in meaning).

Examples:

Why did the mother tell her children not to listen to the birds?
(Answer: Because the birds used foul/fowl language)

What animal is always short of breath?
(Answer: the panther/panter)

What is black and white and red/read all over?
(Answer: a newspaper; a zebra with diaper rash; a penguin at Miami Beach)

The syllepsis conundrum is based on the pun of syllepsis (the use of a word understood differently in relation to the surrounding words).

Examples:

What do you call a dog without any legs?
(Answer: A drag)

What happens if you fail to pay an exorcist?
(Answer: You get repossessed)

What is unreal lunch meat?
(Answer: Phoney baloney)

For similar word play refer to Double Entendre, Nymble, Oxymoron, Paradox, Pun, Riddle, and Wellerism.

BIBLIOGRAPHY

Corbett, Edward P. J. *Classical Rhetoric for the Modern Student.* 2d ed. New York: Oxford University Press, 1971.
Dudeney, Henry Ernest. *300 Best Word Puzzles.* New York: Charles Scribner's Sons, 1968.
Eckler, A. Ross. *Word Recreations: Games and Diversions from "Word Ways."* New York: Dover, 1979.
Espy, Willard R. *The Game of Words.* New York: Grosset & Dunlap, 1972.
Hindman, Darwin A. *1800 Riddles, Enigmas and Conundrums.* New York: Dover, 1963.
Loyd, Samuel. *Sam Loyd's Cyclopedia of 5000 Puzzles, Tricks and Conundrums with Answers.* New York: Pinnacle Books, 1976.
Preminger, Alex, Frank J. Warnker, and O. B. Hardison, Jr., eds. *Encyclopedia of Poetry and Poetics.* Princeton: Princeton University Press, 1965.
Shipley, Joseph T. *Playing with Words.* Englewood Cliffs, N.J.: Prentice-Hall, 1960.
————. "Word and Letter Games." In *Encyclopaedia Britannica: Macropaedia.* 1979.
Thaler, Mike. "Reading, Writing and Riddling." In *Learning* 2, no. 9 (April/May 1983): 59–60.

CONVERGENCE is a sentence guessing game for two players.

Each player writes a four-word sentence, which the other player attempts to guess by announcing another four-word sentence. The player whose sentence is being guessed then tells his opponent whether each of the words in the guessed sentence is alphabetically before, the same as, or after the word in the same position in the sentence being guessed:

One player writes down the sentence: You cross the bridge.
The other player guesses: I hate the news.
The first player says: before, after, same, after.

The two players continue in this manner, alternating guesses at each other's sentence until one guesses the correct sentence.

Refer to Giotto for a similar game.

BIBLIOGRAPHY

Parlett, David. *Botticelli and Beyond: Over 100 of the World's Best Word Games.* New York: Pantheon Books, 1981.

COUNTDOWN VERSES involve the replacing of literal meanings of syllables with visual repeats; they are a form of Pun.

Here are two examples:

Today = day-day
Misfortune = mis-tune-tune-tune-tune

For similar word play refer to Pun and Rebus.

BIBLIOGRAPHY

Espy, Willard R. *An Almanac of Words at Play*. New York: Clarkson N. Potter, Inc., 1975.

COUNTING OUT RHYMES. See COUNTING RHYMES.

COUNTING RHYMES, or counting out rhymes, involve the combination of rhyme and counting.

A number of children's games use variations on counting rhymes, some of which can be traced back as far as the first century A.D. Often these rhymes are used to determine who is "it" or when whoever is "it" is about to begin "seeking."

Here are two examples:

"One Potato, Two Potatoes"

Generally the participants stand in a circle and hold out both fists. One player counts off fists: "One potato, two potatoes, three potatoes, four; five potatoes, six potatoes, seven potatoes more." Whoever gets his fist hit on "more" removes his fist from the next round. The counting out continues until only one fist is left. That person is "it." Sometimes the rhyme ends with the line: "O-U-T spells out and out you do go."

"Matthew, Mark, Luke and John"

Matthew, Mark, Luke and John
Saddle the cat and I'll get on,
Give me the switch and I'll be gone,
Out goes he.

For other word play involving numbers refer to ABC Words, ACE Words, Centurion, Cipher, Code, Crypt-Arithmetic, Flat, Numwords, and Oulipo Algorithms.

For other word play involving acting out rhymes refer to Acting Out Rhymes, Ball Bouncing Rhymes, Game Rhymes, Hand Clapping Rhymes, Jump Rope Rhymes, Mnemonics, Nursery Rhymes, and Tongue Twister.

BIBLIOGRAPHY

Abrahams, Roger D., ed. *Jump-Rope Rhymes: A Dictionary*. Austin: University of Texas Press, 1969.

Abrahams, Roger D., and Lois Rankin, eds. *Counting-Out Rhymes: A Dictionary*. Austin: University of Texas Press, 1980.

Espy, Willard R. *A Children's Almanac of Words at Play*. New York: Clarkson N. Potter, Inc., 1982.

Laubach, David C. *Introduction to Folklore*. Rochelle Park, N.J.: Hayden Book Co., 1980.

Opie, Peter, and Iona Opie. *Children's Games in Street and Playground*. 1969. Reprint. New York: Oxford University Press, 1979.

_____. *The Lore and Language of Schoolchildren*. 1959. Reprint. New York: Oxford University Press, 1980.

_____. *The Oxford Dictionary of Nursery Rhymes*. 1951. Reprint. New York: Oxford University Press, 1983.

_____. *The Oxford Nursery Rhyme Book*. 1955. Reprint. New York: Oxford University Press, 1984.

Shipley, Joseph T. *Playing with Words*. Englewood Cliffs, N.J.: Prentice-Hall, 1960.

Sutton-Smith, Brian. *The Folkgames of Children*. Austin: University of Texas Press, 1972.

Volland, P. F. *Mother Goose*. Chicago: P. F. Volland & Co., 1915. Reprint. New York: Rand McNally & Co., 1982.

CRAMBO, also known as rhyme in time and rhymoriginals, is a rhyming game.

The word "crambo" is derived from Latin for "bubble-and-squeak." The Latin phrase *crambe repetita* means literally "cabbage served up again." The game has developed a reputation for "distasteful repetition."

One player states a short phrase, for example: "Pie makes me high." Each of the other players in turn must come up with a phrase roughly equal in syllables and with a similar end rhyme, for example: "Never say die"; or "I'll sadly cry"; or "Learn how to fly." Players lose when they fail to come up with a new rhyme.

Gyles Brandreth, *Indoor Games* (1977), calls this game rhyme in time and admonishes players not to begin a round with an end rhyme of "orange," since there is no known rhyme for "orange" in English.

In *The World's Best Indoor Games* (1981), Brandreth also offers the following variation. One player thinks of a word and then gives the other players a different word that rhymes with the word he has thought up. The other players have three guesses each to come up with the word.

For similar word play refer to Charades and Dumb Crambo.

BIBLIOGRAPHY

Brandreth, Gyles. *Indoor Games*. London: Hodder & Stoughton, Ltd., 1977.

_____. *The World's Best Indoor Games*. New York: Pantheon Books, 1981.

Parlett, David. *Botticelli and Beyond: Over 100 of the World's Best Word Games.* New York: Pantheon Books, 1981.

Shipley, Joseph T. *Playing with Words.* Englewood Cliffs, N.J.: Prentice-Hall, 1960.

CRASH. See GIOTTO.

CRAZY GRAMMAR is the application of standard grammatical rules to exceptions to those rules for the purpose of humor.

Here is an example:

If a teacher is someone who teaches and an eater is someone who eats, wouldn't a pigger be someone who pigs and a header be someone who heads (assuming a teacher has something to teach and an eater has something to eat)?

Refer to Abbreviations for other artificial ways of inverting standard rules of grammar and spelling.

BIBLIOGRAPHY

Espy, Willard R. *A Children's Almanac of Words at Play.* New York: Clarkson N. Potter, Inc., 1982.

CROAKERS are verbs used as Puns.

Here are some examples:

"We've taken over the government," the general <u>cooed.</u>

"That joke was so funny I nearly <u>died</u> from laughing," the old man said, as he was being rushed to the hospital.

I <u>kept turning over a new leaf,</u> but all I ever found was dry grass.

For similar word play refer to Pun, Tom Swifties, and Wellerism.

BIBLIOGRAPHY

Brandreth, Gyles. *The Joy of Lex: How to Have Fun with 860,341,500 Words.* New York: Quill, 1983.

Espy, Willard R. *An Almanac of Words at Play.* New York: Clarkson N. Potter, Inc., 1975.

Fuller, John G. *Games for Insomniacs; or, A Lifetime Supply of Insufferable Brain Twisters.* New York: Doubleday, 1966.

CROSS-BREED is the mixing of syllables from the names of various animals.

The idea is to combine the first syllable(s) of the name of one animal with the final syllable(s) of the name of another animal: kangafish, hippobird, dogephant.

For similar word play refer to Animalistics, Confusing and Confounding Cats, and Pun.

BIBLIOGRAPHY

Fuller, John G. *Games for Insomniacs; or, A Lifetime Supply of Insufferable Brain Twisters,* New York: Doubleday, 1966.

CROSSING JOKES are a form of Conundrum.
Here are some examples:

Cross Alexander the Great with a grape and what do you get?
(Answer: Alexander the Grape)

Cross Albert Einstein with a pig and what do you get?
(Answer: Alboar Einswine)

For more detailed discussion of Conundrum and Pun refer to those entries.

BIBLIOGRAPHY

Espy, Willard R. *A Children's Almanac of Words at Play.* New York: Clarkson N. Potter, Inc., 1982.
———. *The Game of Words.* New York: Grosset & Dunlap, 1972.

CROSSWORD PUZZLE, also called scorewords, wordsquares, and wordsworth, is a puzzle in which words corresponding to numbered clues are put into a grid of horizontal and vertical squares to form intersecting words.

On April 18, 1924, Simon & Schuster published the first book of such puzzles, *The Crossword Puzzle Book.* Since then the crossword puzzle with its many variations has become the most published of all the language puzzles. Nearly all of the major newspapers and many national book publishers and magazines include crossword puzzles in their publications.

The National Puzzlers' League has developed the cryptic crossword (see Extras) and Forms (puzzles similar to crosswords but having solutions printed in geometrical shapes; see Forms).

The basic form of a crossword puzzle consists of a grid of squares which players fill up as letters are called out by each player in turn. Whoever makes the most and longest words wins. The words are often scored on some form of up-and-down and crossing words format (sometimes scores are given for diagonal words). Some variations allow words within words or overlapping words.

The standard form today consists of a numbered grid already set (dead squares indicated) to take the words, which are arrived at by solving numbered clues; it is usually played solitaire.

A standard crossword puzzle game has two players taking turns filling up an open grid with interconnecting words (one point for each additional letter used). Gyles Brandreth, *World's Best Indoor Games,* calls this form ''crossword'' and establishes a grid of nine squares by nine squares.

He describes another version, which he calls ''crosswords,'' where each player draws a grid of five squares across and down (more if desired). Each player in turn then calls out a letter. All players enter that letter in their grid wherever they want. Once the letter has been entered it cannot be moved. The aim is to form words across or down. The game ends when all the squares have been filled. One point is scored for each letter contained in a valid word (one-letter words, proper nouns, foreign words, and abbreviations do not count). One bonus point is scored for words that completely fill a row or column. Points can only be scored for one word when two or more words share letters in the same row or column, e.g., a row containing "house" cannot score for both "house" and "us."

Anagram charades is played in the same manner, except that an anagram is substituted for each listed clue.

Ernst Theimer has published charade crosswords in the August 1970, August 1971, August 1983, and May 1984 issues of *Word Ways: The Journal of Recreational Linguistics*. According to Theimer, the words sought in a charade crossword are not directly defined by the clues, but, rather, are buried in a sentence as a charade. For example, the word "nisi" is contained in the following sentence: "An artistic man is impossible to live with." This seems slightly more difficult than a normal crossword puzzle, but it is made much more difficult by removing the word (nisi) from the clue sentence and rewriting the sentence with the remaining letters in their original order: "An artistic mam possible to live with." The number of letters removed is indicated at the end of the sentence. To be technically correct, the word to be determined from the clue sentence must fit inside a word of the clue and must be a part of at least two separate words.

For similar word play refer to Across-tic, Acrostic, Alphacross, Alphawords, Arrow of Letters, Black Squares, Flat, Forms, Last Word, Lynx, Magic Word Squares, Puzzling Squares, Quizl, Ragaman, SCRABBLE, SCRABBLE-GRAM, and Scramble.

BIBLIOGRAPHY

Borgmann, Dmitri A. *Beyond Language: Adventures in Word and Thought.* New York: Charles Scribner's Sons, 1967.

_____. *Language on Vacation: An Olio of Orthographical Oddities.* New York: Charles Scribner's Sons, 1965.

Brandreth, Gyles. *Indoor Games.* London: Hodder & Stoughton, Ltd., 1977.

_____. *The Joy of Lex: How to Have Fun with 860,341,500 Words.* New York: Quill, 1983.

_____. *More Joy of Lex: An Amazing and Amusing Z to A and A to Z of Words.* New York: William Morrow and Co., 1982.

_____. *The World's Best Indoor Games.* New York: Pantheon Books, 1981.

Espy, Willard R. *A Children's Almanac of Words at Play.* New York: Clarkson N. Potter, Inc., 1982.

Hart, Harold H. *Grab a Pencil.* New York: Hart Publ. Co., 1958.

Morris, William, and Mary Morris. *The Word Game Book.* New York: Harper & Brothers, 1959.

Parlett, David. *Botticelli and Beyond: Over 100 of the World's Best Word Games*. New York: Pantheon Books, 1981.
Sharp, Richard, and John Piggott. *The Book of Games*. New York: Galahad Books, 1977.
Theimer, Ernst. "Another Charade Crossword." *Word Ways: The Journal of Recreational Linguistics* 17, no. 2 (May 1984): 117–119.

CROW FLIGHT. See MEANDER.

CRYPT. See CRYPTOGRAM.

CRYPTARITHM. See CRYPT-ARITHMETIC.

CRYPTARITHMIE. See CRYPT-ARITHMETIC.

CRYPT-ARITHMETIC, also called cryptarithmie, cryptarithm, alphametic, and arithmetical restoration, is the replacing of digits by letters or other symbols.

The word "crypt-arithmetic" (cryptarithmie) was first applied to this form of mathematical word play by M. Vatriquent in the May 1931 issue of *Sphinx,* a Belgian magazine of recreational mathematics. Maurice Kraitchik, editor of *Sphinx* from 1931 to 1939, however, says that better examples can be found previous to 1932 in *La Mathématique des Jeux*. Maxey Brooke, *150 Puzzles in Crypt-Arithmetic* (1969), claims that crypt-arithmetic is a descendent of arithmetical restoration, which was probably invented in India during the Middle Ages.

For the purpose of language recreation, the idea is to replace numbers with letters, or rather the digits representing numbers with letters:

$$\begin{array}{ccc} A & A & B \\ \times\ \underline{BC} & +\ \underline{B} & \times\ \underline{C} \end{array} \qquad (F - C) - B = A$$

(answer: A = 1, B = 2, C = 3, F = 6)

For similar word play refer to ABC Words, ACE Words, Centurion, Cipher, Code, Cryptic Quotes, Flat, Oulipo Algorithms.

BIBLIOGRAPHY

Borgmann, Dmitri A. *Language on Vacation: An Olio of Orthographical Oddities*. New York: Charles Scribner's Sons, 1965.
Brooke, Maxey. *150 Puzzles in Crypt-Arithmetic*. 2d ed., rev. New York: Dover, 1969.

CRYPTIC CROSSWORD. See EXTRAS.

CRYPTIC QUOTES is a mathematical substitution cipher where secret quotations are revealed by matching up letters with corresponding numerals. Statements are made in which the letters in certain words are replaced by numerals.

By solving what these words are, the player discovers which numerals stand for which letters:

The Secret	_ _ _ _ _ _ _ _ _
Quotation:	1 2 3 4 5 6 7 8 9

The clues:

1. Whatever you 6-2-4. (answer: say)
2. 5-7-9 is closely related to a monkey. (answer: ape)
3. D 8-3 before 1. (answer: is, E)
Answer: Easy as pie.

For similar word play refer to Cipher, Code, Crossword Puzzle, Crypt-Arithmetic, and Cryptoglyphics.

BIBLIOGRAPHY

Brooke, Maxey. *150 Puzzles in Crypt-Arithmetic.* 2d ed., rev. New York: Dover, 1969.
Gaines, Helen Fouché. *Cryptanalysis: A Study of Ciphers and Their Solution.* New York: Dover, 1939.

CRYPTOGLYPHICS are Codes or Ciphers using symbols or pictures to represent letters of the alphabet. An example is contained in ''The Gold Bug'' by Edgar Allan Poe.

For more deatiled discussion refer to Cipher and Code.

BIBLIOGRAPHY

Brooke, Maxey. *150 Puzzles in Crypt-Arithmetic.* 2d ed., rev. New York: Dover, 1969.
Gaines, Helen Fouché. *Cryptanalysis: A Study of Ciphers and Their Solution.* New York: Dover, 1939.
Poe, Edgar Allan. ''The Gold Bug.'' 1843. Reprint. *Eighteen Best Stories by Edgar Allan Poe,* ed. Vincent Price and Chandler Brossard. New York: Dell, 1984.

CRYPTOGRAM, also called cryptowords, is a Code or Cipher where letters are substituted for other letters.

Cryptogram is one of the National Puzzlers' League's major puzzle forms. They define it as a coded message in which every letter is replaced throughout the entire message by another letter, no letter standing for itself, no letter representing more than one other letter. Original word divisions are kept, and capitalized words are indicated with an asterisk.

The following rules apply:

1. All cryptograms shall contain from seventy-five to ninety letters, at least eighteen of which are different.

2. No more than six of the letters may be used only once.

3. The words should be found in *Webster's New International Dictionary*, second or third edition.

4. No more than four words should be capitalized.

5. The cryptic message must be a complete and coherent statement, grammatically correct.

Dmitri Borgmann, *Beyond Language: Adventures in Word and Thought* (1967), points out that ETAOIN SHRDLU (an entry in *Webster's New International Dictionary*) is often used by cryptographers to help in decoding substitution ciphers, because ETAOIN SHRDLU represents the twelve most commonly used letters of the alphabet.

For similar word play refer to Cipher, Code, and Flat.

BIBLIOGRAPHY

Borgmann, Dmitri A. *Beyond Language: Adventures in Word and Thought*. New York: Charles Scribner's Sons, 1967.
Eckler, A. Ross. *Word Recreations: Games and Diversions from "Word Ways."* New York: Dover, 1979.
Espy, Willard R. *The Game of Words*. New York: Grosset & Dunlap, 1972.
Gaines, Helen Fouché. *Cryptanalysis: A Study of Ciphers and Their Solutions*. New York: Dover, 1939.

CRYPTOWORDS. See CRYPTOGRAM.

CURTAILMENT. See FLAT.

D

DAFFY DEFINITIONS, also called daft definitions and daffynitions, is the defining of words by Puns, generally by the pun of paronomasia.

Here are four examples:

Oh say = a common Mexican name.
Datum = the stomach.
Harmony = a woman's cash.
Cheetah = an animal that never plays fair.
Baroque = an eighteenth-century poor man.

Visual daffynitions use pictures to show humorous meanings for common words or phrases; they are visual puns.

For a more in-depth discussion of pun and for similar word play, refer to Pun. For similar word play involving visual daffynitions refer to Rebus. For similar word play involving definitions refer to Dictionary Definitions Game.

BIBLIOGRAPHY

Espy, Willard R. *The Game of Words*. New York: Grosset & Dunlap, 1972.
Parlett, David. *Botticelli and Beyond: Over 100 of the World's Best Word Games*. New York: Pantheon Books, 1981.

DAFFYNITIONS. See DAFFY DEFINITIONS.

DAFT DEFINITIONS. See DAFFY DEFINITIONS.

DEAR DEPARTED is a phrase used by Willard R. Espy, *A Children's Almanac of Words at Play,* for humorous epitaphs for members of various professions.

Here are some examples:

A poker player: "Just bluffing."
A taxi driver: "End of the line."
A salesman: "All sold out."
A baseball player: "Strike three."

For similar word play refer to Pun.

BIBLIOGRAPHY

Espy, Willard R. *A Children's Almanac of Words at Play*. New York: Clarkson N. Potter,
    Inc., 1982.

DECAPITATION. See BEHEADING.

DEFECTIVE DETECTIVE involves the solving of detective novel titles.
    The game is discussed by David Parlett, *Botticelli and Beyond: Over 100 of
the World's Best Word Games*. The title is taken from an Erle Stanley Gardner
novel, *The Case of the Defective Detective*.
    One player gives a clue to an alliterative Gardner-type novel title. Whoever
guesses the title first scores a point and sets the next clue:

Clue: scared relatives
Title: *The Case of the Horrified Heirs*

Clue: mother's loving sister
Title: *The Case of the Amorous Aunt*

Clue: good looking poor
Title: *The Case of the Beautiful Beggar*

Clue: separated swinger
Title: *The Case of the Dancing Divorcee*

For similar word play refer to Book Conversation and MADvertisements.

BIBLIOGRAPHY

Parlett, David. *Botticelli and Beyond: Over 100 of the World's Best Word Games*. New
    York: Pantheon Books, 1981.

DEGREES is a game based on the three degrees of comparison (good, better,
best; bad, worse, worst).
    Joseph T. Shipley created this game and discusses it in his book *Playing with
Words* (1960). The idea is to apply Synonyms for the three degrees of comparison for "I," "you," and "he":

<u>I</u> am a creative writer. (bad)
<u>You</u> have journalistic abilities. (worse)
<u>He</u> writes dissertations. (worst)

BIBLIOGRAPHY

Shipley, Joseph T. *Playing with Words*. Englewood Cliffs, N.J.: Prentice-Hall, 1960.

DELETION. See FLAT.

DIALOGUE GAMES include the use of words; in general, they are children's games built around verses.

Brian Sutton-Smith, *The Folkgames of Children* (1972), has compiled a number of games played by New Zealand children in the nineteenth and twentieth centuries which revolve around words. He divides these games into two general categories: those in which the central character represents a fearsome person, such as a witch or a ghost, who captures or steals children; and those in which the central player represents an old woman, who is teased by the other players. He discusses the following games: ghost in the garden; mother, mother the pot boils over; honey pots; who goes round my stone wall; hen and chickens (fox and geese); the old lady (or woman) from Botany Bay; and Old Mother Gray.

Gyles Brandreth, *The World's Best Indoor Games* (1981), discusses a number of similar English games, including oranges and lemons, ring a ring of roses, three blind mice, and the farmer's in his den, all of which have been Americanized, e.g., oranges and lemons has become London Bridge.

Although they never use this term, Iona and Peter Opie have a very complete discussion of dialogue games in *Children's Games in Street and Playground* (1979). Here is one that is played throughout Great Britain:

The King of Barbarees

There are a King, a Queen, a Princess, a Captain of the Guard, some soldiers, and a Castle (two children holding hands). The King tells the Captain of the Guard to march round the Castle singing: "Will you surrender, will you surrender, The King of the Barbarees?"

The Castle replies: "We won't surrender, we won't surrender, The King of the Barbarees."

The Captain says: "I'll tell the King, I'll tell the King, the King of the Barbarees."

The Castle replies: "You can tell the King, you can tell the King, the King of the Barbarees."

The Captain goes back to the King and, stamping his foot, says: "They won't surrender, they won't surrender, the King of the Barbarees."

The King says, "Take two of my trusty soldiers."

The soldiers follow the Captain and the rhyme is repeated: "Will you surrender, will you surrender, the King of the Barbarees?"

This is all repeated with the Princess, the Queen, and finally the King. Then the King says: "We'll break down your gates," and the rhyme is gone through again. Then, with the King going first, each of the players in turn runs at the Castle and tries to break through the two players holding hands (the Castle). If no one can break through, the Castle wins.

For similar word play refer to Acting Out Rhymes, Ball Bouncing Rhymes, Counting Rhymes, Game Rhymes, Hand Clapping Rhymes, Jump Rope Rhymes, Nursery Rhymes, and Skipping Rhymes.

BIBLIOGRAPHY

Brandreth, Gyles. *The World's Best Indoor Games*. New York: Pantheon Books, 1981.
Opie, Peter, and Iona Opie. *Children's Games in Street and Playground*. 1969. Reprint. New York: Oxford University Press, 1979.
Sutton-Smith, Brian. *The Folkgames of Children*. Austin: University of Texas Press, 1972.

DIAMANTES is a form of poetry or word puzzle often used to introduce children to the language arts; it is word play involving Antonyms.
The following rules apply:

Lines 1 and 7 are one-word antonyms.
Line 2 is two adjectives describing the word in line 1.
Line 6 is two adjectives describing the word in line 7.
Line 3 is three participles describing the word in line 1.
Line 5 is three participles describing the word in line 7.
Line 4 is four nouns, the first two referring to line 1, the second two to line 7:

man

strong   insensitive

demanding   deserving   desiring

beast   superior/superior   flower

deluding   defeating   delighting

sensitive   weak

woman

For similar word play refer to Alliteration, Alphabent, Alphabetical Adjectives, Alphabet Poetry, Alphabet Pyramids, Alphabet Word Chain, Animal Alphabet, Antonym, Lanterne, and Single-Rhymed Alphabet.

BIBLIOGRAPHY

Van Allen, Roach, and Claryce Allen. *Language Experience Activities*. 2d ed. Boston: Houghton Mifflin Co., 1982.

DICTIONARY. See ACROSTICALS.

DICTIONARY DEFINITIONS GAME, also called fictionary dictionary, is the creation of definitions for nouns; it served as the basis for a television show titled "Call My Bluff."

Each player starts with a piece of paper and a pen. One player reads off nouns in the dictionary until one is found that no one knows. Each player makes up a definition for that word. One player mixes the real definitions together with the created definitions and reads all of the definitions out loud. The players guess which is the correct definition, receiving one point for each correct vote.

Variations are numerous. Each person may have a dictionary to himself, or a dictionary may be passed around so that each player can pick out a separate word. Then all the players make up definitions for the word they have chosen, attempting to fool the other players into believing the wrong definition.

For similar word play refer to Daffy Definitions and Suspended Sentences.

BIBLIOGRAPHY

Eckler, A. Ross. *Word Recreations: Games and Diversions from "Word Ways."* New York: Dover, 1979.

Espy, Willard R. *The Game of Words.* New York: Grosset & Dunlap, 1972.

Fuller, John G. *Games for Insomniacs; or, A Lifetime Supply of Insufferable Brain Twisters.* New York: Doubleday, 1966.

Parlett, David. *Botticelli and Beyond: Over 100 of the World's Best Word Games.* New York: Pantheon Books, 1981.

Sharp, Richard, and John Piggott. *The Book of Games.* New York: Galahad Books, 1977.

DICTIONARY DIGEST is an alphabet game created by William and Mary Morris, *The Word Game Book*.

The names of all of the players are listed on a scorecard in the order in which they are seated. The first person then names as many words as he can that begin with the letter A in two minutes. Each player takes a turn, working through the alphabet (the letters J, Q, U, V, X, Y, and Z are omitted).

Variant forms of the same word do not count as additional words.

For other alphabet games refer to Alphabent, Alphabetical Adjectives, Alphabet Poetry, Alphabet Word Chain, Animal Alphabet, and Single-Rhymed Alphabet.

BIBLIOGRAPHY

Morris, William, and Mary Morris. *The Word Game Book.* New York: Harper & Brothers, 1959.

DIGRAMS is a game based on words that have the same two consecutive letters (not to be confused with digraphs, where two letters express a single sound).

The game is played by thinking of a digram (e.g., "tl") and seeing who can come up with the most words containing it (e.g., little, brittle, battle, cattle, bottle, spittle).

For similar word play refer to Stepladders and Trigrams.

BIBLIOGRAPHY

Parlett, David. *Botticelli and Beyond: Over 100 of the World's Best Word Games.* New York: Pantheon Books, 1981.

DONKEY. See GHOST AND SUPERGHOST.

DOUBLE ACROSTIC. See ACROSTIC.

DOUBLE CENTURION. See CENTURION.

DOUBLE-DACTYL, also known as hechtascalande, higgledy-piggledy, niminy-piminy, and reduplication, is a strict verse form based on the poetic dactyl foot (three syllables: stressed, unstressed, unstressed) used for humorous word play.

The verse form called higgledy-piggledy was created by Anthony Hecht, John Hollander, and Paul Pascal in 1951. It consists of eight lines, two four-line stanzas:

First line = a nonsense double-dactyl
Second line = the name of the subject
Sixth line = one double-dactyl word
Fourth and eighth lines = rhyme and are curtailed double-dactyls

Lament of the Playful Elf

Picking and packing, a
Curse on you Santa Claus;
Elves are for frolicking,
Santa, that's me!

Toys are for children, I
Know that's the way it is;
Elves should be busy, but
That's just not me.

For similar word play refer to Clerihew, Limerick, and Stinky Pinky.

BIBLIOGRAPHY

Espy, Willard R. *An Almanac of Words at Play.* New York: Clarkson N. Potter, Inc., 1975.
_____. *The Game of Words.* New York: Grosset & Dunlap, 1972.
_____. *Say It My Way: How to Avoid Certain Pitfalls of Spoken English Together with a Decidedly Informal History of How Our Language Rose (or Fell).* New York: Doubleday, 1980.

Hecht, Anthony, and John Hollander. *Jiggery Pokery.* New York: Atheneum, 1966.
Shipley, Joseph T. *Playing with Words.* Englewood Cliffs, N.J.: Prentice-Hall, 1960.

DOUBLE ENTENDRE, a form of punning, is the use of terms with double meanings, especially when one of the meanings is risqué.

C. C. Bombaugh, *Gleanings for the Curious,* includes a number of examples. The author of the following is unknown, but Bombaugh claims that it originally appeared in a Philadelphia newspaper. It can be read three different ways: in its entirety; only up to the comma in each line; and only from the comma in each line:

Revolutionary Verses

Hark! hark! the trumpet sounds, the din of war's alarms,
O'er seas and solid grounds, doth call us all to arms;
Who for King George doth stand, their honors soon shall shine;
Their ruin is at hand, who with the Congress join.
The acts of Parliament, in them I much delight,
I hate their cursed intent, who for the Congress fight,
The Tories of the day, they are my daily toast,
They soon will sneak away, who Independence boast;
Who non-resistance hold, they have my hand and heart.
May they for slaves be sold, who act a Whiggish part;
On Mansfield, North, and Bute, may daily blessings pour,
Confusion and dispute, on Congress evermore;
To North and British lord, may honors still be done,
I wish a block or cord, to General Washington.

Double entendre is one of the standard features of any James Bond movie, witness some of the names: Octopussy, Goldfinger, and Mrs. Moneypenny.

Eugene Ulrich, "Double Entendre Headlines," quotes a number of possibly ambiguous headlines based on double entendre, such as "Reagan Sees Red over Arms Control Treaty."

For similar word play refer to Conundrum, Equivocally Speaking, and Pun.

BIBLIOGRAPHY

Bombaugh, C. C. *Gleanings for the Curious.* 1890. Reprint. *Oddities and Curiosities of Words and Literature,* ed. Martin Gardner. New York: Dover, 1961.
Espy, Willard R. *The Game of Words.* New York: Grosset & Dunlap, 1972.
Ulrich, Eugene. "Double Entendre Headlines." *Word Ways: The Journal of Recreational Linguistics* 17, no. 2 (August 1984): 136–137.

DOUBLE TIEGRAMS is an amusement based on Acrostics.

Two words with the same number of letters are chosen: e.g., John and Mary.

One is listed down the left side of the paper and the other is listed down the right side:

J	M
O	A
H	R
N	Y

The object is to find words which join the two listed words together.

J		M	(JAM)
O	M E G	A	(OMEGA)
H	E A	R	(HEAR)
N	A	Y	(NAY)

Rules may vary. It may be established that the words must all have the same number of letters (e.g., "jugum," "omega," "humor," and "nobby"). It may be played as a game with points awarded for the number of letters used.

Refer to Acrostics for similar word play.

BIBLIOGRAPHY

Shipley, Joseph T. *Playing with Words*. Englewood Cliffs, N.J.: Prentice-Hall, 1960.

DOUBLETONES, a game based on Puns, was created by Joseph T. Shipley, *Playing with Words* (1960).

Each player starts with two sheets of paper. On one he writes all of the words he can think of with dual meanings (in three minutes). On the other he writes two sentences for each of five of the words he has thought of, leaving a blank where the word would appear. The players exchange papers and attempt to come up with each other's words.

Refer to Pun for similar word play.

BIBLIOGRAPHY

Shipley, Joseph T. *Playing with Words*. Englewood Cliffs, N.J.: Prentice-Hall, 1960.

DOUBLETS, also called letter by letter, letter change, transmutations, word alchemy, and word ladders, is Lewis Carroll's term for a form of word play based on Anagrams that requires mutating from one word to another by changing one letter at a time without altering the other letters or their positions, and thus creating a word at each stage of the process:

mouse / house / horse / forse / forge / gorge / gorse / goose

Willard R. Espy has adapted this activity to a form of light verse. The verse is built around doublets, and the words that make up the chain are left blank. It is up to the reader to fill in the missing words.

For similar word play refer to Anagram, Espygram, Flat, and Meander.

BIBLIOGRAPHY

Borgmann, Dmitri A. *Language on Vacation: An Olio of Orthographical Oddities*. New York: Charles Scribner's Sons, 1967.
Dudeney, Henry Ernest. *300 Best Word Puzzles*. New York: Charles Scribner's Sons, 1968.
Espy, Willard R. *A Children's Almanac of Words at Play*. New York: Clarkson N. Potter, Inc., 1982.
_____. *The Game of Words*. New York: Grosset & Dunlap, 1972.
Parlett, David. *Botticelli and Beyond: Over 100 of the World's Best Word Games*. New York: Pantheon Books, 1981.

DROODLES. See REBUS.

DUMB CRAMBO is a variation on Crambo; it was the original name for acting out Charades.

Players divide into teams. One team leaves the room. The other team chooses a word.

The first team returns. The second team announces a word that rhymes with the word it has chosen. The first team is allowed three chances to guess the word, but it must present its guesses in mime—no speaking is allowed. If anyone on the team speaks, the team forfeits its turn.

Teams exchange roles and play continues. The winning team is the team with the most correct guesses when the players decide to quit.

For similar word play refer to Charades and Crambo.

BIBLIOGRAPHY

Brandreth, Gyles. *The World's Best Indoor Games*. New York: Pantheon Books, 1981.
Parlett, David. *Botticelli and Beyond: Over 100 of the World's Best Word Games*. New York: Pantheon Books, 1981.

E

ECHOES are repetitions of similar sounding syllables.

In Greek mythology, Echo was a nymph who wasted away for love of Narcissus until only her voice was left. According to Joseph T. Shipley, the Greek word "echo" means sound (according to *Webster's New Twentieth Century Dictionary*, a "reverberated sound"), and therefore the myth grew from the meaning of the word rather than the other way around. The myth is told in Ovid's *Metamorphoses*, Book 3, lines 379–400.

Echoes form the basis for echo verse, of which three examples follow:

Jack<u>son's</u> <u>sons</u>
My <u>low</u> esteem—my <u>lowest</u>
<u>Errol</u>, Roland <u>and</u> <u>Andrew</u>

C. C. Bombaugh, *Gleanings for the Curious* (1890), includes the following example, which he claims comes from *The Progress of Queen Elizabeth:*

Well, Echo, tell me yet,
  How might I come to see
This comely Queen of whom we talk?
  Oh, were she now by thee!
                  By thee.
By me? oh, were that true,
  How might I see her face?
How might I know her from the rest,
  Or judge her by her grace?
                  Her grace.

Well, then, if so mine eyes
  Be such as they have been,
Methinks I see among them all
  This same should be the Queen.
                    The Queen.

Bombaugh also includes the following song written by Joseph Addison:

Echo, tell me, while I wander
  O'er this fairy plain to prove him,
If my shepherd still grows fonder,
  Ought I in return to love him?
                    Love him, love him.

If he loves, as is the fashion,
  Should I churlishly forsake him?
Or, in pity to his passion,
  Fondly to my bosom take him?
                    Take him, take him.

Thy advice, then, I'll adhere to,
  Since in Cupid's chains I've led him,
And with Henry shall not fear to
  Marry, if you answer, "Wed him."
                    Wed him, wed him.

For similar word play refer to Chains, Heads and Tails, and Life Sentence.

BIBLIOGRAPHY

Bombaugh, C. C. *Gleanings for the Curious.* 1890. Reprint. *Oddities and Curiosities of Words and Literature,* ed. Martin Gardner. New York: Dover, 1961.

Espy, Willard R. *An Almanac of Words at Play.* New York: Clarkson N. Potter, Inc., 1975.

————. *The Game of Words.* New York: Grosset & Dunlap, 1972.

McKechnie, Jean L., et al., ed. *Webster's New Twentieth Century Dictionary of the English Language: Unabridged.* 2d ed. New York: World Publishing Co., 1971.

Ovid (Publius Ovidius Naso). *Metamorphoses,* trans. Rolfe Humphries. Bloomington: Indiana University Press, 1955.

Perrine, Laurence. "Echo." In *Encyclopedia of Poetry and Poetics.* Princeton: Princeton University Press, 1965.

Shipley, Joseph T. *Dictionary of Word Origins.* New York: Philosophical Library, 1945.

ELISION. See FLAT.

EMBLEMATIC POETRY, also called concrete poetry, picture poems, and shape poetry, is poetry that looks like its subject matter.

   According to C. C. Bombaugh, *Gleanings for the Curious* (1890), emblematic poetry was popular during the seventeenth century. George Wither (1588–1677) wrote the following:

Farewell,
Sweet groves, to you!
You hills that highest dwell,
And all you humble vales, adieu!
You wanton brooks and solitary rocks,
My dear companions all, and you my tender flocks!
Farewell, my pipe! and all those pleasing songs whose moving strains
Delighted once the fairest nymphs that dance upon the plains.
You discontents, whose deep and over-deadly smart
Have without pity broke the truest heart,
Sighs, tears, and every sad annoy,
That erst did with me dwell,
And others joy
Farewell!

Bombaugh also includes the following, which he claims came from the Christian monks of the Middle Ages:

The Cross

Blest they who seek,
While in their youth,
With   spirit   meek,
The   way   of   truth.
To them the Sacred Scriptures now display,
Christ as the only true and living way:
His precious blood on Calvary was given
To make them heirs of endless bliss in heaven.
And e'en on earth the child of God can trace
The glorious blessings of his Saviour's face.
For them He bore
His Father's frown,
For them He wore
The   thorny   crown;
Nailed to the cross,
Endured   its   pain,
That his life's loss
Might be their gain.
Then haste to choose
That   better   part—
Nor   dare   refuse
The Lord your heart,
Lest He declare,—
"I know you not;"
And   deep   despair
Shall be your lot.
Now look to Jesus who on Calvary died,
And trust on Him alone who there was crucified.

For similar word play refer to Looks Like Poetry, Pictonym, Rebus, and ZOO-LULU.

BIBLIOGRAPHY

Bombaugh, C. C. *Gleanings for the Curious*. 1890. Reprint. *Oddities and Curiosities of Words and Literature,* ed. Martin Gardner. New York: Dover, 1961.
Espy, Willard R. *An Almanac of Words at Play*. New York: Clarkson N. Potter, Inc., 1975.
————. *A Children's Almanac of Words at Play*. New York: Clarkson N. Potter, Inc., 1982.
————. *The Game of Words*. New York: Grosset & Dunlap, 1972.
Gensler, Kinereth, and Nina Nyhart. *The Poetry Connection: An Anthology of Contemporary Poems with Ideas to Stimulate Children's Writing*. New York: Teachers & Writers, 1978.

ENDLESS TALES, also called shaggy dog stories, are stories that never end; they have no point other than to see how long the audience will put up with them before realizing it is being taken in.

For similar word play see Round.

BIBLIOGRAPHY

Espy, Willard R. *A Children's Almanac of Words at Play*. New York: Clarkson N. Potter, Inc., 1982.

ENIGMA is a Riddle or Pun based on an obscure or ambiguous allusion; it is one of the established Flats of the National Puzzlers' League.

Here are two famous examples:

The riddle of the sphinx (the riddle Oedipus solved to rid the city of Thebes from the Sphinx):

A thing whose feet are two and four and three, and moves most slowly when on most feet does go.

Answer: Man—he crawls on four feet as a baby, walks on two feet as an adult and uses a cane as a third foot in old age.

The riddle of Samson (Samson had killed a lion and later found that a hive of bees had made honey in the lion's carcass. He posed the riddle to the Philistines, who agreed to let him go if he could ask them a riddle that they could not solve):

Out of the eater came something to eat;
Out of the strong came something sweet.

Answer: A honeycomb in the body of a dead lion.

For similar word play refer to Flat, Pun, and Riddle.

BIBLIOGRAPHY

Eckler, A. Ross. *Word Recreations: Games and Diversions from "Word Ways."* New York: Dover, 1979.

Laubach, David C. *Introduction to Folklore*. Rochelle Park, N.J.: Hayden Book Co., 1980.

Taylor, Archer. *English Riddles from Oral Tradition*. Los Angeles: University of California Press, 1951.

———. *The Literary Riddle Before 1600*. Los Angeles: University of California Press, 1948.

ENIGMATIC REBUS. See FLAT.

EPIGRAM. See PROVERB.

EQUIVOCALLY SPEAKING, also called equivoque, is the radical change in the meaning of a passage by making a slight change in it. Often as slight as a change of a comma, it might be as drastic as the reading of every other line. It is a form of Charades; if the meaning is risqué it is also an example of Double Entendre.

C. C. Bombaugh includes the following équivoque, a copy of a letter written by Cardinal Richelieu to the French ambassador at Rome, in *Gleanings for the Curious* (1890):

First read the letter as you would normally, then read only the first column.

Sir,—Mons. Compigne, a Savoyard by birth, / a Friar of the order of Saint Benedict, is the man who will present to you / as his passport to your protection, this letter. He is one of the most / discreet, the wisest and the least meddling persons that I have ever known / or have had the pleasure to converse with. He has long earnestly solicited me / to write to you in his favor, and to give him a suitable character, / together with a letter of credence; which I have accordingly granted to / his real merit, rather I must say, than to his importunity; for, believe me, Sir, / his modesty is only exceeded by his worth, I should be sorry that you should be / wanting in serving him on account of being misinformed of his real character; / I should be afflicted if you were as some other gentlemen have been, / misled on that score, who now esteem him, and those among the best of my friends; / wherefore, and from no other motive I think it my duty to advertise you / that you are most particularly desired, to have especial attention to all he does, / to show him all the respect imaginable, nor venture to say any thing before him, / that may either offend or displease him in any sort; for I may truly say, there is / no man I love so much as M. Compigne, none whom I should more regret to see / neglected, as no one can be more worthy to be received and trusted in decent society. / Base, therefore, would it be to injure him. And I well know, that as soon as you / are made sensible of his virtues, and shall become acquainted with him / you will love him as I do; and then you will thank me for this my advice. / The assurance I entertain of your Courtesy obliges me to desist from / urging this matter to you further, or saying any thing more on this subject. / Believe me, Sir etc. RICHELIEU.

For similar word play refer to Charades and Double Entendre.

BIBLIOGRAPHY

Bombaugh, C. C. *Gleanings for the Curious*. 1890. Reprint. *Oddities and Curiosities of Words and Literature,* ed. Martin Gardner. New York: Dover, 1961.
Espy, Willard R. *An Almanac of Words at Play.* New York: Clarkson N. Potter, Inc., 1975.
_____. *The Game of Words.* New York: Grosset & Dunlap, 1972.

EQUIVOQUE. See EQUIVOCALLY SPEAKING.

ESPYGRAM is Willard R. Espy's term for light verse containing Anagrams.

Though Arthur Swann had already written similar verses for *Saturday Review,* Espy was the one who made them famous, first publishing them in *Punch* and then in *The Game of Words* (1974).

The espygram is built around an anagram. The words which are anagrams of each other are then omitted. The puzzler must figure them out:

The lion shook his _____ again;
The _____ boy called a _____;
"_____, _____, _____ again,"
His mother cried, "It's not a game."

(Answer: mane, mean, name, amen, amen, amen)

For similar word play refer to Anagram, Doublets, and Missing Words.

BIBLIOGRAPHY

Espy, Willard R. *The Game of Words.* New York: Grosset & Dunlap, 1974.
Worden, Mark. "The Life and Times of Willard Espy (A Play on Words in Three Acts)." *Writer's Digest* 64 (April 1984): 34–37.

ESPYRAMID. See PROGRESSIVE ANAGRAM.

EUPHEMAKEN is a game based on euphemy, the substituting of a pleasant word for a dangerous or unpleasant one, e.g., "darn" for "damn," "Jehovah" for "God," "Odds bodikins" for "God's Little Body" (the Host).

The game goes as follows. Each player lists five disagreeable qualities:

rude, smelly, crude, loud, greedy

Next to each word the players write another word with the same denotative meaning but with complimentary associations:

rude: rugged
smelly: scented
crude: earthy
loud: grandiose
greedy: acquisitive

Finally the players write a sentence for each word, five pairs of sentences:

He was so rude to her that she finally slapped him.
She was attracted to his rugged individualism.

He was smelly from playing football.
The room was scented with strawberry incense.

It's crude to eat chicken with your hands.
He had an earthy attractiveness.

The music was too loud.
The music was grandiose.

He was greedy when it came to money.
He had an acquisitive disposition and learned quickly.

For similar word play refer to Pun.

BIBLIOGRAPHY

Espy, Willard R. *An Almanac of Words at Play.* New York: Clarkson N. Potter, Inc., 1975.
_____. *The Game of Words.* New York: Grosset & Dunlap, 1972.
Lewis, Norman, ed. *The New Roget's Thesaurus of the English Language in Dictionary Form.* Lib. ed. New York: G. P. Putnam's Sons, 1978.
Shipley, Joseph T. *Playing with Words.* Englewood Cliffs, N.J.: Prentice-Hall, 1960.
Spears, Richard A. *Slang and Euphemism: A Dictionary of Oaths, Curses, Insults, Sexual Slang and Metaphor, Racial Slurs, Drug Talk, Homosexual Lingo, and Related Matters.* Middle Village, N.Y.: Jonathan David Publishers, Inc., 1981.

EXPANDING WORDS. See PROGRESSIVE ANAGRAM.

EXTRAS is a term used by the National Puzzlers' League to denote puzzles not included in their other classifications (Anagrams and antigrams, Flats, Forms, Cryptograms, and Kreweland Unusual). See Flat for a brief discussion of the National Puzzlers' League.

Some of the more common types of extras are anaquotes, cryptic crosswords, knight's-tour crypts, and piecemeals.

An anaquote (similar to a Constructapo) is a short quotation divided into successive three-letter groups which are arranged alphabetically (often with the final group only one or two letters long); the lengths of the original words and the correct punctuation are given; the author's name usually appears at the end of the quotation and is included in the alphabetized groupings. Here is an example:

(2 2, 2 3 2 2: 4 2 3 8: *1. *11)
AKE ARE ATI EOR EQU EST ETH ION NOT SPE STH TOB TOB WSH.
(The answer: To be, or not to be: that is the question. William Shakespeare)

A cryptic crossword is a small Crossword Puzzle where the definitions have two parts: 1) a Synonym of the answer; and 2) a cryptic clue to it; generally the clues take the form of Transposals ("tone" = "note"), Hidden Words ("I know him well" = "whim"), phonetic connections ("bear" = "bare"), charade ("meat" = "me - at"), reversals ("not" = "ton"), secondary definition ("belfry" = "refuge"), or word deletion ("Leander" = "and leer").

A knight's-tour crypt consists of a grid, usually in the shape of a rectangle, with each square containing a single letter or mark of punctuation. The idea is to move from letter to letter as a knight would move in a game of chess (two squares in one direction and one square in a right-angle direction, or one and then two, forming an L shape) to spell out the message.

A piecemeal puzzle consists of words of a given length in which the final two or three letters of each word overlap the first two or three letters of another word. The solution words are divided into groups of two (sometimes three) letters and the groups alphabetized. By placing these groups in a geometric pattern (generally a square) the solver can sort out the original words. For example, AN CH DE IR MO NI SM ST can be rearranged to form

MO	NI	SM
DE		IR
ST	AN	CH

For similar word play refer to Anagram, Constructapo, Cryptogram, Flat, Forms, and Kreweland Unusual.

BIBLIOGRAPHY

"Mini-Sample." *The Enigma* (July 1978).
Nightowl, Treesong, Merlin, Hap, et al. *Guide to "The Enigma."* Buffalo, N.Y.: National Puzzlers' League, 1977.

F

FAMOUS NAME PUZZLES are a form of word play where clues are given to help solve letters which in turn spell out a famous name.

Here is an example:

1. My first letter is in "to<u>y</u>s" and "<u>s</u>ick"	S
2. My second letter is in "not" and "new"	N
3. My third letter is in "hot" and "box"	O
4. My fourth letter is in "hope" and "sock"	O
5. My fifth letter is in "pot" and "pill"	P
6. My sixth letter is in "my" and "fly"	Y

For similar word play refer to Anagram.

BIBLIOGRAPHY

Espy, Willard R. *A Children's Almanac of Words at Play*. New York: Clarkson N. Potter, Inc., 1982.

FANCY FAIRY TALES are familiar stories told using fancy words in place of ordinary words.

Here is an example, a fancy telling of Grimm's "Little Show-White":

Once upon a millennium in the half way point between the extremes of the season when the leaves fall from the perennial plants having permanent, woody, self-supporting stems, when the flakes of precipitation in the form of ice crystals hexagonal in form were descending like one of the horny structures forming the principal covering of birds from the stratosphere, a female sovereign supported her body by her buttocks at an opening to admit the light sewing, and the frame of the opening to let in the light was constructed of ebony, etc.

For similar word play refer to Cliché and Hackneyed Images.

BIBLIOGRAPHY

Grimm, Jakob, and Wilhelm Grimm. *Grimm's Household Tales,* Vol. 1. Trans. Margaret
    Hunt. London: George Bell and Sons, 1884. Reprint. Detroit: Singing Tree Press,
    1968.

FICTIONARY DICTIONARY. See DICTIONARY DEFINITIONS GAME.

FIND THE PHRASE. See REBUS.

FIND THE QUESTION. See WHAT IS THE QUESTION?

FIRST LETTERS is an alphabet game, a form of Alphabent. Fifteen letters of
the alphabet are chosen at random. Each player then must write a sentence using
the fifteen letters at the beginning of fifteen consecutive words:

a, b, e, g, h, m, n, p, t, c, s, w, o, p, r
A boy elephant got his mother new panties to catch some wise, old, purple rat.

For similar word play refer to Alphabetical Adjectives, Alphabet Word Chain,
A to Z Banquet, I Gave My Love, I Love My Love, I Packed My Bag, I Went to
Market, and Travelling Alphabet.

BIBLIOGRAPHY

Brandreth, Gyles. *Indoor Games.* London: Hodder & Stoughton, Ltd., 1977.

FLAT is a term used by the National Puzzlers' League (NPL) to designate any
word puzzle in verse whose solution can be printed as a single row of letters.
    The National Puzzlers' League traces its history back to July 4, 1883, when a
small group of people interested in word puzzles gathered at Pythagoras Hall in
New York City and founded the Eastern Puzzlers' League. In 1920 the name was
changed to the National Puzzlers' League. The stated goals of the league are to
provide entertainment, to raise the standards of puzzling, and to establish friend-
ships among members. The league publishes *The Engima* and holds semiannual
or annual meetings when possible.
    Flats are just one of the categories of puzzles the NPL deals with. Others
include Anagrams, antigrams, Forms, crypts, Extras, and Kreweland Unusual.
    The following rules apply to flats:

1. All of the puzzle answers ("keywords" in NPL language) must be defined in both the
    second and the third edition of *Webster's New International Dictionary* or must be
    noted as "only in NI2" (the second edition) or "only in NI3" (the third edition), or on
    rare occasions "not in NI." Rare, dialect, obsolete, archaic, foreign, and slang words
    may be used but must be identified as such. Reformed spellings are not allowed.

2. The number of letters in the keyword(s) must be given in parentheses; if a phrase, the number of letters in each word plus any punctuation must be given. Apostrophes and hyphens must be retained; capital letters must be preceded by asterisks; phrases must retain their normal punctuation. Thus, "Denver, Colorado" would be identified as (*6, *8); "jack-in-the-box" as (4-2-3-3).

3. All puzzles must be fairly and clearly clued. Though the lines may be a bit vague, enough information must be given to allow for a solution. Only on rare occasions may the keywords be juxtaposed, as this tends to eliminate context clues.

4. Verse must be correct grammatically and metrically and must rhyme (near-rhymes and assonance are not allowed).

5. Each time a keyword appears in a verse it must be replaced by a clue word, i.e., FIRST, LAST, ONE, TWO, ALL.

Numerous puzzles fit under the category of flats, and more are constantly being created. The following list contains the more common types: acrostical enigma, alternade, beheadment, charade, curtailment, deletion, Enigma, head-to-tail shift, heteronym, homoantonym, homonym, homosynonym, letter bank, letter change, linkade, literatim, metathesis, numerical, padlock, Palindrome, Rebus, rebus alternade, repeated letter change, reversal, spoonergram, terminal deletion, Transposal, and word deletion. Examples of these puzzles follow.

Acrostical enigma (formed by dividing the keyword into groups of two or more successive letters which in turn are added to the first two or more letters of successive couplets to form a word which the couplet refers to or is a Synonym of, the final couplet or quatrain expressing a clue to the entire keyword:

(9)
A. Prudent not and fresh as rain,
   impudent! He would not restrain!
B. Sated, throbbing rapidly,
   Expand, contract repeatedly.
C. Strumming one phrase, then another,
   singing two or three together.
D. Loci type quick and very fast,
   The speed, the careless speed, can't last.
A trait of personality
   That thoughtless people often be.
(Answer: impulsive; imprudent, pulsate, sistrum, velocity)

Alternade (either a binade, formed by taking successive alternating letters from the keyword and dividing it into two words, or a trinade, formed by taking every third letter from the keyword to form three words; a less rigid form of alternade is a word lock, which allows for no regular pattern of letter separation, except that the letters must remain in the same order as in the original word [appear; ape, par]); a binade:

(5; 3, 2)
How can I FIRST a value
on someone as TOTAL as you?
SECOND all know how rare it is
to find someone honest and true.
(Answer: sweet; set, we)

Beheadment (formed by removing the keyword's first letter to form a new word):

(5, 4)
She was just a dumb ONE
With a lot of TWO.
(Answer: cluck, luck)

Charade (formed by dividing the keyword into two or more words):

(6; 3, 3)
He likes to eat corn-on-the-ONE;
You might say he's a corn-cob TWO;
He eats it with butter and salt;
He's in a high calorie rut.
(Answer: cobnut; cob, nut)

Curtailment (formed by removing the keyword's final letter to create a new word):

(8, 7)
The ONE was pulled by a dirty old man,
The TWO propelled by a man with a tan.
(Answer: handcart, handcar)

Deletion (formed by removing a letter from the middle of one word to create another word):

(5, 4)
He was eating his TWO of peas,
With a ONE fork and a plastic plate;
But halfway through he had to sneeze;
Lord only knows what became of the peas.
(Answer: metal, meal)

Enigma (a riddle):

(4)
I'm found in potatoes and needles and frogs,
But never in oranges or apples or logs.
(Answer: eyes)

Head-to-tail shift (a transposal where the head letter of one keyword is re-moved and placed at the end of the other keyword):

(5)
He will often ONE
To bake some TWO,
But end up making
Chocolate hearts.
(Answer: start/tarts)

Heteronym (formed from two keywords having the same spelling but different meanings and pronunciations):

(8; 4, 4)
We had to ONE
When we sang the song,
Because each verse ended
With TWO, dang, dong.
(Answer: grinding; grin, ding)

Homoantonym (formed by choosing two keywords or phrases which are hom-onymous to a pair of antonyms):

(5 / 4; homonymous to 5 / 4)
TWO, ONE, and everywhere,
THREE petals fill the air,
I FOUR the wind blow through the trees,
And feel them in my hair.
(Answer: there/here; their/hear)

Homonym (formed from two keywords with the same sound):

(5, 6', 5)
It isn't fair
For them to eat ONE;
After all,
TWO only small,
Not different,
Just not tall,
They deserve THREE own fair share.
(Answer: there, they're, their)

Homosynonym (formed by choosing two keywords or phrases which are hom-onymous to synonyms):

(3 / 3; 3 / 1)
Each TWO opens and FOUR ONE the THREE.
(Answer: see/eye; sea/I)

Letter bank (formed by taking a short word which has no repeated letters and creating longer words which have all the letters of the short word, repeated as often as necessary, and no other letters):

(4, *9)
The ONE were set in TWO
To catch a fish as big as me.
(Answer: nets, Tennessee)

Letter change (formed by changing a certain letter in one word to create another word):

(first letter change; 5)
If you hit your ONE
On the bottom of that pool,
You'll TWO;
Don't be such a fool!
(Answer: crown, drown)

Linkade (formed by dividing a keyword into two or more words which share a common letter or letters at their junctures):

(6; 3, 4)
The TWO was flat
And so was the spare,
So down we ONE
All lost in despair.
(Answer: satire; sat, tire)

Literatim (formed from the sounds of the letters of the keyword taken separately or in combination):

(4)
M2 2s s4 that you've made some 1
And frosted cakes for us to 4-1;
2 must b4 right, 2 know 2 3,
Come take a seat and let's begin.
(Answer: time)

Metathesis (a transposal formed by interchanging two letters of one keyword to form another keyword):

(5)
I drink a ONE of vinegar each day
To keep the surgeon's TWO away.
(Answer: cruet, curet)

Numerical (formed by substituting numbers for the letters of the keyword consecutively, making two shorter anagrams of the word, offering a couplet clue to the entire word, and offering a couplet clue to each of the shorter words, which are represented by their numerical equivalents):

(7; 4, 3)
TOTAL: I taste delicious freshly made,
      And often start a kitchen raid.
3-5-4-6: People take me on a hike
      To carry food and drink and light.
1-2-7: People use me to play pool,
      They say I'm warped, but they're the fool.
(Answer: cupcake, pack, cue)

Padlock (formed by combining the non-overlapping parts of two words to create a third):

(5 / 3 / 4)
I TWO my sights on winning,
But the men in the THREE
Could see I was ONE,
And my troubles were just beginning.
(Answer: ten*se* / *set* / *t*ent)

Palindrome (formed from a phrase or a sentence that reads the same forward as it does backward; consonants are replaced by blanks):

_ O _ _ E _ _ E _ E _ _ E _ _ O _
How much does it weigh
When the tret's away?
(Answer: not ten level net ton)

Rebus (formed by using letters, figures, or other symbols to represent words or phrases; a phonetic rebus employs sound rather than spelling for some or all of its components [e.g., "i" for "eye"]; an enigmatic rebus is one in which some of the components are not given and must be derived from clues in the verse; a suber is a reversed rebus); a rebus:

(1, 4', 5, 3)
IC& ST& U
I thought that you loved me true,
But you ran around and made me feel blue;
I try to forgive, I try to forget;
But all I can say is ALL!
(Answer: I can't stand you)

Rebus alternade (a complex form combining the rebus and the alternade); a rebus trinade:

(6, 6, 6: 'S M IC IC HX I OH I ON LG)
I went to ONE with boys and girls,
Where TWO was the golden rule;
So with a girl I tried to mix,
An THREE and I a fool.
(Answer: School, mixing, icicle)

Repeated letter change (formed by replacing a repeated letter in a word with another letter throughout the word):

(4 / 4)
He put a ONE in his mulligan stew,
And then, for flavor,
Stuck a TWO in it too.
(Answer: beet / boot)

Reversal (a transposal where one keyword is the reverse of the other):

(3)
The ONE was on the grass the day we TWO;
The ONE was gone before we went to bed.
(Answer: dew, wed)

Switchback or backswitch (formed by changing the first letter of a keyword and turning around the remaining letters to form the other word):

(4 / 4)
He drank a ONE,
And it made him feel free;
But his freedom was short;
He fell out of a TWO.
(Answer: beer, tree)

Spoonergram (formed by exchanging the initial sound(s) of two words or syllables in the answer):

(2 3, 2 3)
ONE we'd TWO by the end of the day,
So when the rain came we had nothing to say.
(Answer: we bet, be wet)

Terminal deletion (formed by removing both the first and the final letters of the keyword to form a new word; in transdeletion, a letter is removed from a word and the remaining letters are rearranged to form a new word at least three times [e.g., mater, team, eat, at], avoiding beheadment and curtailment); a terminal deletion:

(5, 3)
He never learned to TWO a boat,
He never learned to swim;
He'll ONE, he'll ONE, he'll ONE for sure,
If he ever goes fishing again.
(Answer: drown, row)

Transposal (formed by arranging the letters of one keyword in a new order to form a second keyword; transpogram is a variation where entire words are interchanged); a transposal:

(*6, 6)
ONE believed that man evolved
From the same beasts as chimpanzees,
But all the laughter he received
Entrapped him in controversies;
He turned his pain and doubt TWO,
To struggle where none other sees.
(Answer: Darwin, inward)

Word deletion (formed by removing a shorter word from the middle of a longer word and joining the two ends of the longer word to form another word):

(*7; 3, 4)
ALL loved Hero,
ONE watched him from year to year,
But Hero thought ALL's look
Was nothing more than a TWO.
(Answer: Leander; and, leer)

For similar word play refer to Anagram, Beheading, Charades, Enigma, Extras, Head-to-Tail Shift, Kreweland Unusual, Palindrome, Rebus, Spoonerism, and Transposal.

BIBLIOGRAPHY

Borgmann, Dmitri A. *Beyond Language: Adventures in Word and Thought*. New York: Charles Scribner's Sons, 1967.
———. *Language on Vacation: An Olio of Orthographical Oddities*. New York: Charles Scribner's Sons, 1965.
Eckler, A. Ross. *Word Recreations: Games and Diversions from "Word Ways."* New York: Dover, 1972.
The Enigma (all issues). Buffalo, N.Y.: National Puzzlers' League, 1883–present.
McKechnie, Jean L., et al. *Webster's New Twentieth Century Dictionary of the English Language: Unabridged*. 2d ed. New York: World Publishing Co., 1971.

"Mini-Sample." *The Enigma* (July 1978).

Nightowl, Treesong, Merlin, Hap, et al. *Guide to "The Enigma."* Buffalo, N.Y.: National Puzzlers' League, 1977.

Word Ways: The Journal of Recreational Linguistics.

FOLK RIDDLE. See POPULAR RIDDLE.

FORM-A-WORD is a general term for word play based on groups of words containing the same smaller word.

Here is an example:

1. You drink this PUN. (punch)
2. This PUN is part of a famous form of puppet show. (Punch-and-Judy)
3. This PUN is what you do to a sentence. (punctuate)

For similar word play refer to Anagram, Animalistics, Confusing and Confounding Cats, Cross-breed, Flat, and Galaxy of Gals.

BIBLIOGRAPHY

Fuller, John G. *Games for Insomniacs; or, A Lifetime Supply of Insufferable Brain Twisters.* New York: Doubleday, 1966.

Morris, William, and Mary Morris. *The Word Game Book.* New York: Harper & Brothers, 1959.

FORMS is a term used by the National Puzzlers' League to designate puzzles similar to Crossword Puzzles but having solutions printed in geometrical shapes, with no black squares or bars allowed.

Some of the more common geometrical shapes are: connected word squares (two separate word squares which share one common line of letters), pentagons, right star (the words beginning from the top of the star and running down the right side, and from the left point of the star and running across), left star (the key word running down the right side of the star), pyramid, diamond, left rhomboid, right rhomboid, enneagons, left windmill, right windmill, inverted pyramid, truncated pyramid, half squares, left lattice, and right lattice.

The form is denoted a "double" if the words across and down are different (requiring separate definitions). A progressive word square is built from successive words which vary by only one letter (see Doublets). Enigmatic forms have cryptic or phonetic solutions (see cryptic crossword under Extras).

Here is an example of a diamond form:

```
          A
        A N A
      A R O S E
    A N O T H E R
      A S H E N
        E E N
          R
```

For similar word play refer to Crossword Puzzle, Doublets, Extras, and Flat.

BIBLIOGRAPHY

The Enigma. Buffalo, N.Y.: National Puzzlers' League, 1883–present.
"Mini-Sample." *The Enigma* (1978).
Nightowl, Treesong, Merlin, Hap, et al. *Guide to "The Enigma."* Buffalo, N.Y.: National Puzzlers' League, 1977.

FRACTURED BOOK-REVIEWS is a name used by John G. Fuller for a punning game involving book critiques.

The idea is to take the title of a famous book and offer a one-line critique of it based on a Pun of its title.

Here is an example:

Stephen King, *Firestarter:* This should be a red hot seller.

For similar word play refer to Book Conversation, Captions Courageous, Conundrum, Defective Detective, Headlines, MADvertisements, Pun, and Subject Matter.

BIBLIOGRAPHY

Fuller, John G. *Games for Insomniacs; or, A Lifetime Supply of Insufferable Brain Twisters.* New York: Doubleday, 1966.

FRACTURED GEOGRAPHY is a name used by John G. Fuller for the combining of a real or fictional town with a state Abbreviation to form a Pun, e.g., Church, Mass.; Bent, Kan.; Sing, La.; and Bad Luck, Ill.

For similar word play refer to Abbreviations, Conundrum, Fractured Book-Reviews, Fractured Industry, Jumbled Geography, and Pun.

BIBLIOGRAPHY

Fuller, John G. *Games for Insomniacs; or, A Lifetime Supply of Insufferable Brain Twisters.* New York: Doubleday, 1966.

FRACTURED INDUSTRY is a name used by John G. Fuller for the combining of well-known Proverbs or quotations with the words of industry or advertising.

The idea is to find a quotation or proverb which will form a humorous combination with a common product:

"Friends, Romans, countrymen, lend me your ears" (a quotation from *Julius Caesar*), for a business selling cotton swabs.

Fuller suggests a game based on this form of word play. Each player is provided with a common list of popular quotations written down the left side of a piece of paper. Enough space is left on the right side of the paper for the players to list company names that match the quotations. Space may also be left for the players to come up with their own quotations.

The players with the most or best (as voted on by all) quotations score an established number of points.

For similar word play refer to Conundrum, Fractured Book-Reviews, Fractured Geography, Invent-a-Name, Portmanteau, Proverb, and Pun.

BIBLIOGRAPHY

Fuller, John G. *Games for Insomniacs; or, A Lifetime Supply of Insufferable Brain Twisters*. New York: Doubleday, 1966.

G

GALAXY OF GALS is an amusement created by William and Mary Morris, *The Word Game Book* (1959), for a form of word play requiring the completing of words beginning with "gal," e.g., Four quarts equal a gal _____ (gallon).

For similar word play refer to Animalistics, Confusing and Confounding Cats, Cross-breed, Form-a-Word, and Quiz That Man.

BIBLIOGRAPHY

Morris, William, and Mary Morris. *The Word Game Book.* New York: Harper & Brothers, 1959.

GAME RHYMES, also called play rhymes, are a form of word play associated with games, generally children's playground games.

One example, quoted by Peter and Iona Opie in *Children's Games in Street and Playground,* comes from Mactaggart's *Gallovidian Encyclopedia* (1824), page 300, where it appeared under the title "King and Queen o' Cantelon":

Two boys stand between two "doons" or places of safety and attempt to catch the rest of the players when they run from one doon to the other, after being called forth with the following rhyme:

"King and Queen o' Cantelon,
How mony mile to Babylon;
Six or seven, or a lang eight,
Try to win there wi' candle-light."

For similar word play refer to Acting Out Rhymes, Ball Bouncing Games, Counting Rhymes, Dialogue Games, Hand Clapping Rhymes, Jump Rope Rhymes, Nursery Rhymes, and Skipping Rhymes.

BIBLIOGRAPHY

Abrahams, Roger D. *Jump-Rope Rhymes: A Dictionary*. Austin: University of Texas Press, 1969.

Abrahams, Roger D., and Lois Rankin. *Counting-Out Rhymes: A Dictionary*. Austin: University of Texas Press, 1980.

Opie, Peter, and Iona Opie. *Children's Games in Street and Playground*. 1969. Reprint. New York: Oxford University Press, 1979.

————. *The Lore and Language of Schoolchildren*. 1959. Reprint. New York: Oxford University Press, 1980.

Sutton-Smith, Brian. *The Folkgames of Children*. Austin: University of Texas Press, 1972.

GHOST AND SUPERGHOST, also called donkey, were originally called wraiths because the children who played them considered those who lost so far beyond the pale that they were ghosts; it is a word-building game.

The first player announces a letter or letters of a potential word of four or more letters. Each player in turn adds a letter to the end of the letters, the letters together in the sequence they are announced forming a potential word, but not completing a word.

Players may be challenged for two reasons: 1) for having completed a word; and 2) for having added a letter which prevents the forming of a valid word. If the challenged player cannot form a word, he becomes a third of a ghost. If the challenged player can form a word, the challenger becomes a third of a ghost. Once a player has lost three times, he becomes all ghost and loses the game.

Here is an example:

First player: The   (less than four letters)
Second player: Ther
Third player: Theri
First player: Challenges the third player.
Third player: Theriac—a compound of sixty-four drugs used by people of the time of Classical Greece as an antidote for poison.
First player loses and becomes a third of a ghost. The second player starts another word.

Superghost follows the same rules as ghost except that letters may be added to either end of the word:

First player: The
Second player: Othe
Third player: Rothe
First player: Brothe
Second player cannot add a letter and becomes a third of a ghost.

Anaghost combines ghost and anagrams. In this version letters need not be added sequentially, and if the letters form an anagram of a word the player announcing those letters becomes a third of a ghost. Also, in anaghost even a word of less than four letters is not allowed:

First player: r
Second player: tr
Third player: tmr
first player: ytmr
Second player challenges. First player forms "myrtle." Second player becomes a third of a ghost.

See the entry for Ultraghost, also called license plate game, for a related game. For other similar word play refer to Acromania, Anagram, Crossword Puzzle, and Flat.

BIBLIOGRAPHY

Brandreth, Gyles. *Indoor Games*. London: Hodder & Stoughton, Ltd., 1977.
_____. *The Joy of Lex: How to Have Fun with 860,341,500 Words*. New York: Quill, 1983.
Eckler, A. Ross. *Word Recreations: Games and Diversions from "Word Ways."* New York: Dover, 1979.
Espy, Willard R. *The Game of Words*. New York: Grosset & Dunlap, 1972.
Morris, William, and Mary Morris. *The Word Game Book*. New York: Harper & Brothers, 1959.
Parlett, David. *Botticelli and Beyond: Over 100 of the World's Best Word Games*. New York: Pantheon Books, 1981.
Sharp, Richard, and John Piggott. *The Book of Games*. New York: Galahad Books, 1977.
Shipley, Joseph T. "Word and Letter Games." In *Encyclopaedia Britannica: Macropaedia*. 1979.

GIOTTO, also called jotto and wordpower, is a word guessing game similar to Convergence; it is a language game equivalent of the number game bull and cow, and of Meirovit's deductive game using colored pegs, mastermind.

Each player writes down a key word of an agreed length (five letters works well). The object is to guess the other player's word. This is done by calling out a word of an equal number of letters. The other player states how many letters of the hidden word appear in the called-out word, regardless of position.

Players may or may not decide to consider an anagram a winning call (e.g., the key word is "notes"; the called-out word is "tones").

Crash is a slight variation on Giotto where only the letters corresponding to letters in the same position are indicated as "crashes," e.g., the key word is "notes"; the called out word is "names"; there are three crashes (n, e, s).

In wild crash the players may keep changing the key word as long as it does not falsify previous answers.

For similar word play refer to Convergence, Shaffe's Game, and Uncrash.

BIBLIOGRAPHY

Eckler, A. Ross. *Word Recreations: Games and Diversions from "Word Ways."* New York: Dover, 1979.
Parlett, David. *Botticelli and Beyond: Over 100 of the World's Best Word Games.* New York: Pantheon Books, 1981.
Sharp, Richard, and John Piggott. *The Book of Games.* New York: Galahad Books, 1977.

GNOME. See PROVERB.

GOLDWYNNER is word play named after motion picture magnate Samuel Goldwyn, who was famous for his Boners or Irish Bulls; it is accidental word play based on Puns.

For instance, Goldwyn said, "Our comedies are not to be laughed at."

Joseph T. Shipley collected a number of Goldwynners created by Goldwyn publicity managers. Here are a few:

Include me out!
I'll tell you in two words: I'm possible!
Didn't you hear me keeping still?
I read part of it all the way through.
We have to get some fresh platitudes.
It rolls off my back like a duck.

For similar word play refer to Boner, Conundrum, Irish Bull, and Pun.

BIBLIOGRAPHY

Shipley, Joseph T. *Playing with Words.* Englewood Cliffs, N.J.: Prentice-Hall, 1960.

GUGGENHEIM is a category game involving the playing of five categories games at the same time.

Five categories are chosen (cities, dogs, cars, famous men, holidays, or something similar might serve as the categories). Each player lists the five categories down the side of a sheet of paper, and lists five agreed upon letters across the top of the paper (creating a five by five grid). A time limit is set (say ten minutes). During that time each player attempts to fill his grid by finding an example for each category that begins with the letter in question:

	D	H	M	R	S
Cities	Delaware	Houston	Miami	Richfield	San Diego
Dogs	Doberman pinscher	Hound	Maltese	Retriever	Setter
Cars	Dodge	Honda	Mercury	Rolls Royce	Sedan
Famous Men	Dali	Hoover	Melville	Richard III	Solomon
Holidays	Decoration Day	Holy Days of Obligation	Memorial Day	Rosh Hashanah	St. Valentine's Day

For similar word play refer to Category Puzzles.

BIBLIOGRAPHY

Brandreth, Gyles. *Indoor Games*. London: Hodder & Stoughton, Ltd., 1977.
_____. *The World's Best Indoor Games*. New York: Pantheon Books, 1981.
Morris, William, and Mary Morris. *The Word Game Book*. New York: Harper & Brothers, 1959.
Parlett, David. *Botticelli and Beyond: Over 100 of the World's Best Word Games*. New York: Pantheon Books, 1981.

H

HACKNEYED IMAGES is a form of word play that uses Clichés.

Each player attempts to write as many clichés as he can in a set amount of time (ten minutes).

For similar word play refer to Cliché and Fancy Fairy Tales.

BIBLIOGRAPHY

Shipley, Joseph T. *Playing with Words.* Englewood Cliffs, N.J.: Prentice-Hall, 1960.

THE HAIRY APE is word play involving word grouping.

The title comes from Joseph Shipley, *Playing with Words,* and is taken from Eugene O'Neill's play of the same name.

The object is to take four words (three of which are related in some way) and pick out the word that does not belong.

Various forms of this game have been common material on I.Q. tests, possibly because it fits the multiple choice format so well.

Since the words can be related in many ways other than by meaning (e.g., they may be Antonyms, Synonyms, ABC Words, and so on), the games can become very sophisticated.

Refer to Flat for various combinations that can be made and applied to The Hairy Ape.

BIBLIOGRAPHY

Shipley, Joseph T. *Playing with Words.* Englewood Cliffs, N.J.: Prentice-Hall, 1960.

HAND CLAPPING RHYMES are verses said to the clapping of hands; they are a form of Acting Out Rhymes; other hand, arm, and leg movements often accompany the hand clapping.

Here are two examples from a school playground in Havre, Montana:

Eni, meni, pasadeni,
Oom pa papadeni,
Education, liberation,
I love you tutti fruitti,
Down by the roller coaster,
Sweet, sweet, sweet baby,
Never wanna let you go;
Shimrock, shimrock,
Shimmy shimmy shimrock,
Eat a piece of candy,
Yummy, yummy,
Jump out the window,
Crazy, crazy,
Won't do the dishes,
Lazy, lazy,
Eni, meni, pasadeni,
Oom pa papaleni,
Education, liberation,
I love you tutti fruitti.

Say, say, oh, playmate
Come out and play with me;
Bring your dollies three,
Climb up my apple tree,
Slide down my rainbow
Into my cellar door,
And we'll be jolly friends
Forever more, more, mo, mo more.
Say, say, oh, enemy
Come out and fight with me;
Bring your weapons three,
Climb up my poison tree,
Slide down my razor blade
Into my cellar door,
And we'll be enemies
Forever more, more, mo, mo, more.

For similar word play refer to Acting Out Rhymes, Ball Bouncing Rhymes, Counting Rhymes, Dialogue Games, Jump Rope Rhymes, Nursery Rhymes, and Skipping Rhymes.

BIBLIOGRAPHY

Abrahams, Roger D., and Lois Rankin. *Counting-Out Rhymes: A Dictionary.* Austin: University of Texas, 1980.
Opie, Peter, and Iona Opie. *Children's Games in Street and Playground.* 1969. Reprint. New York: Oxford University Press, 1979.

_____. *The Lore and Language of Schoolchildren*. 1959. Reprint. New York: Oxford University Press, 1980.
Sutton-Smith, Brian. *The Folkgames of Children*. Austin: University of Texas Press, 1972.

HANDS-ACROSS-THE-SEA is William and Mary Morris's name for word play involving the differences in English English and American English. Willard R. Espy includes such word play under the headings fractured foreigners and hobson-jobson.

According to Espy, the term "hobson-jobson" comes from the English substitution of the common surnames Hobson and Jobson for the Mohammedans' ritual cry of mourning at the feast of Muharram, "O Hasan! O Hasan!" It has since come to mean any corruption of a foreign expression.

The object of Hands-Across-the-Sea is to match American and English words or phrases:

American	English
Car hood	Bonnet
Car trunk	Boot
Apartment	Flat
Elevator	Lift
Ice cream cone	Cornet of ice

BIBLIOGRAPHY

Espy, Willard R. *An Almanac of Words at Play*. New York: Clarkson N. Potter, Inc., 1975.
_____. *The Game of Words*. New York: Grosset & Dunlap, 1972.
Morris, William, and Mary Morris. *The Word Game Book*. New York: Harper & Brothers, 1959.

HANGMAN, also called PROBE, is a classic game of word deduction.

One player takes the role of the "hangman." He thinks of a word and draws a line of dashes, one for each letter of the word.

The other player or players take turns guessing the correct letters of the word. If they guess a letter correctly, the hangman fills in the appropriate dash or dashes. If they guess incorrectly, the hangman draws in a part of the figure of a hanged man. There are generally thirteen parts to the hanged man. It does not really matter whether the parts are the eyes, nose, mouth, ears, hands, or sections of the scaffolding, as long as they total thirteen (the number can also be varied— eleven is sometimes used).

If the players guess the correct word before the thirteen parts of the hanged man are filled in, they win. If not, the hangman wins.

There are numerous variations. For instance, one point may be given the hangman for each part of the hanged man he has managed to fill in, and thus a running score is kept to whatever total is agreed upon.

Also, if a player guesses a wrong word, another part of the hanged man may be added, thus penalizing bad guesses.

For other word deduction word play refer to Anagram, Charades, Cipher, Code, Espygram, Flat, and Hidden Names.

BIBLIOGRAPHY

Brandreth, Gyles. *Indoor Games*. London: Hodder & Stoughton, Ltd., 1977.
————. *The World's Best Indoor Games*. New York: Pantheon Books, 1981.
Eckler, A. Ross. *Word Recreations: Games and Diversions from "Word Ways."* New York: Dover, 1979.
Parlett, David. *Botticelli and Beyond: Over 100 of the World's Best Word Games*. New York: Pantheon Books, 1981.
Sharp, Richard, and John Piggott. *The Book of Games*. New York: Galahad Books, 1977.

HEADLINES involves the writing of humorous newspaper headlines.

David Parlett, *Botticelli and Beyond: Over 100 of the World's Best Word Games,* developed this game as a variation of Consequences. Each player needs a pencil and a piece of paper. On the top of his paper, he writes a personal-description phrase, e.g., sad, blue-eyed, lovesick. He then folds over the paper to hide the phrase, and passes his paper to the left. The same process is repeated for the following:

1. Type of person (drunk, policeman, store owner)

2. Transitive verb in present tense (hijacks, entreats, shoots)

3. Object of the verb (dog, President, babysitter)

4. Place of occurrence (bathroom, park, airplane)

Once each of the steps is filled in, the resulting headlines are read out loud:

Sad drunk hijacks dog from bathroom.
Blue-eyed policeman entreats President in park.
Love-sick store owner shoots babysitter on airplane.

For similar word play refer to Book Conversation, Captions Courageous, Consequences, Conundrum, Defective Detective, MADvertisements, Pass It On, Pun, and Subject Matter.

BIBLIOGRAPHY

Espy, Willard R. *The Game of Words*. New York: Grosset & Dunlap, 1972.
Parlett, David. *Botticelli and Beyond: Over 100 of the World's Best Word Games*. New York: Pantheon Books, 1981.

HEADS AND TAILS is a form of Chains.

Players choose a category, e.g., dogs. Each player in turn must name a type of dog which has not previously been mentioned and which begins with the final letter of the previous dog named, e.g., shepherd—dachshund. A player loses when he fails to come up with a name in an established amount of time.

David Parlett offers two possible variations. In the first, anyone who lists a name with the same first and final letters (e.g., dachshund) must drop out; in the second, a timer is set, and the player answering last before the timer goes off wins.

For similar word play refer to Chains, Echoes, Head to Tail, and Life Sentence.

BIBLIOGRAPHY

Parlett, David. *Botticelli and Beyond: Over 100 of the World's Best Word Games.* New York: Pantheon Books, 1981.

HEAD TO TAIL is a form of word play involving Chains.

A two-word compound is chosen, e.g., nighthawk, roadside, peanut butter. The object is to create as long a connected chain of compounds as possible, e.g., peanut butter, butterball, ballgame, gameboard, and so on.

If played as a game, a time limit may be set. An extra challenge requires that the chain eventually circle back on the first word.

For similar word play refer to Chains, Echoes, Heads and Tails, and Life Sentence.

BIBLIOGRAPHY

Borgmann, Dmitri A. *Language on Vacation: An Olio of Orthographical Oddities.* New York: Charles Scribner's Sons, 1965.
Parlett, David. *Botticelli and Beyond: Over 100 of the World's Best Word Games.* New York: Pantheon Books, 1981.

HEAD-TO-TAIL SHIFT. See FLAT.

HECHTASCALANDE. See DOUBLE-DACTYL.

HETERONYM. See PUN.

HE WHO HESITATES. See AD LIB.

HIDDEN NAMES is a form of Buried Words where the buried word is the name of a person, place, or thing:

The bears will be around again next spring. (bear)

Refer to Buried Words, Cipher, Code, and Flat for similar word play.

BIBLIOGRAPHY

Espy, Willard R. *The Game of Words.* New York: Grosset & Dunlap, 1972.
Phillips, Hubert. *Word Play.* New York: Ptarmigan Books, 1945.

HIDDEN SENTENCE CODE is a Code where the message is decoded by moving from one letter to another in a grid:

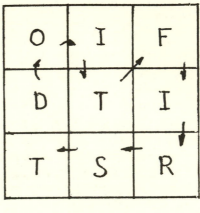

"Do it first."

For more in-depth discussion of Cipher and Code, refer to those entries. Refer to Hidden Word Search for similar word play.

BIBLIOGRAPHY

Adler, Irving, and Peggy Adler. *The Adler Book of Puzzles and Riddles, or Sam Loyd Up to Date*. New York: John Day Co., 1962.
Borgmann, Dmitri A. *Beyond Language: Adventures in Word and Thought*. New York: Charles Scribner's Sons, 1967.
———. *Language on Vacation: An Olio of Orthographical Oddities*. New York: Charles Scribner's Sons, 1965.
Brandreth, Gyles. *Indoor Games*. London: Hodder & Stoughton, Ltd., 1977.
———. *The World's Best Indoor Games*. New York: Pantheon Books, 1981.
Dudeney, Henry Ernest. *300 Best Word Puzzles*. New York: Charles Scribner's Sons, 1968.
Eckler, A. Ross. *Word Recreations: Games and Diversions from "Word Ways."* New York: Dover, 1979.
Espy, Willard R. *The Game of Words*. New York: Grosset & Dunlap, 1972.
Gaines, Helen Fouché. *Cryptanalysis: A Study of Ciphers and Their Solution*. New York: Dover, 1939.

HIDDEN WORDS involves finding words within other words.
    Here is an example:

Find ten words that contain "son."
Answer: reason, season, treason, song, sonar, sonnet, sonic, sonority, sonata, sonde.

For similar word play refer to Animalistics, Buried Words, Confusing and Confounding Cats, Cross-breed, Form-a-Word, Galaxy of Gals, and Hidden Names.

BIBLIOGRAPHY

Espy, Willard R. *The Game of Words*. New York: Grosset & Dunlap, 1972.
Gardner, Martin. *Perplexing Puzzles and Tantalizing Teasers*. New York: Simon & Schuster, 1969.
Phillips, Hubert. *Word Play*. New York: Ptarmigan Books, 1945.

HIDDEN WORD SEARCH, also called secret message squares and word search, is a form of word play requiring the finding of words in a grid when the letters of each word must be in squares that touch each other (in secret message squares the letters need not necessarily touch):

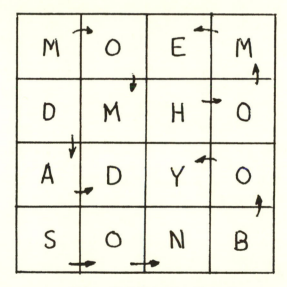

"Mom, Dad, Son, Boy, Home."

For similar word play refer to Cipher, Code, Flat, Hidden Sentence Code, and Hidden Words.

BIBLIOGRAPHY

Espy, Willard R. *The Game of Words*. New York: Grosset & Dunlap, 1972.
Gaines, Helen Fouché. *Cryptanalysis: A Study of Ciphers and Their Solution*. New York: Dover, 1939.
Phillips, Hubert. *Word Play*. New York: Ptarmigan Books, 1945.

HIGGLEDY-PIGGLEDY. See DOUBLE-DACTYL.

HINKY-PINKY. See STINKY PINKY.

HOBBY-HORSE is a quick-response game.

One player starts by asking the other players in turn: "What's your hobby, (made up name)?" The player asked must quickly come up with a hobby (made up hobbies are accepted) that has words beginning with the same letters as the made up name. Anyone who fails to come up with a hobby immediately is either eliminated or loses a point:

Questioner: "What's your hobby, Mandy Pandy?"
Possible correct answers: "Making Pies," or "Murdering Pandas," or "Mixing
    Pancakes," or "Mending Potatoes."

For similar word play refer to Ad Lib, Monosyllables, Railroad Carriage Game, and Word Associations.

BIBLIOGRAPHY

Parlett, David. *Botticelli and Beyond: Over 100 of the World's Best Word Games.* New
    York: Pantheon Books, 1981.

HOBSON-JOBSON. See HANDS-ACROSS-THE-SEA.

HOITY-TOITIES is word play involving finding or creating words which rhyme within themselves (e.g., "harum-scarum" and "hodge-podge").

Refer to ABC Words, ACE Words, Ad Lib, and Hobby-Horse for similar word play.

BIBLIOGRAPHY

Espy, Willard R. *The Game of Words.* New York: Grosset & Dunlap, 1972.

HOMOANTONYM. See FLAT.

HOMOGRAPH. See PUN.

HOMONYM. See PUN.

HOMONYMBLES. See PUN.

HOMOPHONE. See PUN.

HOMOPHONE CARTOONS. See PUN.

HOMOPHONICS. See PUN.

HOMOSYNONYM. See FLAT.

HOMOSYNTAXISM is a term used by the Oulipo (see Möbius Strip for a discussion of the Oulipo) for the changing of all of the words of a passage while retaining the same syntax.

For similar word play refer to Cento, Constructapo, Oulipo Algorithms, and Slygram.

BIBLIOGRAPHY

Eckler, A. Ross. *Word Recreations: Games and Diversions from "Word Ways."* New York: Dover, 1979.
Gardner, Martin. "Mathematical Games: The flip-strip sonnet, the lipogram and other mad modes of wordplay." *Scientific American* 236, no. 2 (February 1977): 121–125.

HYPOCHONDRIAC is an alphabet game.

The first player begins with the sentence: I went to the hospital because I had _____ (some problem beginning with A, e.g., aches, appendicitis).

The next player must add a health problem beginning with B (e.g., blisters): I went to the hospital because I had aches and blisters. This continues through the alphabet.

For similar word play refer to Alphabent, Alphabetical Adjectives, Alphabet Word Chain, A to Z Banquet, First Letters, I Gave My Love, I Love My Love, I Packed My Bag, I Went to Market, and Travelling Alphabet.

BIBLIOGRAPHY

Parlett, David. *Botticelli and Beyond: Over 100 of the World's Best Word Games.* New York: Pantheon Books, 1981.

I

I GAVE MY LOVE is alphabet word play.

The first player starts with "I gave my love some _____" (something beginning with the letter A). The next player repeats this and adds something beginning with B. The process continues through the alphabet.

For similar word play refer to Alphabetical Adjectives, Alphabet Word Chain, A to Z Banquet, First Letters, Hypochondriac, I Love My Love, I Packed My Bag, I Went to Market, and Travelling Alphabet.

BIBLIOGRAPHY

Morris, William, and Mary Morris. *The Word Game Book.* New York: Harper & Brothers, 1959.

I LOVE MY LOVE is alphabet word play.

The first player begins:

"I love my love with an A, announces (A) _____, because she is (A) _____. I took her to (A) _____ and treated her to (A) _____ and (A) _____. Her name is (A) _____ and she comes from (A) _____."

The idea is to fill the blanks with words beginning with the letter A. The next player must do the same for B, and so on.

A variation involves memory:

"I love my love with an A because she is (A) _____. I love my love with a B because she is [repeat the word used for A] and (B) _____. I love my love with a C because she is [repeat the word used for A and the word used for B] and (C) _____." This continues through the alphabet.

For similar word play refer to Alphabetical Adjectives, Alphabet Word Chain, A to Z Banquet, First Letters, Hypochondriac, I Gave My Love, Initial Answers, I Packed My Bag, I Went to Market, and Travelling Alphabet.

BIBLIOGRAPHY

Brandreth, Gyles. *The World's Best Indoor Games.* New York: Pantheon Books, 1981.
Parlett, David. *Botticelli and Beyond: Over 100 of the World's Best Word Games.* New York: Pantheon Books, 1981.

IMPOSSIBLE RHYMES are a form of word play involving the need to stretch the limits of rhyme, often employing assonance, to create purposely awkward rhymes.

Refer to Clerihew for similar word play.

BIBLIOGRAPHY

Espy, Willard R. *An Almanac of Words at Play.* New York: Clarkson N. Potter, Inc., 1975.
———. *A Children's Almanac of Words at Play.* New York: Clarkson N. Potter, Inc., 1982.
———. *The Game of Words.* New York: Grosset & Dunlap, 1972.

IMPROBABLE OPPOSITES involves the substitution of a syllable of a word that is opposite in meaning to the original syllable, e.g., popular/momular, fungus/sadgus.

For similar word play refer to Agile Antonyms.

BIBLIOGRAPHY

Borgmann, Dmitri A. *Language on Vacation: An Olio of Orthographical Oddities.* New York: Charles Scribner's Sons, 1965.
Espy, Willard R. *The Game of Words.* New York: Grosset & Dunlap, 1972.
Morris, William, and Mary Morris. *The Word Game Book.* New York: Harper & Brothers, 1959.

INCANTATIONS are spells or Charms purported to have magic powers.

The word comes from Latin *incantatio,* to chant a magic formula (*in* meaning "in" and *cantare* meaning "to sing or chant"); thus, an incantation is something sung or chanted into something else.

The following incantation is included in Shakespeare's *Macbeth,* act 4, sc. 1, lines 4–38:

First Witch: Round about the caldron go:
    In the poisoned entrails throw.
    Toad, that under cold stone
    Days and nights has thirty-one
    Swelt'red venom sleeping got,
    Boil thou first i' th' charmèd pot.

All: Double, double, toil and trouble;
    Fire burn and caldron bubble.

Second Witch: Fillet of a fenny snake,
    In the caldron boil and bake;
    Eye of newt and toe of frog,
    Wool of bat and tongue of dog,
    Adder's fork and blindworm's sting,
    Lizard's leg and howlet's wing,
    For a charm of pow'rful trouble,
    Like a hell-broth boil and bubble.

All: Double, double, toil and trouble;
    Fire burn and caldron bubble.

Third Witch: Scale of dragon, tooth of wolf,
    Witch's mummy, maw and gulf
    Of the ravined salt-sea shark,
    Root of hemlock digged i' th' dark,
    Liver of blaspheming Jew,
    Gall of goat, and slips of yew
    Slivered in the moon's eclipse,
    Nose of Turk and Tartar's lips,
    Finger of birth-strangled babe
    Ditch-delivered by a drab,
    Make the gruel thick and slab:
    Add thereto a tiger's chaudron,
    For th' ingredients of our caldron.

All: Double, double, toil and trouble;
    Fire burn and caldron bubble.

Second Witch: Cool it with a baboon's blood,
    Then the charm is firm and good.

Incantations are common in children's word and game play. Here are three that Peter and Iona Opie gathered and quoted in *The Lore and Language of Schoolchildren:*

In Swansea they say:

Step on a beetle, it will rain;
Pick it up and bury it, the sun will shine again.

In Market Rasen, a ladybird is considered good luck, and if someone finds one he
    says:

Ladybird, ladybird, fly away home,
Your house is on fire, your children are gone,
Except the little one under a stone,
Ladybird, ladybird, fly away home.

In England in general, it is believed that the future can be foretold according to the
    number of magpies seen:

One for sorrow,
Two for mirth,
Three for a wedding,
Four for a birth.

For similar word play refer to Acting Out Rhymes, Ball Bouncing Rhymes, Charms, Counting Rhymes, Game Rhymes, Hand Clapping Rhymes, Jump Rope Rhymes, Mnemonics, Nursery Rhymes, and Tongue Twister.

BIBLIOGRAPHY

Evans, Robert O. "Incantation." In *Encyclopedia of Poetry and Poetics,* ed. Alex Preminger. Princeton: Princeton University Press, 1965.
Opie, Peter, and Iona Opie. *The Lore and Language of Schoolchildren.* 1959. Reprint. New York: Oxford University Press, 1980.
Partridge, Eric. *Origins: A Short Etymological Dictionary of Modern English.* New York: Greenwich House, 1983.
Shakespeare, William. *Macbeth.* In *The Complete Signet Classic Shakespeare.* New York: Harcourt Brace Jovanovich, Inc., 1963.
Shipley, Joseph T. *Dictionary of Word Origins.* New York: Philosophical Library, 1945.
Sutton-Smith, Brian. *The Folkgames of Children.* Austin: University of Texas Press, 1972.

INFLATED RHETORIC is word play popularized by Victor Borge and Willard R. Espy where numbers or words which have the same sound as numbers are increased by one, e.g., "Once upon a time" becoming "Twice upon a time."

This is a form of punning; see Pun for similar word play.

BIBLIOGRAPHY

Espy, Willard R. *The Game of Words.* New York: Grosset & Dunlap, 1972.

INFLATION is a game combining mathematics and language.

Each letter of the alphabet is assigned a number (A = 1, B = 2, C = 3, and so on) and the players must create three-letter words whose letters add up to ever increasing totals.

The first player writes down a word whose value is not more than ten (e.g., ADD = 9). Each player in turn then takes one letter from the previous word and creates a three-letter word with higher numerical value than the previous word (e.g., ADD = 9; DOG = 26; GOT = 42). The winner is the player who creates the word with the highest total.

For similar word play refer to ABC Words, ACE Words, Centurion, Cipher, Code, Crypt-Arithmetic, Flat, Numwords, and Oulipo Algorithms.

BIBLIOGRAPHY

Parlett, David. *Botticelli and Beyond: Over 100 of the World's Best Word Games.* New York: Pantheon Books, 1981.

INITIAL ANSWERS is a game where players must respond to questions in turn with words that begin with the same letters as the players' initials.

One player is chosen questioner and asks the other players in turn any question he wishes. If the player asked does not respond properly in a short amount of time, he loses and becomes the questioner for the next round.

For similar word play refer to Adverbs, Aesop's Mission, Alphabetical Adjectives, Alphabet Poetry, Alphabet Word Chain, A to Z Banquet, Botticelli, Charades, First Letters, Hypochondriac, I Gave My Love, I Love My Love, Initial Game, I Packed My Bag, I Went to Market, Leading Lights, Name that Gov't Agency, Travelling Alphabet, and What Do They Stand For?

BIBLIOGRAPHY

Brandreth, Gyles. *The World's Best Indoor Games.* New York: Pantheon Books, 1981.

INITIALETTES. See CATEGORY PUZZLES.

INITIAL GAME involves guessing the name of a famous person from clues beginning with the same letters as his initials, e.g., <u>M</u>ovie <u>M</u>ouse = <u>M</u>ickey <u>M</u>ouse; it is similar to Botticelli.

For similar word play refer to Adverbs, Aesop's Mission, Alphabetical Adjectives, Alphabet Poetry, Alphabet Word Chain, A to Z Banquet, Charades, First Letters, Hypochondriac, I Gave My Love, I Love My Love, Initial Answers, Initial Goals, I Packed My Bag, I Went to Market, Leading Lights, and Travelling Alphabet.

BIBLIOGRAPHY

Brandreth, Gyles. *The World's Best Indoor Games.* New York: Pantheon Books, 1981.
Shipley, Joseph T. *Playing with Words.* Englewood Cliffs, N.J.: Prentice-Hall, 1960.

INITIAL GOALS is a question and answer game involving the initials of the players' names.

Each player writes his three initials across the top of a sheet of paper. He then must use words beginning with those three initials to answer questions posed by other players in turn. If the player cannot come up with an acceptable answer in two minutes, he is out of the game.

For similar word play refer to Adverbs, Aesop's Mission, Alphabetical Adjectives, Alphabet Poetry, Alphabet Word Chain, A to Z Banquet, Botticelli, Charades, First Letters, Hypochondriac, I Gave My Love, I Love My Love, Initial Answers, Initial Game, I Packed My Bag, I Went to Market, and Travelling Alphabet.

BIBLIOGRAPHY

Shipley, Joseph T. *Playing with Words.* Englewood Cliffs, N.J.: Prentice-Hall, 1960.

INITIAL SENTENCES. See ACROMANIA.

INQUISITION is a conversation game.

The object is to continue a conversation using only questions (the questions must have some logical relationship to the previous conversation):

First Player: How are you?
Second Player: What's it to you?
First Player: Why so defensive?
Second Player: Can't you tell?
First Player: Am I supposed to be a mind reader?
Second Player: Aren't you?
and so on.

The conversation continues until one player cannot think of a suitable question.

For a similar game refer to Railroad Carriage Game.

BIBLIOGRAPHY

Parlett, David. *Botticelli and Beyond: Over 100 of the World's Best Word Games.* New York: Pantheon Books, 1981.

INVENT-A-NAME is the creating of names for imaginary new ideas, inventions, discoveries, and so on, e.g., metamap, a map for exploring metaphysics; aquacouch, a couch for resting under water.

For similar word play refer to Conundrum, Fractured Book-Reviews, Fractured Geography, Fractured Industry, Portmanteau, and Pun.

BIBLIOGRAPHY

Fuller, John G. *Games for Insomniacs; or, A Lifetime Supply of Insufferable Brain Twisters.* New York: Doubleday, 1966.
Morris, William, and Mary Morris. *The Word Game Book.* New York: Harper & Brothers, 1959.
Shipley, Joseph T. *Playing with Words.* Englewood Cliffs, N.J.: Prentice-Hall, 1960.

INVERSIONS is Scott Kim's term for symmetric lettering, including upside down lettering and mirror reflection lettering, and pivots around a point lettering (letters rotated around a center). According to Scott Kim, Scott Morris of *Omni* magazine uses the term ''designatures'' to describe the same activity.

Here is an example:

For similar word play refer to Alphabet Poetry, Animal Alphabet, Emblematic Poetry, Flat, Looks Like Poetry, Palindrome, Rebus, Riddle, Spine Poetry, Typitoons, and ZOO-LULU.

BIBLIOGRAPHY

Bombaugh, C. C. *Gleanings for the Curious*. 1890. Reprint. *Oddities and Curiosities of Words and Literature,* ed. Martin Gardner. New York: Dover, 1961.
Borgmann, Dmitri A. *Beyond Language: Adventures in Word and Thought.* New York: Charles Scribner's Sons, 1967.
Espy, Willard R. *A Children's Almanac of Words at Play.* New York: Clarkson N. Potter, Inc., 1982.
Kim, Scott. *Inversions: A Catalog of Calligraphic Cartwheels.* Peterborough, N.H.: BYTE Books, McGraw Hill, 1981.

INVERTED ZOO is word play involving the replacing of animal names that have been used in a figurative sense with words pertaining to humans:

Instead of "to ape," "to man."
Instead of "robin red," "human red."

For similar word play refer to Pun.

BIBLIOGRAPHY

Fuller, John G. *Games for Insomniacs; or, A Lifetime Supply of Insufferable Brain Twisters.* New York: Doubleday, 1966.

I PACKED MY BAG is an alphabet game.
One player begins with "I went to (A)_____ and in my bag I packed an (A)_____." The next player continues with "I went to (B)_____ and in my bag I packed a (B)_____."
This continues through the alphabet, players being eliminated whenever they cannot quickly come up with words to fill the blanks.
In another version the list continues to accumulate: "I went to (A)_____ and in my bag I packed an (A)_____;" "I went to (A)_____ and (B)_____ and in my bag I packed an (A)_____ and a (B)_____"; and so on.
For similar word play refer to Alphabent, Alphabetical Adjectives, Alphabet Word Chain, A to Z Banquet, First Letters, Hypochondriac, I Gave My Love, I Love My Love, I Went to Market, and Travelling Alphabet.

BIBLIOGRAPHY

Brandreth, Gyles. *Indoor Games.* London: Hodder & Stoughton, Ltd., 1977.
_____. *The World's Best Indoor Games.* New York: Pantheon Books, 1981.
Parlett, David. *Botticelli and Beyond: Over 100 of the World's Best Word Games.* New York: Pantheon Books, 1981.

IRISH BULL, also called bull, is a statement that makes no sense and often contradicts itself, e.g., "A man is never a man when he's a man."
C. C. Bombaugh, *Gleanings for the Curious* (1890), quotes a definition by Samuel Taylor Coleridge (1771–1834): "A bull consists in a mental juxtaposition of incongruous ideas, with the sensation, but without the sense, of connec-

tion.'' The term "Irish bull" comes from Obadiah Bull, an early nineteenth century Irish solicitor in London.

Sir Boyle Roche (1743–1807), a Dublin politician, was well known for them:

Half of the lies our opponents tell about us are not true.
A man cannot be in two places at once unless he is a bird.
I marvel at the strength of human weakness.

Bombaugh includes a number of examples in his book. The following he claims to have found in Maria Edgeworth's *Essay on Irish Bulls:*

The following resolutions were passed by the Board of Councilmen in Canton, Mississippi:—
1. Resolved, by this Council, that we build a new Jail.
2. Resolved, that the new Jail be built out of the materials of the old Jail.
3. Resolved, that the old Jail be used until the new Jail is finished.

The following two examples come from John Milton (1608–1674), *Paradise Lost,* Book 4:

Adam, the goodliest man of men <u>since born</u>
<u>His sons</u> —the fairest of <u>her daughters, Eve</u>

and

The loveliest pair
That ever <u>since</u> in love's embraces met.

The following examples are from Dr. Samuel Johnson (1709–1784), *A Dictionary of the English Language: in Which the Words are Deduced from Their Originals, and Illustrated in Their Different Significations by Examples from the Best Writers* (1755, rev. 1773):

A garret is "a room on highest floor in the house" and a cock-loft is "the room over the garret."

Every monumental inscription should be in Latin; for that being a <u>dead</u> language, it will always <u>live</u>.

The following two examples come from William Shakespeare (1564–1616):

Turn from the glittering bribe your scornful eye,
Nor sell for gold what gold can never buy.

I will strive with things impossible,
Yea, get the better of them.

(*Julius Caesar,* act 2, sc. 1)

The following comes from John Dryden (1631–1700):

A horrid silence never invades the ear.

For similar word play refer to Accidental Language, Back Slang, Boner, Burlesque, Cliché, Conundrum, Malapropism, Oxymoron, Parody, Pun, Spoonerism, and Wellerism.

BIBLIOGRAPHY

Bombaugh, C. C. *Gleanings for the Curious.* 1890. Reprint. *Oddities and Curiosities of Words and Literature,* ed. Martin Gardner. New York: Dover, 1961.

Daiches, David; Malcolm Bradbury; and Eric Mottram. *The Avenel Companion to English and American Literature.* New York: Avenel Books, 1981.

Espy, Willard R. *A Children's Almanac of Words at Play.* New York: Clarkson N. Potter, Inc., 1982.

————. *The Game of Words.* New York: Grosset & Dunlap, 1972.

Shipley, Joseph T. *Playing with Words.* Englewood Cliffs, N.J.: Prentice-Hall, 1960.

IRREVERSIBLES are words that are a combination of two other words which, when reversed, have a different meaning.

Here are some examples:

overcome / come over
over run / run over
out going / going out
overall / all over
outride / ride out

Irreversibles can serve as a puzzle in which a single person attempts to collect as many as possible, or as many starting with the same letter as possible (as in the example above), or as many of a certain length as possible. Irreversibles can also serve as a game in which players compete (a time limit should be set).

For similar word play refer to Anagram.

BIBLIOGRAPHY

Shipley, Joseph T. *Playing with Words.* Englewood Cliffs, N.J.: Prentice-Hall, 1960.

ISOGRAM, also called a nonpattern word, is a word that uses no letter of the alphabet more than once, e.g., "advent."

Dmitri Borgmann, *Language on Vacation: An Olio of Orthographical Oddities* (1965), describes a game involving such words. One person lists the number of letters in the word and a short clue. The other player or players attempt to solve the word.

For similar word play refer to Alphabent, Alphawords, and Pangram.

BIBLIOGRAPHY

Borgmann, Dmitri A. *Language on Vacation: An Olio of Orthographical Oddities.* New York: Charles Scribner's Sons, 1965.

ISOSCELES WORDS. See PROGRESSIVE ANAGRAM.

I SPY is a deductive guessing game.

One player sees something and says "I spy something _____" (the blank is filled by whatever type of clue the players agree to use, e.g., a color, the first letter of the word, the size, the shape, the use).

The other players attempt to guess what it is, either by naming possible objects, words, phrases, and so on, or by locating it in space—to which the spy replies "hot" (close) or "cold" (far away).

Complex versions of the game may involve Anagrams, reversals, and so on. For example, the spy sees a clock; the players must guess "lock" because of an established rule allowing or requiring Beheading.

For other deductive word play refer to Backenforth, Botticelli, Clue Words, Password, and Twenty Questions.

BIBLIOGRAPHY

Brandreth, Gyles. *The World's Best Indoor Games.* New York: Pantheon Books, 1983.
Parlett, David. *Botticelli and Beyond: Over 100 of the World's Best Word Games.* New York: Pantheon Books, 1981.
Sharp, Richard, and John Piggott. *The Book of Games.* New York: Galahad Books, 1977.

I WENT TO MARKET is an alphabet game.

Players in turn repeat the phrase "I went to market and I bought _____," successively filling in the blank with successive letters of the alphabet.

A more difficult version requires the players to retain each word, thus creating an ever increasing alphabetical list:

I went to market and bought an apple.
I went to market and bought an apple and a banana.
I went to market and bought an apple and a banana and a carrot.
And so on.

For similar word play refer to Alphabent, Alphabetical Adjectives, Alphabet Word Chain, A to Z Banquet, First Letters, Hypochondriac, I Gave My Love, I Love My Love, I Packed My Bag, and Travelling Alphabet.

BIBLIOGRAPHY

Brandreth, Gyles. *The World's Best Indoor Games.* New York: Pantheon Books, 1981.

J

JEU DE MOTS. See PUN.

JOBBERS. See PUN.

JOKE is something done to provoke humor; it may be a Riddle where the teller is expected to give the answer, usually based on a Pun.

According to Joseph T. Shipley, *Dictionary of Word Origins,* the word "joke" came from Jove, the great player of practical jokes among the Roman gods.

Here is an example:

Quasimodo (the hunchback in Victor Hugo's *Notre Dame de Paris* whose job is to ring the bells) decides he needs to hire a helper. So he hangs an ad on the wall outside the bell tower.

After a few days a man applies for the job, but he doesn't have any arms.

"How can you be a bell ringer, if you have no arms?" asks Quasimodo.

"I just run, jump up, and hit it with my face," the man replies.

"What!" Quasimodo says. "That's ridiculous! Don't you hurt yourself?"

"No," the man replies. "Watch." He runs, jumps, and rings the bell.

"Aren't you hurt?" Quasimodo asks.

"No," the man replies. "Watch, I'll do it again." He runs, jumps, and rings the bell.

"This is amazing," Quasimodo says. "I'll tell you what—if you can do it one more time without hurting yourself, the job is yours."

The man runs, jumps, and misses the bell. He goes right out the window, down four stories, and smashes into the ground.

A crowd of people gathers around him. Quasimodo rushes down the stairs. The people ask Quasimodo, "Do you know this man? Do you know his name?"

"No," Quasimodo says, "but his face rings a bell."

For similar word play refer to Knock-knock, Pun, and Riddle.

BIBLIOGRAPHY

Shipley, Joseph T. *Dictionary of Word Origins*. New York: Philosophical Library, 1945.

JOTTO. See GIOTTO.

JUMBLED GEOGRAPHY consists of Puns on the names of states or Abbreviations of places, e.g., the cleanest state is <u>Wash</u>ington.

For similar word play refer to Abbreviations, Conundrum, Fractured Geography, and Pun.

BIBLIOGRAPHY

Espy, Willard R. *A Children's Almanac of Words at Play*. New York: Clarkson N. Potter, Inc., 1982.

JUMBLES are mixed-up words, or puzzles in which words are unscrambled to find letter clues to a mystery word.

Here is an example:

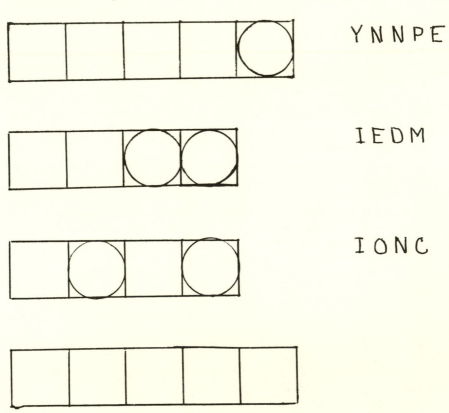

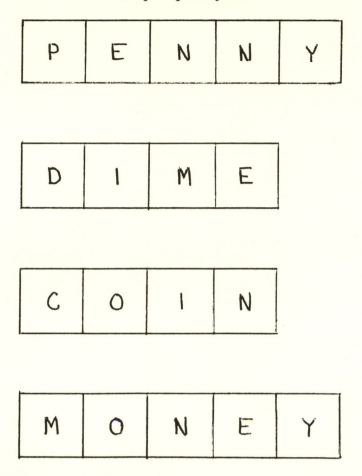

For similar word play refer to Anagram.

BIBLIOGRAPHY

Hart, Harold H. *Grab a Pencil.* New York: Hart Publ. Co., 1958.

JUMP ROPE RHYMES are verses to accompany the jumping of a rope.

Here are some examples from the Havre, Montana, elementary school playgrounds:

Teddy Bear, Teddy Bear, turn around,
Teddy Bear, Teddy Bear, touch the ground;
Teddy Bear, Teddy Bear, go upstairs,
Teddy Bear, Teddy Bear, say your prayers;
Teddy Bear, Teddy Bear, turn out the light,
Teddy Bear, Teddy Bear, say goodnight.

Cinderella.
Dressed in yella,
Went upstairs to kiss her fella;
Made a mistake
And kissed a snake;
How many doctors did it take?

Fudge, fudge,
Call the judge,
Mommy's got a brand new baby;
Wrap it up in tissue paper,
Send it down the elevator—
First floor—stop!
Second floor—miss!
Third floor—turn around!
Fourth floor—touch the ground!
Fifth floor—get out of town!

For similar word play refer to Acting Out Rhymes, Ball Bouncing Rhymes, Counting Rhymes, Dialogue Games, Hand Clapping Rhymes, Nursery Rhymes, and Skipping Rhymes.

BIBLIOGRAPHY

Abrahams, Roger D. *Jump-Rope Rhymes: A Dictionary.* Austin: University of Texas, 1969.
Opie, Peter, and Iona Opie. *Children's Games in Street and Playground.* 1969. Reprint. New York: Oxford University Press, 1979.
_____. *The Lore and Language of Schoolchildren.* 1959. Reprint. New York: Oxford University Press, 1980.
Sanches, Mary, and Barbara Kirshenblatt-Gimblett. *Speech Play.* Philadelphia: University of Pennsylvania, 1976.
Shipley, Joseph T. *Playing with Words.* Englewood Cliffs, N.J.: Prentice-Hall, 1960.

JUST A MINUTE. See AD LIB.

K

KEYWORD. See PASSWORD.

KEY WORDS. See WORD HUNT.

KNIGHT'S-TOUR CRYPT. See EXTRAS.

KNOCK-DOWNS. See WORD KNOCK-DOWNS.

KNOCK-KNOCK is a formal Joke pattern generally involving a play on the sound of a word or its dual meanings; it is a form of Pun.

Here is an example:

"Knock-knock."
"Who's there?"
"Harry."
"Harry who?"
"Harry up and answer the door."

For similar word play refer to Conundrum, Joke, and Pun.

BIBLIOGRAPHY

Espy, Willard R. *A Children's Almanac of Words at Play*. New York: Clarkson N. Potter, Inc., 1982.

Gardner, Martin. *Perplexing Puzzles and Tantalizing Teasers*. New York: Simon & Schuster, 1969.

Parlett, David. *Botticelli and Beyond: Over 100 of the World's Best Word Games*. New York: Pantheon Books, 1981.

KOLODNY'S GAME is an inductive game named after its inventor, David Greene Kolodny, involving the attempt to discover the rules of the game.

The players attempt to come up with the rule(s) of the game by asking the creator questions to which the creator must answer either ''yes'' or ''no.'' The answer, just to make things more complicated, refers to the form of the question rather than the content.

For example, one rule of the game may be that all questions with less than five words are answered ''yes'' and all questions with five or more words are answered ''no'':

Is this a word game? (five words)
No.
Are anagrams used? (three words)
Yes.
And so on.

For other word guessing games refer to Aesop's Mission, Botticelli, Charades, and Outsider.

BIBLIOGRAPHY

Fixx, James. *Games for the Super-intelligent.* New York: Doubleday, 1972.
Parlett, David. *Botticelli and Beyond: Over 100 of the World's Best Word Games.* New York: Pantheon Books, 1981.

KREWELAND UNUSUAL is a phrase used by the National Puzzlers' League to denote puzzles which do not fall into their other categories of puzzles, not even the general category of Extras. (See FLAT for a brief discussion of the National Puzzlers' League.)

L

LAMPOON is a sharp attack or scurrilous, personal satire.

"Lampoon" comes from the imperative of the Old French *lamper, lampons,* which means "let's drink." *Lampons* was used as the refrain for a drinking song and slid into the modern "lampoon." Since such songs were generally ribald and often abusive, when the term was adopted into English it became "to lampoon," to ridicule.

Lampoons were very popular during the Restoration and the eighteenth century, and along with this popularity they gained a number of critics. As Robert C. Elliott, "Lampoon," indicates, John Dryden (1631–1700), a great lampooner in his own right, condemned the form as unlawful: "We have no moral right on the reputation of other men."

Elliott also distinguishes a lampoon from a satire on the grounds that a lampoon is personal, motivated by malice, and unjust. Though the term dates only to the seventeenth century, lampooning occurs as early as written poetry.

In the mid-1970s an after dinner activity based on lampooning became popular. Strange as it may seem, the activity consisted of friends saying the most cutting things they could think of to each other—no true malice intended. The object was to top the previous lampoon—a "how far do you dare go" word play.

Refer to Burlesque and Parody for similar word play.

BIBLIOGRAPHY

Elliott, Robert C. "Lampoon." In *Encyclopedea of Poetry and Poetics,* ed. Alex Preminger. Princeton: Princeton University Press, 1965.

Lewis, Norman, ed. *The New Roget's Thesaurus of the English Language in Dictionary Form.* Lib. ed. New York: G. P. Putnam's Sons, 1978.

Partridge, Eric. *Origins: A Short Etymological Dictionary of Modern English*. New York: Greenwich House, 1983.
Shipley, Joseph T. *Dictionary of Word Origins*. New York: Philosophical Library, 1945.

LANTERNE is a form of Emblematic Poetry written in the shape of a lantern.

Line 1 is one syllable, line 2 two syllables, line 3 three syllables, line 4 four syllables, and line 5 one syllable:

A

Big Boy

From Brooklyn

Got off the Train

Fast

For similar word play refer to Emblematic Poetry.

BIBLIOGRAPHY

Carlson, Ruth Kearney. *Sparkling Words*. Geneva, Ill.: Paladin House Publ., 1979.
Van Allen, Roach, and Claryce Allen. *Language Experience Activities*. 2d ed. Boston: Houghton Mifflin Co., 1982.

LAST AND FIRST is a chain game involving categories.

A category is chosen, e.g., dogs, soups, movies; players in turn must choose a word belonging to the category that begins with the final letter of the previous word chosen.

Whenever a player cannot think of a word quickly, he must drop out of the game. The game continues until only one player remains, who is the winner.

Here is a sample:

The category chosen is "dogs."

First Player: Boston Terrier
Second Player: Russian Wolfhound
Third Player: Dandie Dinmont
First Player: Toy Poodle
Second Player: Drops out (cannot think of a name)
Third Player: English Foxhound
First Player: Doberman Pinscher
Third Player: Drops out (cannot think of a name)
First Player wins.

For similar word play refer to Category Puzzles, Chains, Echoes, Guggenheim, and Heads and Tails.

BIBLIOGRAPHY

Brandreth, Gyles. *The World's Best Indoor Games*. New York: Pantheon Books, 1981.

LAST WORD is the title of two different word games.

The first game is also called Up the Dictionary. The second game was created by Sid Sackson, *A Gamut of Games* (1969), and is based on Anagrams.

It is played on a grid of eleven by eleven or thirteen by thirteen squares. The nine center squares are filled in with random letters:

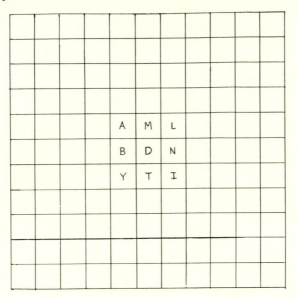

Each player in turn adds a letter to any square adjacent to one already containing a letter and claims the longest anagrammatized word that can be made in any direction from it using only consecutive lines of letters.

The players thus far have scored as follows:

First: Male (4 pts.)
Second: Line (4 pts.)
First: Aline (4 pts. × 4 pts. from his first word = 16 pts.)
Second: Saline (5 pts. × 4 pts. from his first word = 20 pts.)
First: Safe (4 pts. × 16 from his first two words = 64 pts.)
Second: Realm (5 pts. × 20 from his first two words = 100 pts.)

As indicated, scoring is done by multiplying the lengths of all the words a player makes. The game ends when a letter has been placed in at least one square next to each of the four edges of the grid:

							E			
							O			
					N	O	T	E		
					A					
				A	M	L	E	R	A	T
				B	D	N	O	T		
				Y	T	I				
P	A	S	T	O		E				
		C	A	T		A				
						S				
						F				

For similar word play refer to Across-tic, Acrostic, Alphacross, Alphawords, Arrow of Letters, Black Squares, Crossword Puzzle, Flat, Forms, Lynx, Magic Word Squares, Ragaman, SCRABBLE, and Scramblegram.

BIBLIOGRAPHY

Parlett, David. *Botticelli and Beyond: Over 100 of the World's Best Word Games.* New York: Pantheon Books, 1981.
Sackson, Sid. *A Gamut of Games.* New York: Random House, 1969.

LEADING LIGHTS is word play involving description and the use of initials.

The object is to find two-word descriptions for famous people; the two words must begin with the same letters as the initials of the person's name, e.g., Babe Ruth = Baseball Righthander; Shirley Temple = Star Treatment.

For similar word play refer to Adverbs, Aesop's Mission, Alphabetical Adjectives, Alphabet Poetry, Alphabet Word Chain, A to Z Banquet, Botticelli, Charades, First Letters, Hypochondriac, I Gave My Love, I Love My Love, Initial Answers, Initial Game, Initial Goals, I Packed My Bag, I Went to Market, and Travelling Alphabet.

BIBLIOGRAPHY

Brandreth, Gyles. *The World's Best Indoor Games*. New York: Pantheon Books, 1981.

LETTER-ADDS is word play involving the discovery of famous sayings, Proverbs, and Clichés by adding a letter removed from a string of words.

Here is an example:

arlytobdarlytorismaksamanhalthywalthyandwis.

The letter removed is e.

The following saying is one of Benjamin Franklin's from *Poor Richard's Almanack:*

Early to bed
Early to rise
Makes a man
Healthy, wealthy, and wise.

For similar word play refer to Cliché, Lipogram, and Proverb.

BIBLIOGRAPHY

Espy, Willard R. *A Children's Almanac of Words at Play*. New York: Clarkson N. Potter, Inc., 1982.

LETTER BANK. See FLAT.

LETTER BY LETTER. See DOUBLETS.

LETTER CHANGE is also called Doublets, Letter by Letter, and Word Alchemy. See DOUBLETS; FLAT.

LETTER REBUS. See FLAT.

LETTER STRIKE is a letter search game.

A reasonably long word is chosen, and everyone takes pencil and paper and searches through the newspaper to find all of the letters contained in that word.

BIBLIOGRAPHY

Brandreth, Gyles. *Indoor Games*. London: Hodder & Stoughton, Ltd., 1977.

LETTER-TOONS. See REBUS.

LETTER WORDS. See REBUS.

LICENSE PLATE GAME is a name used for two separate games. See CAR GAME; ULTRAGHOST.

LIFE SENTENCE is a variation on Heads and Tails.

The idea is to produce plausible sentences as a string of words connected by identical last and first letters. Each player contributes a word in turn:

Sometimes someone eats something godawful lousy.

For similar word play refer to Chains, Echoes, Heads and Tails, and Head to Tail.

BIBLIOGRAPHY

Parlett, David. *Botticelli and Beyond: Over 100 of the World's Best Word Games*. New York: Pantheon Books, 1981.

LIMERICK is a nonsense poem, generally beginning "There was . . . "; it is usually five anapestic lines in length, the first, second, and fifth lines three feet long and in rhyme, the third and fourth lines two feet long and in rhyme. (Occasionally it is four lines in length, the third line a tetrameter with invariable internal rhyme.) The final line in either version is usually a repetition or varied repetition of the first line. The poem is often risqué.

Edward Lear is the accepted master of the form; the following is a sample from his *Book of Nonsense* (1846):

There was an Old Man of the Dee,
Who was sadly annoyed by a Flea;
When he said, "I will scratch it,"
They gave him a hatchet,
Which grieved that Old Man of the Dee.

Because of his mastery of the limerick, some have credited Lear with having originated it. However, examples can be found in *The History of Sixteen Won-*

derful Old Women, published by J. Harris in 1821, and in *Anecdotes and Adventures of Fifteen Gentlemen,* published by John Marshall in 1822 and possibly written by R. S. Sharp (it is cited by Lear as having given him the idea). Some have pushed the origin back to a group of Nursery Rhymes, *Mother Goose Melodies for Children* (1719). Others suggest that the limerick was an old French form brought to the town of Limerick, Ireland, by returning veterans of the French war. The etymology of the term (never used by Lear) is unknown.

Alfred Lord Tennyson, Algernon Charles Swinburne, Rudyard Kipling, Robert Louis Stevenson, and W. S. Gilbert all employed the limerick, and in the twentieth century such poets as Morris Bishop began changing the form—often using the final line as a surprise ending, rather than simply as a repeat of the first line. Here are two samples of my own:

There was a young woman in red,
Who walked through the woods to a bed;
Her grandma was gone;
The wolf came along;
The woman in red now is dead.

There was a young farmer of Mound,
Who thought that his horse made a sound;
He asked what it said;
Got kicked in the head;
And now he lies under the ground.

Joseph T. Shipley, *Playing with Words,* created a game based on the limerick, the limericksaw. One player states the first line of a possible limerick, and the other players in turn add the remaining lines.

Dmitri A. Borgmann, *Beyond Language: Adventures in Word and Thought,* discusses a similar puzzle, often included in newspapers, where the contestants are asked to supply the final line to a limerick.

For similar word play refer to Bouts Rimés, Double-Dactyl, and Impossible Rhymes.

BIBLIOGRAPHY

Borgmann, Dmitri A. *Beyond Language: Adventures in Word and Thought.* New York: Charles Scribner's Sons, 1967.

Espy, Willard R. *An Almanac of Words at Play.* New York: Clarkson N. Potter, Inc., 1975.

———. *A Children's Almanac of Words at Play.* New York: Clarkson N. Potter, Inc., 1982.

———. *The Game of Words.* New York: Grosset & Dunlap, 1972.

———. *Say It My Way: How to Avoid Certain Pitfalls of Spoken English Together with a Decidedly Informal History of How Our Language Rose (or Fell).* New York: Doubleday, 1980.

Fuller, John G. *Games for Insomniacs; or, A Lifetime Supply of Insufferable Brain Twisters.* New York: Doubleday, 1966.

Gardner, Martin. "Notes." In *Oddities and Curiosities of Words and Literature.* New
     York: Dover, 1961.
Koestler, Arthur. "Humor and Wit." In *Encyclopaedia Britannica: Macropaedia.* 1979.
Preminger, Alex, and Frank J. Warnke. "Limerick." In *Encyclopedia of Poetry and
     Poetics,* eds. Alex Preminger, Frank J. Warnke, and O. B. Hardison, Jr. Prince-
     ton: Princeton University Press, 1965.
Shipley, Joseph T. *Playing with Words.* Englewood Cliffs, N.J.: Prentice-Hall, 1960.

LIMERICKSAW. See LIMERICK.

LINKADE. See FLAT.

LIPOGRAM is a word with a letter purposely deleted, or a composition lacking
a certain letter throughout.

Miguel de Cervantes (1547–1616) wrote five novels omitting one of the
vowels in each; Peter de Riga, a canon of Rheims, wrote a summary of the Bible
in twenty-three sections, excluding a particular letter in each; Pindar wrote an
ode excluding the letter *sigma;* Tryphiodorus wrote an Odyssey excluding successive letters of the alphabet, one for each book; in 1939 E. V. Wright wrote a
150,000-word novel, *Gadsby,* excluding all E's; Gordianus Fulgentius wrote *De
Ætatibus Nundi et Hominis,* excluding successive letters of the alphabet from
each successive chapter; Gregorio Letti delivered a discourse to the Academy of
Humorists at Rome purposely omitting the letter R; in 1957 James Thurber wrote
The Wonderful O as a Parody on the lipogram.

For similar word play refer to Letter-adds and Lost Letter Puzzles.

BIBLIOGRAPHY

Bombaugh, C. C. *Gleanings for the Curious.* 1890. Reprint. *Oddities and Curiosities of
     Words and Literature,* ed. Martin Gardner. New York: Dover, 1961.
Borgmann, Dmitri A. *Language on Vacation: An Olio of Orthographical Oddities.* New
     York: Charles Scribner's Sons, 1965.
Brandreth, Gyles. *The Joy of Lex: How to Have Fun with 860,341,500 Words.* New York:
     Quill, 1983.
Eckler, A. Ross. *Word Recreations: Games and Diversions from "Word Ways."* New
     York: Dover, 1979.
Espy, Willard R. *An Almanac of Words at Play.* New York: Clarkson N. Potter, Inc.,
     1975.
———. *The Game of Words.* New York: Grosset & Dunlap, 1972.
Shipley, Joseph T. *Playing with Words.* Englewood Cliffs, N.J.: Prentice-Hall, 1960.

LITERARY RIDDLE. See RIDDLE.

LITERATIM. See FLAT.

LITTLE AUDREY is a fictional character who is constantly put in horrible
situations and just laughs about them. Such stories may be a form of extended
Pun, a Joke, or a short story with a pun for the final line.

Here is an example:

Little Audrey was kidnapped and tied up to a chair and hidden in the closet. The kidnappers kept her there without food and water or even any light for three days. Then she heard them call her parents and ask for $1 million. Little Audrey just laughed and laughed because she knew she wasn't worth $1 million.

For similar word play refer to Joke, Little Willie, Moron Joke, and Pun.

BIBLIOGRAPHY

Espy, Willard R. *A Children's Almanac of Words at Play*. New York: Clarkson N. Potter, Inc., 1982.

LITTLE MORON JOKE. See MORON JOKE.

LITTLE WILLIE is the name for light verse about a fictional character who is constantly involved in gory disasters (sick humor) that are so outrageous they are funny; it is based on a gruesome Pun or Paradox.
   Here is an example:

Willie cooked his puppy good
And made a meaty meal;
And when his mom saw what he did
How did it make her feel?
"When Willie eats he's very bad
But when he cooks he's better."

For similar humor refer to Joke, Little Audrey, Moron Joke, Nymble, Paradox, and Pun.

BIBLIOGRAPHY

Espy, Willard R. *A Children's Almanac of Words at Play*. New York: Clarkson N. Potter, Inc., 1982.

LOOKS LIKE POETRY is a form of Alphabet Poetry where the letters of the alphabet are sequentially compared to what they look like, e.g., "A looks like a tent; B looks like a pregnant woman; C looks like a sideways bowl," and so on. It is sometimes used to introduce elementary students to poetry.
   For similar word play refer to Alliteration, Alphabet Poetry, Alphabet Pyramids, Alphabet Word Chain, Animal Alphabet, I Gave My Love, I Love My Love, Initial Answers, I Packed My Bag, I Went to Market, Single-Rhymed Alphabet, and Spine Poetry.

BIBLIOGRAPHY

Gensler, Kinereth, and Nina Nyhart. *The Poetry Connection: An Anthology of Contemporary Poems with Ideas to Stimulate Children's Writing*. New York: Teachers & Writers, 1978.

Koch, Kenneth. *Wishes, Lies, and Dreams: Teaching Children to Write Poetry*. New York: Harper & Row, 1980.

LOST LETTER PUZZLES are word puzzles in which some of the letters are missing (usually all of the vowels or consonants). Generally, the idea of the puzzle is to replace the missing letters; it is a form of Lipogram.

Refer to Lipogram for more discussion and examples.

BIBLIOGRAPHY

Eckler, A. Ross. "A Sound-Alike Dictionary." *Word Ways: The Journal of Recreational Linguistics* 17, no. 2 (May 1984): 80–81.

Frank, Alan. "Consonant-Characterized Words." *Word Ways: The Journal of Recreational Linguistics* 17, no. 2 (May 1984): 76–79.

LYNX is a Crossword Puzzle game created by David Parlett, *Botticelli and Beyond: Over 100 of the World's Best Word Games.*

It works best with two players but can be varied to suit more. Players begin by finding an unused crossword puzzle grid or making one up. One player enters a word in one of the shorter lights (a light is a row or column of blanks meant to be filled with a word). The player receives one point for each space filled.

Each player in turn enters a word into the grid so as to fit one light exactly and link properly with crossing words. The standard rules for crossword puzzles are used to determine what words or phrases are acceptable.

After the first word has been entered, each added word must link with one or more existing words in the pattern. Scores are determined by multiplying the number of links (words crossed) by the length of the word entered.

Play continues alternately until one player cannot find another word. If the opponent also cannot play, then the first to say so gets an extra ten points. If the opponent can continue, however, he does, and proceeds to add words until he can no longer play. The first player can no longer play once he has declared that he is done. In this case, no one gets the extra ten points.

Wrong words may either be erased or, especially if entered with a pen, simply left without score. If words are too long or too short, the final letters can either be left off or repeated to fill up the spaces.

If there are three players, play continues until all three declare that they can no longer add a word. (The ten extra points are not awarded when there are more than two players.) Once he has passed, a player is out permanently. Scores are determined by doubling a player's score and adding the undoubled score of the player to the right.

If there are four players, partnerships are formed. No consultation is allowed between partners. As a variation on this, one partner may be required to designate which light his partner must use.

For similar word play refer to Across-tic, Acrostic, Alphacross, Alphawords, Arrow of Letters, Black Squares, Crossword Puzzle, Flat, Forms, Last Word, Magic Word Squares, SCRABBLE, and Scramblegram.

BIBLIOGRAPHY

Parlett, David. *Botticelli and Beyond: Over 100 of the World's Best Word Games.* New York: Pantheon Books, 1981.

M

MACARONICS, mixed or jumbled languages, generally refers to the mixing of Latin and English.

C. C. Bombaugh, *Gleanings for the Curious,* includes the following "A Treatise of Wine" from the commonplace book of Richard Hills, who died in 1535:

The best tree if ye take intent,
   Inter liga fructifera,
Is the vine tree by good argument,
   Dulcia ferens pondera.

Saint Luke saith in his Gospel,
   Arbor fructu noscitur,
The vine beareth wine as I you tell,
   Hinc aliis praeponitur.

The first that planted the vineyard,
   Manet in coeli gaudio,
His name was Noe, as I am learned,
   Genesis testimonio.

God gave unto him knowledge and wit,
   A quo procedunt omnia,
First of the grape wine for to get,
   Propter magna mysteria.

The first miracle that Jesus did,
   Erat in vino rubeo,
In Cana of Galilee it betide,
   Testante Evangelio.

He changed water into wine,
   Aquae rubescunt hydriae,

And bade give it to Archetcline,
  Ut gustet tunc primarie.

Like as the rose exceedeth all flowers,
  Inter cuncta florigera,
So doth wine all other liquors,
  Dans multa salutifera.

David, the prophet, saith that wine
  Laetificat cor hominis,
It maketh men merry if it be fine,
  Est ergo digni nominis.

It nourisheth age if it be good,
  Facit ut esset juvenis,
It gendereth in us gentle blood,
  Nam venas purgat sanguinis.

By all these causes ye should think
  Quae sunt rationabiles,
That good wine should be best of all drink
  Inter potus potabiles.

Wine drinkers all, with great honor,
  Semper laudate Dominum,
The which sendeth the good liquor
  Propter salutem hominum.

Plenty to all that love good wine,
  Donet Deus largius,
And bring them some when they go hence,
  Ubi non sitient amplius.

Though history is filled with attempts of leading writers and grammarians to combine English and Latin—a disaster, since Latin for the most part is based on inflections and English for the most part is not—even the most serious attempts tend to come off as either humorous or embarrassing, pompous at best. This in turn encourages word play. The following is also included in *Gleanings for the Curious* (no author is given):

Τι σοι λεγω, μειρακιον,

Now that this fickle heart is won?
Me semper amaturam te
And never, never, never stray?
Herzschätzchen, Du verlangst zu viel
When you demand so strict a seal.
N'est-ce pas assez que je t'aime
Without remaining still the same?
Gij daarom geeft u liefde niet

If others may not have a treat.
Muy largo es mi corazon,
And fifty holds as well as one.
Non far nell' acqua buco che
I am resolved to have my way;
Im lo boteach atta bi,
I'm willing quite to set you free:
Be you content with half my time,
As half in English is my rhyme.

Ulrich K. Goldsmith, "Macaronic Verse," in *Encyclopedia of Poetry and Poetics,* claims that Tisi degli Odassi, *Carmen maccaronicum* (1488), was probably the inventor of macaronic verse. Teofilo Folengo made it famous in his mock-epic *Maccaroneae* (1517–1521).

For similar word play refer to Pig Latin.

BIBLIOGRAPHY

Bombaugh, C. C. *Gleanings for the Curious.* 1890. Reprint. *Oddities and Curiosities of Words and Literature,* ed. Martin Gardner. New York: Dover, 1961.
Espy, Willard R. *An Almanac of Words at Play.* New York: Clarkson N. Potter, Inc., 1975.
———. *The Game of Words.* New York: Grosset & Dunlap, 1972.
Goldsmith, Ulrich K. "Macaronic Verse." In *Encyclopedia of Poetry and Poetics,* ed. Alex Preminger. Princeton: Princeton University Press, 1965.

MADVERTISEMENTS are humorous advertisements that poke fun at real ads, e.g., "White Bread—the artificially flavored, chemical-packed vanilla bread for vanilla people!"

For similar word play refer to Book Conversation, Conrundrum, Defective Detective, and Pun.

BIBLIOGRAPHY

Fuller, John G. *Games for Insomniacs; or, A Lifetime Supply of Insufferable Brain Twisters.* New York: Doubleday, 1966.
Hart, Harold H. *Grab a Pencil.* New York: Hart Publ. Co., 1958.

MAGIC WORD SQUARES are comprised of a group of words placed on a grid so that they read the same from left to right and from top to bottom:

O	N	E
N	O	T
E	T	H

For similar word play refer to Across-tic, Acrostic, Alphacross, Alphawords, Arrow of Letters, Black Squares, Flat, Forms, Last Word, Lynx, SCRABBLE, and Scramblegram.

BIBLIOGRAPHY

Adler, Irving, and Peggy Adler. *The Adler Book of Puzzles and Riddles, or Sam Loyd Up to Date.* New York: John Day Co., 1962.

Borgmann, Dmitri A. *Beyond Language: Adventures in Word and Thought.* New York: Charles Scribner's Sons, 1967.

Dudeney, Henry Ernest. *300 Best Word Puzzles.* New York: Charles Scribner's Sons, 1968.

Eckler, A. Ross. *Word Recreations: Games and Diversions from "Word Ways."* New York: Dover, 1979.

Espy, Willard R. *The Game of Words.* New York: Grosset & Dunlap, 1972.

Loyd, Samuel. *Sam Loyd's Cyclopedia of 5000 Puzzles, Tricks and Conundrums with Answers.* New York: Pinnacle Books, 1976.

MALAPROPISM is the grotesque and unintentional misuse of one word for another, e.g., pretend for portend, fortuitously for fortunately.

The term is derived from a character in Richard Brinsley Sheridan's play *The Rivals* (1775), Mrs. Malaprop, who constantly used them.

For similar word play refer to Accidental Language, Back Slang, Boner, Burlesque, Cliché, Conundrum, Irish Bull, Parody, Pun, Spoonerism, and Wellerism.

BIBLIOGRAPHY

Brandreth, Gyles. *The Joy of Lex: How to Have Fun with 860,341,500 Words.* New York: Quill, 1983.

Espy, Willard R. *An Almanac of Words at Play.* New York: Clarkson N. Potter, Inc., 1975.

————. *A Children's Almanac of Words at Play.* New York: Clarkson N. Potter, Inc., 1982.

————. *The Game of Words.* New York: Grosset & Dunlap, 1972.

————. *Say It My Way: How to Avoid Certain Pitfalls of Spoken English Together with a Decidedly Informal History of How Our Language Rose (or Fell).* New York: Doubleday, 1980.

MARSUPIALS are smaller Synonyms of larger words contained within those words in correct order, though not necessarily sequentially.

The puzzle takes its name from the order of viviparous, nonplacental animals with a pouch or fold of skin on the female abdomen (e.g., the kangaroo).

Joseph T. Shipley uses this word to refer to word play where all of the larger word is indicated except for the marsupial within it.

f__t___n (fatten, ate)
f____s__ (feast, eat)
m__stica____d (masticated, ate)

For similar word play refer to Anagram, Flat, Middleput, Middletake, Scaffold, and Synonym.

BIBLIOGRAPHY

Shipley, Joseph T. *Playing with Words*. Englewood Cliffs, N.J.: Prentice-Hall, 1960.

MATCH WORDS involves the forming of words from a set arrangement of match sticks.

Here is an example:

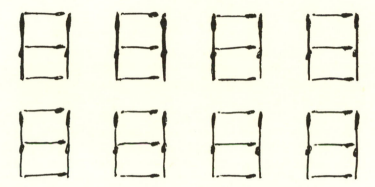

The idea is to remove match sticks until words have been formed:

BIBLIOGRAPHY

Brandreth, Gyles. *The World's Best Indoor Games*. New York: Pantheon Books, 1981.

MEANDER is the name used by Joseph T. Shipley to designate two puzzles based on Doublets.

The first he calls crow flight. The idea is to select two words with the same number of letters and to successively change one letter of the first word (always forming a word) until the second word is reached, e.g., apple, apply, amply.

The second he calls blot and carry (see head-to-tail shift under Flat). The idea is to drop letters (more than one) from the beginning of a word and add them to the end of it, each time forming a new word. If played as a game, whoever makes the longest list wins.

Refer to Doublets and Flat for similar word play.

BIBLIOGRAPHY

Shipley, Joseph T. *Playing with Words*. Englewood Cliffs, N.J.: Prentice-Hall, 1960.

MESOSTICH. See ACROSTIC.

METALLEGES are words formed from the Transposal of two letters in another word, e.g., sit-tis, meat-team, mate-meta.

The metallege is a terminal switch if the two letters switched are the first and final letters of the word, e.g., sit-tis, meat-team.

For similar word play refer to Flat.

BIBLIOGRAPHY

Borgmann, Dmitri A. *Language on Vacation: An Olio of Orthographical Oddities*. New York: Charles Scribner's Sons, 1965.

METATHESIS. See FLAT.

MIDDLEPUT is word play involving finding shorter words within longer words.

The longer word is written on a piece of paper with blanks replacing the letters of the shorter word it contains. Clues may be given for one or both of the words:

me __ __ __ __ e
Clues:
1. A colorless, odorless, flammable gas.
2. Used after comparative adverbs and adjectives (and certain other words) to
    introduce the second member of the comparison.
Answer: methane, than

For similar word play refer to Anagram, Flat, Marsupials, Middletake, and Scaffold.

BIBLIOGRAPHY

Shipley, Joseph T. *Playing with Words*. Englewood Cliffs, N.J.: Prentice-Hall, 1960.

MIDDLETAKE is a game involving the discovery of words where one of the words contains the other within it, e.g., hate-hat.

In the game a clue is offered for both the short and the long word. The winner is the person who gets the most words right:

1. To fire a gun.
2. A black material that adheres to the insides of chimneys.
Answer: shoot, soot

For similar word play refer to Anagram, Flat, Marsupials, Middleput, and Progressive Anagram.

BIBLIOGRAPHY

Shipley, Joseph T. *Playing with Words*. Englewood Cliffs, N.J.: Prentice-Hall, 1960.

MIRROR WRITING. See REFLECTED WRITING.

MISSING WORDS is an Anagram activity that requires supplying anagrams that have been left out of a passage of writing:

He used __ __ __ __ to __ __ __ __ the animal-like players on his __ __ __ __.
Answer: meat, tame, team.

For similar word play refer to Acrosticals, Add-on, Alfabits, Anablank, Ana-game, Cap Me, Category Puzzles, Circular Reversals, Crossword Puzzle, Doublets, Espygram, Flat, Jumbles, Last Word, Marsupials, Middleput, Middletake, Missing Words, Name in Vain, Palindrome, Progressive Anagram, Reversible Anagram, Scaffold, Scramblegram, Word Knock-downs, and Word Ping-Pong.

BIBLIOGRAPHY

Dudeney, Henry Ernest. *300 Best Word Puzzles*. New York: Charles Scribner's Sons, 1968.

MNEMONICS are memory aids, a means of playing with the language for the purpose of remembering something. The cleverness of the word play is precisely what makes mnemonics effective.

The name comes from Mnemosyne, the mother of the Muses, the goddess of memory; memory is still considered by the sages of India and the wise men of Greece to equal wisdom.

Here are two examples:

To remember the days of the week:
Thirty days hath September,
April, June, and November.
All the rest have thirty-one,
Except February, which in fine
Has twenty-eight, in Leap Year twenty-nine.

To remember the lines on the treble clef:
Every good boy does fine (in England: Every good boy deserves favour).

For similar word play refer to Acting Out Rhymes, Ball Bouncing Rhymes, Charms, Counting Rhymes, Game Rhymes, Hand Clapping Rhymes, Incantations, Jump Rope Rhymes, Nursery Rhymes, and Tongue Twister.

BIBLIOGRAPHY

Borgmann, Dmitri A. *Beyond Language: Adventures in Word and Thought*. New York: Charles Scribner's Sons, 1967.

Espy, Willard R. *An Almanac of Words at Play.* New York: Clarkson N. Potter, Inc., 1975.

———. *A Children's Almanac of Words at Play.* New York: Clarkson N. Potter, Inc., 1982.

Opie, Peter, and Iona Opie. *Children's Games in Street and Playground.* 1969. Reprint. New York: Oxford University Press, 1979.

———. *The Lore and Language of Schoolchildren.* 1950. Reprint. New York: Oxford University Press, 1980.

———. *The Oxford Dictionary of Nursery Rhymes.* 1951. Reprint. New York: Oxford University Press, 1983.

Partridge, Eric. *Origins: A Short Etymological Dictionary of Modern English.* New York: Greenwich House, 1983.

Shipley, Joseph T. *Dictionary of Word Origins.* New York: Philosophical Library, 1945.

———. *Playing with Words.* Englewood Cliffs, N.J.: Prentice-Hall, 1960.

MOBIUS STRIP is the writing of a poem by joining lines on a continuous strip of paper that is twisted and joined rubber-band style so that the poem will have opposite meanings when read before and after the twist.

The idea originated with Luc Étienne, a member of the Oulipo (which stands for Ouvroir de Littérature Potentielle—Workshop of Potential Literature).

Since its founding in 1960 by François Le Lionnais and Raymond Queneau, the Oulipo has been one of the most sophisticated groups dealing in word play. Most of its members are French, though at least one member, Harry Mathews, is an American. The Möbius strip is only one of the many forms of word play the group deals with (and it is constantly inventing new forms). Some of the others are Homosyntaxism (the replacing of all of the words of a passage while retaining the syntax), vocabularyclept poetry (the writing of a poem from the alphabetized words of another poem—A. Ross Eckler's term; see Constructapo), snowball sentences (where each word is one letter longer than the previous word), and various forms of algorithms (the replacing of words in accordance with some mathematical formula).

In the Möbius strip, lines of a poem are interwoven by writing half of the poem on one side of a strip and the other half on the other side of it (upside down). The strip is then twisted and joined at the ends.

For similar word play refer to Cento, Constructapo, Homosyntaxism, Monosyllabic Verse, Oulipo Algorithms, Rhopalic, and Slygram.

BIBLIOGRAPHY

Bombaugh, C. C. *Gleanings for the Curious.* 1890. Reprint. *Oddities and Curiosities of Words and Literature,* ed. Martin Gardner. New York: Dover, 1961.

Borgmann, Dmitri A. *Language on Vacation: An Olio of Orthographical Oddities.* New York: Charles Scribner's Sons, 1965.

Eckler, A. Ross. *Word Recreations: Games and Diversions from "Word Ways."* New York: Dover, 1979.

Gardner, Martin. "Mathematical Games: The flip-strip sonnet, the lipogram and other mad modes of wordplay." *Scientific American* (February 1977).

MONOSYLLABIC VERSE is a form of word play requiring the use of only one-syllable words.

Examples can be found in the Bible (Gen. 1: "And God said, 'Let there be light'; and there was light. And God saw that the light was good"), in John Milton's poetry (*Paradise Lost,* Book 8: "But who I was, or where . . . I move and live?"), and in the plays of William Shakespeare (*King Lear,* act 4, sc. 6: "Thou know'st . . . good block?"; and *King John,* act 3, sc. 3: "Good friend . . . But let it go.").

Willard R. Espy, *The Game of Words,* quotes the following from Phineas Fletcher, ca. 1650, which has only one word of more than one syllable:

New light new love, new love new life hath bred;
A light that lives by loves, and loves by light;
A love to Him to whom all loves are wed;
A light to whom the sun is dark as night.
Eye's light, heart's love, soul's only life He is;
Life, soul, love, heart, light, eye and all are His;
His eye, light, heart, love, soul, He all my joy and bliss.

For similar word play refer to Cento, Constructapo, Möbius Strip, and Monosyllables.

BIBLIOGRAPHY

Espy, Willard R. *The Game of Words.* New York: Grosset & Dunlap, 1972.
———. *Say It My Way: How to Avoid Certain Pitfalls of Spoken English Together with a Decidedly Informal History of How Our Language Rose (or Fell).* New York: Doubleday, 1980.

MONOSYLLABLES is a question and answer game allowing only the use of one-syllable words.

Players, without hesitation, must ask and answer questions in succession, using no words of more than one syllable. Anyone who hesitates or uses an incorrect word is out of the game.

For similar word play refer to Ad Lib, Hobby-Horse, Railroad Carriage Game, and Word Associations.

BIBLIOGRAPHY

Brandreth, Gyles. *Indoor Games.* London: Hodder & Stoughton, Ltd., 1977.

MORNINGTON CRESCENT is a game developed by David Parlett out of two BBC Radio 4 games, one of them called Mornington Crescent, the other a variation of Tennis-Elbow-Foot Game.

In the BBC Radio 4 Mornington Crescent activity, someone begins by saying "Mornington Crescent"; others then follow in succession, saying London place names, until someone says "Mornington Crescent" and the activity ends.

In David Parlett's game, the next player must come up with a word which not only has not been said before but also has no connection with the previous word. If anyone can find a legitimate connection, the challenged player is out of the game.

Refer to Tennis-Elbow-Foot Game for a similar game.

BIBLIOGRAPHY

Parlett, David. *Botticelli and Beyond: Over 100 of the World's Best Word Games*. New York: Pantheon Books, 1981.

MORON JOKE, also called little moron joke, is a Joke based on a Pun involving something the moron did.

Here are some examples:

Why did the moron throw <u>butter</u> out the window?
Because he wanted to see a <u>butter</u>fly.

Why did the moron tip-toe past the medicine cabinet?
Because he didn't want to wake the sleeping pills.

Technically, a moron joke is more of a Conundrum, more of a Riddle answered with a pun, than a joke; but these forms of word play overlap, and the definitions vary.

For similar word play refer to Conundrum, Joke, Little Audrey, Little Willie, Nymble, Pun, and Riddle.

BIBLIOGRAPHY

Espy, Willard R. *A Children's Almanac of Words at Play*. New York: Clarkson N. Potter, Inc., 1982.

MOSAIC VERSE. See CENTO.

MUSICAL MESSAGES are messages in which each musical note stands for its letter name; these are somewhat limited since the notes can only go through the letter G, unless each new octave continues the alphabet instead of starting over.

Refer to Cipher and Code for further discussion of this type of word play, and to Telephone Words for a similar puzzle.

Dmitri Borgmann uses the term "piano words" to refer to words which can be played on the piano (i.e., those that have no letters further along in the alphabet than G).

BIBLIOGRAPHY

Borgmann, Dmitri A. *Language on Vacation: An Olio of Orthographical Oddities*. New York: Charles Scribner's Sons, 1965.

NAME IN VAIN is word play involving finding amusing Anagrams for famous names, e.g., Shakespeare = Seek sea harp.

David Parlett offers two possible versions. In the first, everyone agrees on a name, and the object is to be the first to come up with an anagram. In the second, a time limit is set, and the one who comes up with the best anagram wins.

For similar word play refer to Acrosticals, Add-on, Alfabits, Anablank, Anagame, Cap Me, Category Puzzles, Circular Reversals, Crossword Puzzle, Doublets, Espygram, Flat, Jumbles, Last Word, Marsupials, Middleput, Missing Words, Palindrome, Progressive Anagram, Reversible Anagram, Scaffold, Scramblegram, Word Knock-downs, and Word Ping-Pong.

BIBLIOGRAPHY

Parlett, David. *Botticelli and Beyond: Over 100 of the World's Best Word Games.* New York: Pantheon Books, 1981.

NAME THAT GOV'T AGENCY is word play involving initials.

The object is to name the government agency that the listed initials stand for. If played as a game, the player who names the most agencies correctly wins. Penalties may be given for wrong guesses.

For example:

What do the following initials stand for?
FRB
CWA
NHA
FPC
Answers: Federal Reserve Bank; Civil Works Administration; National Housing Agency; Federal Power Commission.

For similar word play refer to Adverbs, Aesop's Mission, Alphabetical Adjectives, Alphabet Poetry, Alphabet Word Chain, A to Z Banquet, Botticelli, Charades, First Letters, Hypochondriac, I Gave My Love, I Love My Love, Initial Answers, Initial Game, I Packed My Bag, I Went to Market, Leading Lights, Travelling Alphabet, and What Do They Stand For?

BIBLIOGRAPHY

Morris, William, and Mary Morris. *The Word Game Book.* New York: Harper & Brothers, 1959.

NECK RIDDLE. See RIDDLE.

NIMBLEBREAK is a game involving the solving of clues based on Puns of paronomasia.

One player gives a clue to the word, and the other player or players attempt to guess the word:

Clue: An animal that never plays fair.
Answer: A cheetah.

For similar word play refer to Conundrum, Double Entendre, Moron Joke, Nymble, and Pun.

BIBLIOGRAPHY

Shipley, Joseph T. *Playing with Words.* Englewood Cliffs, N.J.: Prentice-Hall, 1960.

NIMINY-PIMINY. See DOUBLE-DACTYL.

NUMBER ASSOCIATIONS, also called numbers game, is a game involving quick responses, Clichés, and numbers.

Each player in turn calls out a number. The other players respond with an appropriate phrase (a cliché, a Proverb, a famous saying, and so on) associated with that number:

Seven is called out.
Days in a week is the response.

Nine is called out.
Cloud nine is the response.

The first player to respond with an acceptable phrase scores a point. The player with the most points at the end of the game wins.

For similar word play refer to Aesop's Mission, Botticelli, Charades, Cliché, and Proverb.

BIBLIOGRAPHY

Brandreth, Gyles. *The World's Best Indoor Games.* New York: Pantheon Books, 1981.

NUMBER PLATE GAME. See ULTRAGHOST.

NUMBERS GAME. See NUMBER ASSOCIATIONS.

NUMERICAL. See FLAT.

NUMWORDS is a form of mathematical word play.

Each letter of the alphabet is given a corresponding numeral, e.g., A = 1, B = 2, C = 3, and so on. David Parlett coined the term and discusses two games based on numwords. In the first a number is selected (generally somewhere around 65), and a time limit is established, e.g., two minutes. Each player attempts to come up with words whose numerical value equals the selected number (e.g., 65). The player who comes up with the most words wins. The total value of the letters added together (e.g., 65) is called the wordnum. The object of numwords, then, is to make wordnums.

The second game is a variation on the first. In this game an established word length (e.g., 5 letters) or an initial letter (e.g., H) is agreed upon. The object is to find the lowest and/or highest value numword.

For similar word play refer to ABC Words, ACE Words, Centurion, Cipher, Code, Crypt-Arithmetic, Flat, Inflation, and Oulipo Algorithms.

BIBLIOGRAPHY

Parlett, David. *Botticelli and Beyond: Over 100 of the World's Best Word Games.* New York: Pantheon Books, 1981.

NURSERY RHYMES are verses read to or by (or spoken to or by) children.

Iona and Peter Opie, *The Oxford Dictionary of Nursery Rhymes* (1951), have put together a highly respected collection and study of nursery Rhymes, dividing the rhymes into four areas: Counting Rhymes, Riddles, infant amusements, and lullabies. Rhymes are often grouped in other ways as well: Acting Out Rhymes (similar to infant amusements, e.g., "Patty Cake, Patty Cake"), Ball Bouncing Rhymes (verses to be said while bouncing a ball), Dialogue Games (e.g. "London Bridge" or its English predecessor, "Oranges and Lemons"), Hand Clapping Rhymes (verses meant to accompany the clapping of hands), and Jump Rope Rhymes (e.g., "Lady Bird, Lady Bird, Turn Around").

Nursery rhymes are often the result of historical reality. For instance, Jack Horner, the steward of the Abbot of Glastonbury, was entrusted with the delivery to Henry VIII of a mince pie "in which was baked a plum of great value" (i.e., the deeds of the twelve manors of Glastonbury). On his way Jack took out the deed to the Manor of Mells for himself. Thus, the nursery rhyme:

Little Jack Horner
Sat in a corner
Eating a Christmas Pie;
He stuck in his thumb
And pulled out a plum
And said "What a good boy am I."

Nursery rhymes might also take the form of Tongue Twisters:

Swan swam over the sea,
  Swim, swan, swim!
Swan swam back again,
  Well swum, swan!

A nursery rhyme riddle is generally what would be called a true riddle:

Thirty white horses
Upon a red hill,
Now they tramp,
Now they champ,
Now they stand still.
(Answer: teeth and gums)

"Oranges and Lemons" is what would be called a dialogue game, where words and actions interact:

Oranges and lemons,
Say the bells of St. Clement's.

You owe me five farthings,
Say the bells of St. Martin's.

When will you pay me?
Say the bells of Old Bailey.

When I grow rich,
Say the bells of Shoreditch.

When will that be?
Say the bells of Stepney.

I'm sure I don't know,
Says the great bell at Bow.

Here comes a candle to light you to bed,
Here comes a chopper to chop off your head.

For similar word play refer to Acting Out Rhymes, Ball Bouncing Rhymes, Counting Rhymes, Game Rhymes, Hand Clapping Rhymes, Jump Rope Rhymes, Riddle, and Tongue Twister.

BIBLIOGRAPHY

Abrahams, Roger D. *Jump-Rope Rhymes: A Dictionary*. Austin: University of Texas, 1969.

Abrahams, Roger D., and Lois Rankin. *Counting-Out Rhymes: A Dictionary*. Austin: University of Texas, 1980.

Carpenter, Humphrey, and Mari Prichard. *The Oxford Companion to Children's Literature*. New York: Oxford University Press, 1984.

Laubach, David C. *Introduction to Folklore*. Rochelle Park, N.J.: Hayden Book Co., Inc., 1980.

Opie, Peter, and Iona Opie. *Children's Games in Street and Playground*. 1969. Reprint. New York: Oxford University Press, 1979.

_____. *The Lore and Language of Schoolchildren*. 1959. Reprint. New York: Oxford University Press, 1980.

_____. *The Oxford Dictionary of Nursery Rhymes*. 1951. Reprint. New York: Oxford University Press, 1983.

_____. *The Oxford Nursery Rhyme Book*. 1955. Reprint. New York: Oxford University Press, 1984.

Shipley, Joseph T. *Playing with Words*. Englewood Cliffs, N.J.: Prentice-Hall, 1960.

Sutton-Smith, Brian. *The Folkgames of Children*. Austin: University of Texas Press, 1972.

Volland, P. F. *Mother Goose*. Chicago: P. F. Volland & Co., 1915. Reprint. Rand McNally & Co., 1982.

NYMBLE, also spelled nimble, is a verbal Pun on homonyms; it is a pun of paronomasia.

Here are two examples:

The first comes from William Shakespeare, *Julius Caesar,* act 1, sc. 2, lines 156–157:

"Now it is <u>Rome</u> indeed, and <u>room</u> enough,
When there is in it but one only man.''

The second is a common children's nymble:

"I'm thirsty.''
"How do you do? I'm Friday. Would you like to go out Saturday and have a Sunday?''

For similar word play refer to Conundrum, Joke, Little Audrey, Little Willie, Moron Joke, and Pun.

BIBLIOGRAPHY

Shakespeare, William. *Julius Caesar*. In *The Complete Signet Classic Shakespeare*, ed. Sylvan Barnet. New York: Harcourt Brace Jovanovich, 1963.

Shipley, Joseph T. *Playing with Words*. Englewood Cliffs, N.J.: Prentice-Hall, 1960.

_____. "Word and Letter Games.'' In *Encyclopaedia Britannica: Macropaedia*. 1979.

NYMBLEBREAK is a form of Nymble involving breaking up longer words into smaller words that form homonyms, e.g., cancel = can sell.

For similar word play refer to Conundrum, Nymble, and Pun.

BIBLIOGRAPHY

Shipley, Joseph T. *Playing with Words*. Englewood Cliffs, N.J.: Prentice-Hall, 1960.

NYMPHABET is an alphabetical version of nim.

Nim is any game in which a player removes a number of objects from an original group, the winner being the one who takes the last object, or who forces his opponent to take the last object.

David Parlett created nymphabet as an alphabetical version of this. In nymphabet, the twenty-six letters of the alphabet serve as the original group to be eliminated. Each player in turn writes a word. The first word must begin with A, which is then crossed off the alphabet. If the word contains a B after the A, the B is also crossed off the alphabet. The same is done for each letter of the alphabet in succession:

Able
Both A and B are crossed off the alphabet.

The next player must write a word that begins with the letter of the alphabet next in line that has not been crossed off:

Card
The C and the D are crossed off the alphabet.

This continues until a player is forced to use the Z. David Parlett suggests that the game is most interesting if the writer of the final word loses.

The game can be varied by treating the alphabet as a circle, A following Z, and beginning at any point in the alphabet. It can also be varied by giving points for each new letter used, and either adding or multiplying the points to determine the final score.

For other alphabet word play refer to Alphabent, Alphabetical Adjectives, Alphabet Word Chain, A to Z Banquet, First Letters, Hypochondriac, I Gave My Love, I Love My Love, I Packed My Bag, I Went to Market, and Travelling Alphabet.

BIBLIOGRAPHY

Parlett, David. *Botticelli and Beyond: Over 100 of the World's Best Word Games.* New York: Pantheon Books, 1981.

OILERS is a word game based on tic-tac-toe.

According to David Parlett, it was first described by Dave Silverman in *Word Ways*. Parlett discusses two forms, simple and advanced. In the simple form the following nine words are spaced on a tic-tac-toe grid:

fish	soup	swan
girl	horn	army
knit	vote	chat

The players take words in turn, as if choosing boxes in tic-tac-toe. The winner is the first to take three words sharing a letter in common.

In the advanced form the following sixteen words are spaced on a grid:

ape	day	can	rat
lip	die	tin	rig
hop	dot	one	row
put	bud	sun	rue

Once again, each player chooses words in turn. The first to choose (the "toiler") wins if either player gathers four words sharing a common letter. The opponent (the "spoiler") wins if neither player gathers four words sharing a common letter.

BIBLIOGRAPHY

Eckler, A. Ross. *Word Recreations: Games and Diversions from "Word Ways."* New York: Dover, 1979.

Parlett, David. *Botticelli and Beyond: Over 100 of the World's Best Word Games.* New York: Pantheon Books, 1981.

ORAL ALPHABENT. See ALPHABENT.

ORRIBLE ORIGINS involves the creation of plausible but unlikely origins for well-known phrases, sayings, or titles.

The name comes from David Parlett, who used to listen to Frank Muir and Denis Norden do just that on the BBC.

For similar word play refer to Conundrum, Mornington Crescent, Moron Joke, Pun, and Tennis-Elbow-Foot Game.

BIBLIOGRAPHY

Parlett, David. *Botticelli and Beyond: Over 100 of the World's Best Word Games.* New York: Pantheon Books, 1981.

OULIPO ALGORITHMS involve the replacing of words in a passage in accordance with a mathematical principle.

Jean Lescure invented one called S + 7 (substantif plus seven), which in English would be N + 7 (noun plus seven). The idea is simply to replace every noun in a passage with the seventh noun that follows it in a specified dictionary.

Another algorithm invented by Lescure involves reversing the order of a given type of word (e.g., switching the first and last nouns of a passage, and so on).

For a brief discussion of the Oulipo refer to Möbius Strip. For similar word play refer to ABC Words, ACE Words, Cento, Centurion, Cipher, Code, Constructapo, Crypt-Arithmetic, Flat, Homosyntaxism, Inflation, Numwords, and Slygram.

BIBLIOGRAPHY

Gardner, Martin. "Mathematical Games: The flip-strip sonnet, the lipogram and other mad modes of wordplay." *Scientific American* 236, no. 2 (February 1977).

OUTSIDER is a form of Kolodny's Game; the object is to discover what the game is.

The "outsider," the one person who is not in on the game, seeks to find out what the game is by asking any member of the group questions. The questions must be answered truthfully—according to the rules of the game.

In the specific sense in which James Fixx, *Solve It!*, discusses the game, the rule is simply that each player answers for the player on his left, but there is no reason that other rules cannot be used.

For similar word play refer to Aesop's Mission, Botticelli, Charades, and Kolodny's Game.

BIBLIOGRAPHY

Fixx, James. *Solve It! A Perplexing Profusion of Puzzles.* New York: Doubleday, 1978.

OVERLAPS is a form of word play involving a string of words, each overlapping the previous word, chain style, each containing the same number of letters, and all of them together forming a larger word.

Here is an example:

Washer

was

ash

she

her

For similar word play refer to Chains, Echoes, Flat, Heads and Tails, Last and First, and Tell-A-Tall-Tale.

BIBLIOGRAPHY

Brandreth, Gyles. *The World's Best Indoor Games*. New York: Pantheon Books, 1981.
Hart, Harold H. *Grab a Pencil*. New York: Hart Publ. Co., 1958.

OXYMORON is the conjunction of incongruous or contradictory terms for rhetorical, often humorous, effect.

Edward P.J. Corbett, *Classical Rhetoric for the Modern Student,* states that, through the use of oxymorons, a "writer produces a startling effect, and he may, if his oxymorons are fresh and apt, win for himself a reputation for wit." The following offers a good example:

Here's much to do with hate, but more with love.
Why then, O brawling love! O loving hate!
O anything of nothing first create!
O heavy lightness, serious vanity!
Misshapen chaos of well-seeming forms!
Feather of lead, bright smoke, cold fire, sick health!
Still-waking sleep, that is not what it is!
This love I feel, that feel no love in this.
(William Shakespeare, *Romeo and Juliet,* act 1, sc. 1, c. 1595)

According to Willard R. Espy, *An Almanac of Words at Play,* Erasmus made an oxymoron out of one word, "foolosophers."

The very nature of an oxymoron, its seeming contradiction and seeming aptness, makes it a close ally of Pun, zeugma, and Paradox, all forms of word play involving multiple meanings of a word or phrase. In a denotative sense, it is just as impossible for someone to be "horribly decent" or "terribly well" or "awfully kind" as it is for a person who "cheats" to be a "cheetah." It is just as impossible to speak of "cruel kindness" or "nasty politeness" as it is to say "When she's good she's really good; when she's bad she's better."

This bringing together of seeming opposites highlights the shared similarity to produce a powerful, perhaps the most powerful, expression language is capable of, and is related to simile and metaphor.

For word play similar to or based on oxymoron, refer to Boner, Burlesque, Cliché, Conundrum, Malapropism, Paradox, Parody, Pun, Spoonerism, and Wellerism.

BIBLIOGRAPHY

Corbett, Edward P.J. *Classical Rhetoric for the Modern Student.* 2d ed. New York: Oxford University Press, 1971.

Espy, Willard R. *An Almanac of Words at Play.* New York: Clarkson N. Potter, Inc., 1975.

————. *The Game of Words.* New York: Grosset & Dunlap, 1972.

Preminger, Alex, and Frank J. Warnke. "Oxymoron." In *Encyclopedia of Poetry and Poetics,* ed. Alex Preminger, Frank J. Warnke, and O. B. Hardison, Jr. Princeton: Princeton University Press, 1965.

Shakespeare, William. "Romeo and Juliet." In *The Complete Classic Shakespeare,* ed. S. Bennet. New York: Harcourt Brace Jovanovich, Inc., 1963.

P

PADLOCK. See FLAT.

PALINDROME, also called sotades, is a word, phrase, verse, or sentence that reads the same forward and backward; in Greek it means "a running back again."

According to Howard G. Bergerson, *Palindromes and Anagrams,* the inventor of palindromic verse is alleged to have been Sotades of Maroneia, a Greek poet and satirist of the third century B.C. According to Henry Ernest Dudeney, *300 Best Word Puzzles,* the following palindrome from classical Greece ran around the circular recess where the holy water stoup stood in St. Sophia, Constantinople, until about 1453:

C. C. Bombaugh includes the following example in *Gleanings for the Curious* (1890); The first letter of each successive word is combined to form the first word, the second letter of each successive word is combined to form the second word, and so on; the same is true in reverse:

SATOR AREPO TENET OPERA ROTAS.

Dmitri A. Borgmann, *Beyond Language: Adventures in Word and Thought,* points out that the titles of two of Edgar Allan Poe's poems, "Ulalume" and "Annabel Lee," have strong palindromic qualities.

The National Puzzlers' League includes palindromes in the category known as Flats (see Flat).

Perhaps the most famous sentence palindrome is "Madam, I'm Adam."

A palindrome having an even number of letters is obviously also a form of Anagram, since its last half uses the same letters as its first half.

Here are a few additional examples:

tot, peep, noon, level, eke, tenet, reviver, redder, Hannah, deed, mom, dad.

For similar word play refer to Anagram, Charades, Flat, Phonetic Palindromes, Reversible Anagram, and Sotadic Palindrome.

BIBLIOGRAPHY

Bergerson, Howard W. *Palindromes and Anagrams.* New York: Dover, 1973.

Bombaugh, C. C. *Gleanings for the Curious.* 1890. Reprint. *Oddities and Curiosities of Words and Literature,* ed. Martin Gardner. New York: Dover, 1961.

Borgmann, Dmitri A. *Beyond Language: Adventures in Word and Thought.* New York: Charles Scribner's Sons, 1967.

Borgmann, Dmitri A. *Language on Vacation: An Olio of Orthographical Oddities.* New York: Charles Scribner's Sons, 1965.

————. "The Majestic Palindrome." *Word Ways: The Journal of Recreational Linguistics* 18, no. 1 (Feb. 1985): 3–5.

Costas, Procape S. "Palindrome." In *Encyclopedia of Poetry and Poetics,* ed. Alex Preminger, Frank J. Warnke, and O. B. Hardison, Jr. Princeton: Princeton University Press, 1965.

Dudeney, Henry Ernest. *300 Best Word Puzzles.* New York: Charles Scribner's Sons, 1968.

Eckler, A. Ross. *Word Recreations: Games and Diversions from "Word Ways."* New York: Dover, 1979.

Espy, Willard R. *An Almanac of Words at Play.* New York: Clarkson N. Potter, Inc., 1975.

————. *A Children's Almanac of Words at Play.* New York: Clarkson N. Potter, Inc., 1982.

————. *The Game of Words.* New York: Grosset & Dunlap, 1972.

Gardner, Martin. *Perplexing Puzzles and Tantalizing Teasers.* New York: Simon & Schuster, 1969.

Partridge, Harry B. "Dromes, Phones and Graphs." *Word Ways: The Journal of Recreational Linguistics* 17, no. 4 (November 1984): 206–209.

Shipley, Joseph T. *Playing with Words.* Englewood Cliffs, N.J.: Prentice-Hall, 1960.

————. "Word and Letter Games." In *Encyclopaedia Britannica: Macropaedia.* 1976.

PANGRAM, also called a pangrammatic, is a phrase, sentence, verse, or the like containing all the letters of the alphabet.

The oldest is found in Ezra 7:21. Ausonius, a Roman poet of the fourth century, is also famous for them.

C. C. Bombaugh includes the following example in *Gleanings for the Curious* (1890): "John P. Brady, give me a black walnut box of quite a small size."

Here is one of my own (thirty-nine total letters):

John P. Smith fixed a quiz Cab worked on very long.

For similar word play refer to Acrostic, Alphabent, Alphabetical Adjectives, Alphabet Word Chain, A to Z Banquet, First Letters, Hypochondriac, I Gave My Love, I Love My Love, I Packed My Bag, I Went to Market, Nymphabet, Short Story, and Travelling Alphabet.

BIBLIOGRAPHY
Bombaugh, C. C. *Gleanings for the Curious.* 1890. Peprint. *Oddities and Curiosities of Words and Literature,* ed. Martin Gardner. New York: Dover, 1961.
Borgmann, Dmitri A. *Language on Vacation: An Olio of Orthographical Oddities.* New York: Charles Scribner's Sons, 1965.
Brandreth, Gyles. *The Joy of Lex: How to Have Fun with 860,341,500 Words.* New York: Quill, 1983.
Eckler, A. Ross. *Word Recreations: Games and Diversions from "Word Ways."* New York: Dover, 1979.
Espy, Willard R. *An Almanac of Words at Play.* New York: Clarkson N. Potter, Inc., 1975.
————. *A Children's Almanac of Words at Play.* New York: Clarkson N. Potter, Inc., 1982.
————. *The Game of Words.* New York: Grosset & Dunlap, 1972.
Fuller, John G. *Games for Insomniacs; or, A Lifetime Supply of Insufferable Brain Twisters.* New York: Doubleday, 1966.

PANGRAMMATIC. See PANGRAM.

PARADOX is a statement or proposition seemingly self-contradictory or absurd but in reality expressing a probable truth; it is an extended Pun or Oxymoron:

When Susie's good she's really good,
but when she's bad she's better.

William Van O'Connor, "Paradox," in *Encyclopedia of Poetry and Poetics,* points out that the classical rhetoricians (e.g., Menander, Hermogenes, Cicero, and Quintilian) included paradox among the standard figures of speech. It was popular during the Graeco-Roman period in such forms as paradoxical encomium, *controversiae,* and *suasoriae;* was used to train students in rhetoric during the Middle Ages; and appeared in the literature of the late Middle Ages and Renaissance (e.g., *The Praise of Folly* by Erasmus). During the baroque period, paradox became an important poetic figure (e.g., John Donne, *Paradoxes and Problems*). John Dryden and Alexander Pope both employed paradox, and William Hazlitt referred to neoclassical poetry as "the poetry of paradox." During the twentieth century the term began to be applied to literary criticism (e.g., Cleanth Brooks, *The Well Wrought Urn*).

William Shakespeare includes the following paradox in Sonnet 138:

When my love swears that she is made of truth
I do believe her, though I know she lies.

For a more in-depth discussion of the comparison of paradox to pun, refer to
Pun. For related word play refer to Boner, Burlesque, Cliché, Conundrum,
Malapropism, Oxymoron, Parody, Spoonerism, and Wellerism.

BIBLIOGRAPHY

Corbett, Edward P.J. *Classical Rhetoric for the Modern Student.* 2d ed. New York:
    Oxford University Press, 1971.
Eckler, A. Ross. *Word Recreations: Games and Diversions from "Word Ways."* New
    York: Dover, 1979.
Koestler, Arthur. "Humor and Wit." In *Encyclopaedia Britannica: Macropaedia.* 1979.
O'Connor, William Van. "Paradox." In *Encyclopedia of Poetry and Poetics,* ed. Alex
    Preminger, Frank J. Warnke, and O. B. Hardison, Jr. Princeton: Princeton Uni-
    versity Press, 1965.
Shakespeare, William. "Sonnet 138." In *The Complete Signet Classic Shakespeare,* ed.
    Sylvan Bennet. New York: Harcourt Brace Jovanovich, 1963.

PARODY is a humorous or satirical imitation of a serious piece of literature,
drama, music, or the like; it is an exaggerated imitation of a work of art based on
distortion. "Parody" is derived from the Greek *paródia* (*para,* beside; *aidein,* to
sing).

According to Robert P. Falk and William Beare, "Parody," in *Encyclopedia
of Poetry and Poetics,* parody may be comic (similar to Burlesque) and literary
or critical (a closer following of a writer's work).

Since the beginnings of poetry and drama, parody has served as an emotional
counterpoint (a comic interlude) to tragedy. Examples of such comic parallels to
the main plot can be found throughout the works of William Shakespeare.

Miguel de Cervantes's *Don Quixote* is a classic parody of knight-errantry.
Henry Fielding's *Joseph Andrews* and *Shamela* parodied *Pamela,* a serious novel
by Samuel Richardson.

Aristotle's *Poetics* attributes the origin of parody as art to Hegemon of Thasos,
who used epic style to represent men who were inferior rather than superior to
ordinary men. Polemo, according to Falk and Beare, claims that parody was
invented by Hipponax (sixth century B.C.). Other examples of parody from early
Greece still exist (e.g., *Battle of the Frogs and Mice,* a parody of Homer), but
the greatest parodist of antiquity was Aristophanes; his *Frogs* parodies the styles
of Euripides and Aeschylus.

Parody continued to be a popular form through Roman times, often being used
to make fun of the Christian church, and this use of it persisted through the
Middle Ages and into the Renaissance (e.g., Erasmus's *Praise of Folly* and
Rabelais's *Gargantua and Pantagruel*). Chaucer's *The Rime of Sir Thopas* (par-
odying the grandiose style of medieval romances) is a good example of early
English parodies. Other examples continue to the present day: John Phillips, *The*

Splended Shilling (1705); Duke of Buckingham, *The Rehearsal* (1671); James and Horace Smith, *Rejected Addresses* (1812); Lewis Carroll, "Father William"; Algernon Charles Swinburne, *The Higher Pantheism in a Nutshell;* and numerous parodies by Andrew Lang, Max Beerbohm, Bret Harte, Mark Twain, James Thurber, and E. B. White, many of the twentieth-century ones published in such highly respected magazines as *The New Yorker, Punch,* and *Vanity Fair,* and adopted by such television shows as "Monty Python's Flying Circus" and "Saturday Night Live."

For similar word play refer to Accidental Language, Back Slang, Burlesque, Conundrum, Irish Bull, Lampoon, Malapropism, Pun, Spoonerism, and Wellerism.

BIBLIOGRAPHY

Daiches, David; Malcolm Bradbury; and Eric Mottram. *The Avenel Companion to English and American Literature.* New York: Avenel Books, 1981.
Espy, Willard R. *An Almanac of Words at Play.* New York: Clarkson N. Potter, Inc., 1975.
_____. *The Game of Words.* New York: Grosset & Dunlap, 1972.
Falk, Robert P., and William Beare. "Parody." In *Encyclopedia of Poetry and Poetics,* ed. Alex Preminger, Frank J. Warnke, and O. B. Hardison, Jr. Princeton: Princeton University Press, 1945.
Koestler, Arthur. "Humor and Wit." In *Encyclopaedia Britannica: Macropaedia.* 1979.
Shipley, Joseph T. *Playing with Words.* Englewood Cliffs, N.J.: Prentice-Hall, 1960.

PARONOMASIA. See PUN.

PARONOMASIA CONUNDRUM. See CONUNDRUM.

PASQUINADE is a satire or Lampoon, especially one posted in a public place. Refer to BURLESQUE; LAMPOON; PARODY.

PASS IT ON is a form of group writing.

One person writes a line and half of a second line, folds over the first line, and passes the paper on to another player. The next player finishes the second line and writes the first half of the third line. Once again, the paper is folded over, leaving only the final half-line visible, and passed on. This continues until the story has been written.

For similar word play refer to Bouts Rimés, Bouts Rimés Retournés, Consequences, Headlines, and Pass Rhyme.

BIBLIOGRAPHY

Parlett, David. *Botticelli and Beyond: Over 100 of the World's Best Word Games.* New York: Pantheon Books, 1981.

PASS RHYME is a game of group verse writing.

Each player writes a word, then passes his paper to the player next to him. This is repeated twice. The writer of the fourth word must write a word that rhymes with one of the previous three (unless two of the previous three already rhyme).

The papers are collected, shuffled, and redistributed, one to each player. The players each write a stanza of four lines, each line ending in one of the four selected words, the final word rhyming with one of the previous three words ending a line.

The papers are collected, shuffled, and redistributed again, one to each player. The players in turn read the stanza they have received, and all the players attempt to guess who wrote which rhyme. Finally, the best rhyme is selected.

For similar word play refer to Bouts Rimés, Bouts Rimés Retournés, Consequences, Headlines, and Pass It On.

BIBLIOGRAPHY

Shipley, Joseph T. *Playing with Words.* Englewood Cliffs, N.J.: Prentice-Hall, 1960.

PASSWORD, also called key word, is a word guessing game.

The game works best with five players. One player serves as the "umpire" or "teacher" and passes out the same word to one of the players on each two-player team.

One team begins by having the player who knows the word offer a one-word clue to it (often a Synonym). The other player on the team attempts to guess the secret word. If the guess is correct, the team gets a certain number of points (generally, ten points if guessed on the first clue, and one less point for each additional clue).

If the player does not guess the word, the other team proceeds in the same manner. Clues and guesses are alternated between the two teams until someone guesses the word or until an agreed on number of chances has been given and the word is discarded.

Password has been a popular television game show for a number of years. David Parlett claims to have found it in a schoolteacher's book of language games (which book is not indicated).

For other word guessing activity refer to Adverbs, Aesop's Mission, Botticelli, and Charades.

BIBLIOGRAPHY

Parlett, David. *Botticelli and Beyond: Over 100 of the World's Best Word Games.* New York: Pantheon Books, 1981.

PATCHWORK POETRY AND PATCHWORK VERSE. See CENTO.

PEG PIN CODE. See SUBSTITUTION CODE.

PERMUTATIONAL LANGUAGE is word play, the object of which is the creation of sentences with the greatest number of variations.

Dmitri Borgmann, *Beyond Language: Adventures in Word and Thought,* uses the phrase to indicate a form of word play that pushes recreational language directly into the theories of serious linguistics, most pointedly, Transformational-Generative Grammar (TG).

This form of linguistics exploded upon serious language study when Noam Chomsky published his doctoral dissertation, "Syntactic Structures," in 1957. It directly opposed the then accepted structuralist theories by emphasizing the way language encases meaning rather than excluding meaning from linguistic analysis. Basically, the idea is not to study the final product, the utterance, but the thought process the mind goes through to produce that final utterance.

These theories allow linguists to explain how "Angie likes Meghan" and "Meghan is liked by Angie" come together at some point in the thought process, i.e., mean the same thing.

A discussion of the complexities of modern linguistics is not within the range of this book. However, the puzzle Dmitri Borgmann develops out of this concept is. It involves the fact that words often have multiple meanings (équivoque), e.g., the word "run" may mean "run for office," "run around the block," "run the water," and so on. And it involves the fact that words can be used as different parts of speech.

The object of the puzzle is to create sentences with the greatest number of permutations. Three-word sentences with a total of six possible forms produce the easiest examples of permutational language:

Angie likes Meghan
Angie Meghan likes
Meghan likes Angie
Meghan Angie likes
Likes Meghan Angie
Likes Angie Meghan

For other word play involving multiple meanings refer to Pun and the many types of word play based on puns, especially Charades, Double Entendre, Equivocally Speaking, and Shifty Sentences.

BIBLIOGRAPHY

Baugh, Albert C., and Thomas Cable. *A History of the English Language.* 1957. Reprint. Englewood Cliffs, N.J.: Prentice-Hall, 1978.

Borgmann, Dmitri A. *Beyond Language: Adventures in Word and Thought.* New York: Charles Scribner's Sons, 1967.

Bolton, W. F. *A Living Language: The History and Structure of English.* New York: Random House, 1982.

Chomsky, Noam. "Syntactic Structures." Ph.D. dissertation, University of Pennsylvania, 1957.

Liles, Bruce L. *A Basic Grammar of Modern English*. Englewood Cliffs, N.J.: Prentice-Hall, 1979.
Myers, L. M., and Richard L. Hoffman. *The Roots of Modern English*. 2d ed. Boston: Little, Brown and Co., 1979.

PERVERB, also called pied proverbs, is word play involving Proverbs.

The term is used by Harry Mathews, *Selected Declarations of Dependence* (1976), for the joining of the first half of one proverb to the second half of another proverb:

A rolling stone waits for no man.
It's an ill wind that has a silver lining.
A bird in the hand gets the worm.

For similar word plax refer to Cento, Charms, Constructapo, Homosyntaxism, Incantations, Möbius Strip, Oulipo Algorithms, Shouting Proverbs, Silly Similes, Slygram, and Spicy Proverbs.

BIBLIOGRAPHY

Mathews, Harry. *Selected Declarations of Dependence*. Toronto: Eternal Network, 1976.
Shipley, Joseph T. *Playing with Words*. Englewood Cliffs, N.J.: Prentice-Hall, 1960.

PHONETIC PALINDROMES are phonographically reversible Palindromes; they are words that sound the same whether spelled forward or backward, e.g., kick-kcik.

For similar word play refer to Anagram, Charades, Flat, Palindrome, and Sotadic Palindrome.

BIBLIOGRAPHY

Bergerson, Howard W. *Palindromes and Anagrams*. New York: Dover, 1973.
Bombaugh, C. C. *Gleanings for the Curious*. 1890. Reprint. *Oddities and Curiosities of Words and Literature,* ed. Martin Gardner. New York: Dover, 1961.
Borgmann, Dmitri A. *Beyond Language: Adventures in Word and Thought*. New York: Charles Scribner's Sons, 1967.

PHONETIC REBUS. See FLAT.

PHONETIC REVERSALS are word turn-arounds done by the unit of the syllable or morpheme.

Two Samuel Butler novels, *Erewhon: or Over the Range* (1872; revised 1872, 1901) and *Erewhon Revisited, Both by the Original Discoverer of the Country and His Son* (1901), employ phonetic reversal (Erewhon reversed phonetically is Nowhere).

Here are a few additional examples:

someone—nomos
where—erehw
boyfriend—dneirfyob

For similar word play refer to Phunny Stuph and Pun.

BIBLIOGRAPHY

Borgmann, Dmitri A. *Beyond Language: Adventures in Word and Thought.* New York: Charles Scribner's Sons, 1967.
Daiches, David; Malcolm Bradbury; and Eric Mottram. *The Avenel Companion to English and American Literature.* New York: Avenel Books, 1981.

PHUNNY STUPH is a word search involving the letters ph.

The game is described by James Fixx, *Solve It!* Its object is to find ph words where the ph does not sound like f.

The key is to find words where the p comes at the end of a syllable and the h begins a new syllable, e.g., upheaval, upholster, uphold.

For similar word play refer to Phonetic Reversals and Pun.

BIBLIOGRAPHY

Fixx, James. *Solve It! A Perplexing Profusion of Puzzles.* New York: Doubleday, 1978.

PI is a simplified version of Black Squares.

According to David Parlett, the game was invented by John Shepherd, who first introduced it in the monthly letter of the Knights of the Square Table. Parlett first encountered it in *Games and Puzzles* by Ross Eckler.

The game is played on a squared grid of at least five by five, or twenty-five squares. Each player in turn writes a letter in any square, or challenges the previous player's play.

The loser is the first person unable to move without breaking one of the following two rules:

1. In every row and column three or more consecutive letters must form a word when read in the appropriate direction (top to bottom or left to right).

2. A letter may not be entered which makes it impossible to complete a word of two or more letters by subsequent additions in the same row or column.

A player may challenge his opponent under either of these rules. If the opponent does not prove the existence of a word under rule 1 by reference to a dictionary, the player making the challenge wins (the challenger loses if a word can be made). Similarly, if the challenged player can prove that the letter he has just added can be incorporated into a word of two or more letters, then, under the second rule, he wins; if not he loses.

For similar word play refer to Across-tic, Acrostic, Black Squares, Crossword Puzzle, Forms, Lynx, Magic Word Squares, and SCRABBLE.

BIBLIOGRAPHY

Parlett, David. *Botticelli and Beyond: Over 100 of the World's Best Word Games.* New York: Pantheon Books, 1981.

PICTONYM, also called animated words, is a word written in a way that illustrates something about that word.

Here is an example:

$$D\;D\;C\;A\;V$$
$$D\backslash C/\backslash \Lambda$$

For similar word play refer to Emblematic Poetry, Looks Like Poetry, Rebus, and ZOO-LULU.

BIBLIOGRAPHY

Espy, Willard R. *An Almanac of Words at Play.* New York: Clarkson N. Potter, Inc., 1975.
Kim, Scott. *Inversions: A Catalog of Calligraphic Cartwheels.* Peterborough, N.H.: BYTE Books, McGraw Hill, 1981.

PICTORIAL ACROSTIC. See ACROSTIC.

PICTURE POEMS. See EMBLEMATIC POETRY.

PIDGIN ENGLISH. See PIG LATIN.

PIE. See SCRAMBLEGRAM.

PIECEMEAL. See EXTRAS.

PIED PROVERBS. See PERVERB.

PIG LATIN is word play derived from standard languages by moving the first consonant or consonant cluster of each word to the end of the word and adding the sound "ay" to the end of the word, e.g., og-day atin-lay for "dog Latin."

It is not to be confused with Pidgin English, a simplified form of English used by South Pacific natives and Orientals to communicate with foreigners; the term "pidgin" is said to come from a Chinese mispronunciation of "business"; the two basic forms are Chinese Pidgin and Melanesian Pidgin.

According to Derek Bickerton, Creole developed out of Pidgin languages, the languages used by the children of the slaves and poor laborers pressed into service by the European colonial powers between 1500 and 1900. Creole, as opposed to Pidgin, is not a secondary, simplified language, but the primary language of its users, and thus far more sophisticated.

A continuum, then, exists from pig Latin through Pidgin to Creole: pig Latin is a simple form of word play; Pidgin is a simplified second language; Creole is a primary language, continually growing and changing and developing complexities, as does any language.

For similar word play refer to Macaronics.

BIBLIOGRAPHY

Baugh, Albert C., and Thomas Cable. *A History of the English Language.* 1957. Reprint. Englewood Cliffs, N.J.: Prentice-Hall, 1978.

Bickerton, Derek. "Creole Languages." *Scientific American* 249, no. 1 (July 1983): 116–122.

Bolton, W. F. *A Living Language: The History and Structure of English.* New York: Random House, 1982.

Eckler, A. Ross. *Word Recreations: Games and Diversions from "Word Ways."* New York: Dover, 1979.

Espy, Willard R. *A Children's Almanac of Words at Play.* New York: Clarkson N. Potter, Inc., 1982.

————. *The Game of Words.* New York: Grosset & Dunlap, 1972.

McKechnie, Jean L., et al. *Webster's New Twentieth Century Dictionary of the English Language: Unabridged.* 2d ed. New York: World Publishing Co., 1971.

Myers, L. M., and Richard L. Hoffman. *The Roots of Modern English.* 2d ed. Boston: Little, Brown and Co., 1979.

PLACEMENT CODE. See TRANSPOSITION CODE.

PLAY RHYMES. See GAME RHYMES.

POEM CAPPING. See RENGA.

POPULAR RIDDLE. See RIDDLE.

PORTMANTEAU is a word that combines parts of two different words to form a new word, e.g., breakfast + lunch = brunch; hotel + motor = motel.

Lewis Carroll's "Jabberwocky" is filled with portmanteaus (e.g., chortle, chuckle, snort). James Joyce also created numerous portmanteaus (perhelps, bungelars, murmoirs, hyacinsses, heliotrollops).

For similar word play refer to Abbreviations, Fractured Geography, Fractured Industry, Invent-a-Name, and Pun.

BIBLIOGRAPHY

Brandreth, Gyles. *The Joy of Lex: How to Have Fun with 860,341,500 Words.* New York: Quill, 1983.

Carroll, Lewis. *Alice's Adventures in Wonderland.* 1865. Reprint. New York: New American Library, 1960.

_____. *Through the Looking Glass*. 1872. Reprint. New York: New American Library, 1960.
Espy, Willard R. *Have a Word on Me: A Celebration of Language*. New York: Simon & Schuster, 1981.
Joyce, James. *Finnegans Wake*. 1939. Reprint. New York: Viking Press, 1982.
_____. *Ulysses*. 1922. Reprint. New York: Random House, 1934.
McKechnie, Jean L., et al. *Webster's New Twentieth Century Dictionary of the English Language: Unabridged*. 2d ed. New York: World Publishing Co., 1971.
Shipley, Joseph T. *Playing with Words*. Englewood Cliffs, N.J.: Prentice-Hall, 1960.

PREFIXES is a game involving a word search.

The object of the game is to come up with as many words with the same prefix as possible. The player who finds the most is the winner (generally, a time limit is set).

A prefix is a syllable, a group of syllables, or another word attached to the beginning of a word. A common practice in Latin is to join prefixes (*prae*, "in front"; *fixus*, "attached") to other words, and since Latin is an important source of English words, Latin prefixes are abundant and thus a good source for choosing the prefix to begin the game. Here are the more common Latin prefixes: ab (abs), ad, ante, bene, bi (bis), circum, con, contra, de, dis, ex, extra, in, inter, intra, intro, male, multi, non, ob, per, post, prae, pro, re (red), se, semi, sub, super (sur), trans (tra), ultra, un (uni).

For similar word play refer to Animalistics, Confusing and Confounding Cats, Cross-breed, Form-a-Word, Galaxy of Gals, Hidden Names, Shifting, Spare the Prefix, and Suffixes.

BIBLIOGRAPHY

Brandreth, Gyles. *Indoor Games*. London: Hodder & Stoughton, Ltd., 1977.
Parlett, David. *Botticelli and Beyond: Over 100 of the World's Best Word Games*. New York: Pantheon Books, 1981.
Ullman, B. L., and Albert I. Suskin. *Latin for Americans*. New York: Macmillan Co., 1965.

PRIME-RHYMES. See STINKY PINKY.

PROBE. See HANGMAN.

PROGRESSIVE ANAGRAM, also called isosceles words, transadditions, transmutations, and word pyramids, is a form of Anagram word play where a letter is added to (or subtracted from) each successive word, e.g., i, it, tin, into, niton, nation.

Harold H. Hart, *Grab a Pencil,* discusses a form of progressive anagram he calls blankie. Each blankie is a short story with certain words replaced by blanks (one blank for each letter of the word). The key word (the word that all of the other words must be contained within) is set down in capital letters. Each of the progressive anagrams must contain the letters of the previous word:

TAVERN

__ man checked his mail box __ __ the post office before stopping at a nearby cafe to get something to __ __ __. His clothes were __ __ __ __ and clean, but he ate like a __ __ __ __ __, spilling food all over his clothes. When he got home, his wife asked him if he had been drinking at the local __ __ __ __ __ __.
(Answers: a, at, eat, neat, raven, tavern)

Expanding words comes from Henry Ernest Dudeney, *300 Best Word Puzzles*. It is identical to blankie, except that the key word is not given:

__ boy got sick __ __ school one day because he ate a __ __ __. He said "I'll never do that again; I __ __ __ __ the taste."
(Answers: a, at, hat, hate)

The Espyramid comes from Willard R. Espy. His version of progressive anagram incorporates blankie into light verse:

__ boy was late for school one day
And had to leave __ __ eight;
He took his seat and __ __ __ and __ __ __.
"Your baseball __ __ __ __ can wait;
We'll use them as the wanted __ __ __ __ __
Or build __ __ __ __ __ __ walls."
a
at
sat
bats
baits
abatis

In an Espyramid the progression may also be inverted, moving from the larger word to the smaller one.

For similar word play refer to Acrosticals, Add-on, Alfabits, Anablank, Ana-game, Anagram, Building Blocks, Build-ups, Cap Me, Category Puzzles, Cir-cular Reversals, Crossword Puzzle, Doublets, Espygram, Flat, Jumbles, Last Word, Marsupials, Middleput, Missing Words, Name in Vain, Palindrome, Reversible Anagram, Scaffold, Scramblegram, Stairway, Word Knock-downs, and Word Ping-Pong.

BIBLIOGRAPHY

Borgmann, Dmitri A. *Language on Vacation: An Olio of Orthographical Oddities*. New York: Charles Scribner's Sons, 1965.

Dudeney, Henry Ernest. *300 Best Word Puzzles*. New York: Charles Scribner's Sons, 1968.

Espy, Willard R. *A Children's Almanac of Words at Play*. New York: Clarkson N. Potter, Inc., 1982.

_____. *The Game of Words*. New York: Grosset & Dunlap, 1972.

Hart, Harold H. *Grab a Pencil*. New York: Hart Publ. Co., 1958.
Worden, Mark. "The Life and Times of Willard Espy (A Play on Words in Three Acts)."
      Writer's Digest 64 (April 1984): 34–37.

PROVERB is a short saying, generally expressed in a witty or clever manner, that expresses some form of wisdom.

According to Joseph T. Shipley, *Dictionary of Word Origins,* "proverb" comes from "verb," the most important word in an English sentence. "Verb" once meant "word" (Latin *verbum,* meaning "word," as in *Verbum sapienti satis est*). By placing "pro" in front of "verb," a word is created that means "before verb," pre-word. Thus, a proverb is something that comes before words, a truth that words cannot express.

According to Daniel G. Hoffman, "Proverb," in *Encyclopedia of Poetry and Poetics,* proverbs are among the oldest poetic works in Sanskrit, Hebrew, Germanic, and Scandinavian literatures. He distinguishes between learned proverbs (those long current in literature) and popular proverbs. The two major sources of learned proverbs (as of most western literature and thought) are the Bible and the classical Greek and Roman thinkers (e.g., Aristophanes, Theophrastus, Lucian, and Plautus). Erasmus, *Adagia* (1500), was a major force in reacquainting Europe with the classical proverbs; and proverbs are common in Chaucer (e.g., *Tale of Melibeus*), John Lyly (*Euphues*), Franklin (*The Way to Wealth*), Goethe ("Sprichwörtliches"), and the plays of Shakespeare. Through time, in fact, the term proverb was so overused that it took on connotations of a commonplace or a Cliché.

David Parlett, *Botticelli and Beyond: Over 100 of the World's Best Word Games,* describes a game titled proverbs that goes as follows:

One player is designated "Roof Mender" and is sent upstairs to repair the roof. While he is out of the room, the other players agree on a proverb or popular saying.

The Roof Mender is then allowed back into the room. His task is to solve the proverb; however, the only information he is given is the number of words it contains.

He does this by asking questions. The answers to his questions must be plausible and must contain words from the proverb. The first answer must contain the first word of the proverb, the second answer must contain the second word of the proverb, and so on.

Though the connotations may vary slightly, the four terms proverb, gnome, aphorism, and maxim are denotatively interchangeable. A gnome is a short, pithy expression of a general truth; an aphorism is a terse saying embodying a general truth; and a maxim is a concise expression of a general truth.

In addition to Parlett's game, a number of other forms of word play have been included under the four designations. In one of them, each player must think of, look up, or create a list of aphorisms (e.g., "when you're hot you're hot"; "seeing is believing"; "a stitch in time saves nine"). The players then write down the first or second half of each aphorism on separate sheets of paper, and allow the other players a certain amount of time to guess the complete aphorism. One point is awarded for each correct guess.

An apothegm or apophthegm varies from a proverb in being more of a short instructive remark than an expression of a general truth. "Apophthegm" comes from the classical Greek *apophthegma*, "spoken out."

An epigram varies from a proverb in displaying a personal, specific quality rather than imparting a general truth. Epigrams were an important form of classical Greek expression (the term "epigram" comes from the Greek *epigramma*, "inscription"), and coarse, satirical examples can be found in the works of Martial and other Roman writers. An epigram often takes the form of a couplet or a quatrain, such as the following by Matthew Prior (1664–1721), quoted by Alex Preminger and Frank J. Warnke in "Epigram," in *Encyclopedia of Poetry and Poetics:*

Sir, I admit your general rule,
That every poet is a fool:
But you yourself may serve to show it,
That every fool is not a poet.

Though proverbs are generally shorter than a quatrain, they can be longer, as the following from the King James Bible indicates (Proverbs 3:13–18):

Happy is the man who finds wisdom,
   and the man who gets understanding,
for the gain from it is better than
   gain from silver and its profit better than gold.
She is more precious than jewels,
   and nothing you desire can compare with her.
Long life is in her right hand;
   in her left hand are riches and honor.
Her ways are ways of pleasantness,
   and all her paths are peace.
She is a tree of life to those who lay
   hold of her;
Those who hold her fast are called
   happy.

For similar word play refer to Charms, Fractured Industry, Incantations, Perverb, Shouting Proverbs, and Spicy Proverbs.

BIBLIOGRAPHY

Brandreth, Gyles. *The World's Best Indoor Games*. New York: Pantheon Books, 1981.
Daiches, David; Malcolm Bradbury; and Eric Mottram. *The Avenel Companion to English and American Literature*. New York: Avenel Books, 1981.

Gardner, Martin. *Perplexing Puzzles and Tantalizing Teasers.* New York: Simon & Schuster, 1969.

Hoffman, Daniel G. "Proverb." In *Encyclopedia of Poetry and Poetics,* ed. Alex Preminger. Princeton: Princeton University Press, 1965.

King James Bible, 1611. Reprint. King James Version. Camden, N.J.: Thomas Nelson, Inc., 1970.

McKechnie, Jean L., et al., eds. *Webster's New Twentieth Century Dictionary of the English Language: Unabridged.* 2d ed. New York: World Publishing Co., 1971.

Parlett, David. *Botticelli and Beyond: Over 100 of the World's Best Word Games.* New York: Pantheon Books, 1981.

Partridge, Eric. *Origins: A Short Etymological Dictionary of Modern English.* New York: Greenwich House, 1983.

Preminger, Alex, and Frank J. Warnke. "Epigram." In *Encyclopedia of Poetry and Poetics,* eds. Alex Preminger, Frank J. Warnke, and O. B. Hardison, Jr. Princeton: Princeton University Press, 1965.

Sherzer, Joel. "Saying Is Inventing: Gnomic Expressions in *Molloy.*" In *Speech Play,* ed. Barbara Kirshenblatt-Gimblett. Philadelphia: University of Pennsylvania, 1976.

Shipley, Joseph T. *Dictionary of Word Origins.* New York: Philosophical Library, 1945.

Smith, George William. *The Oxford Dictionary of English Proverbs,* ed. F. P. Wilson. 3d ed. Oxford, Eng.: Clarendon Press, 1970.

PUN, in French *jeu de mots,* is a play on the dual meanings of a word or words that sound alike or the use of a word in two different contexts.

According to Stephen F. Fogel, "Pun," in *Encyclopedia of Poetry and Poetics,* an anonymous treatise on rhetoric, *Rhetorica ad Herennium,* distinguishes three forms of pun: *traductio* (the use of the same word in different connotations or a balancing of homonyms), *adnominatio* (the repetition of a word with slight changes—prefixes, suffixes, letter or sound transpositions), and *significatio* (a figure of speech depending on similarity of sound and disparity of meaning).

According to Edward P.J. Corbett, *Classical Rhetoric for the Modern Student,* there are three contemporary classifications of pun: puns of paronomasia ("the use of words alike in sound but different in meaning," e.g., "Casting my perils before swains" [Marshall McLuhan, quoted by Corbett, p. 482]); puns of antanaclasis ("the repetition of a word in two different senses," e.g., "Your argument is sound, nothing but sound" [Benjamin Franklin, quoted by Corbett, p. 482]); and puns of syllepsis ("the use of a word understood differently in relation to two or more other words, which it modifies or governs," e.g., "Here thou, great Anna! whom three realms obey / Dost sometimes counsel take—and sometimes tea" [Alexander Pope, quoted by Corbett, p. 483]).

Fogel includes a fourth contemporary classification along with the three discussed by Corbett, asteismus. In asteismus, one speaker replies to another, using the latter's words in a different sense, e.g., "Cloten: 'Would he had been one of my rank!' Lord: 'To have smell'd like a fool' " (Shakespeare, *Cymbeline,* act 2, sc. 1, line 17, quoted by Fogel, p. 681).

Asteismus, however, though an obvious form of punning, is not a separate type of pun with paronomasia, antanaclasis, and syllepsis, but rather is a form of antanaclasis or syllepsis, depending on how it is used. Perhaps that is why Corbett does not include it in his system of classification.

Both Corbett's and Fogel's systems of classification are valuable and suggestive of a number of poetic techniques. Nevertheless, they may also suggest unreal limitations on the uses of such juxtapositions of word meanings. Arthur Koestler, "Humor and Wit," in *Encyclopaedia Britannica: Macropaedia,* though limiting puns even more than Corbett and Fogel (allowing them to include only the word play which consists of "two disparate strings of thought tied together by an acoustic knot . . . an association based on pure sound"), nevertheless extends the use of puns in word games by integrating them into a more encompassing form of humor. He states:

From the play on sounds—puns and Spoonerisms—an ascending series leads to the play on words and so to the play on ideas. When Groucho Marx says of a safari in Africa, "We shot two bucks, but that was all the money we had," the joke hinges on the two meanings of the word buck.

The disagreement comes from whether or not to limit puns to sounds or to include all linguistic play involving an inclusion of multiple meanings in one expression. Corbett would probably classify Groucho Marx's statement as a pun of syllepsis. Richard Lederer would agree: "Punning is largely the trick of combining two or more ideas within a single word or expression" ("Primer of Puns," *English Journal,* October 1981). Apparently Koestler, however, would turn to Corbett's definition of a Paradox as the correct category, because, "it involves not so much a 'turn' of meaning in juxtaposed words as a 'turn' of meaning in the whole statement" (Corbett, p. 492). Wherever the distinguishing lines are drawn, puns are a major form of word play.

Jesus Christ (Matt. 16:18) punned on the name of Simon Peter: "And I say also unto thee, That thou art Peter, and upon this rock I will build my church; and the gates of hell shall not prevail against it." In Greek, Peter (*petro*) means rock. Jesus, then, made a pun of antanaclasis.

Shakespeare's plays are filled with puns. In *Romeo and Juliet,* the dying Mercutio says, "Look for me tomorrow, and you will find me a grave man." Hilaire Belloc wrote: "When I'm dead, I hope it will be said, 'His sins were scarlet, but his books were read.'"

A number of terms are used to describe the various types of puns. A homophone is a word pronounced the same as another word (although not necessarily spelled the same) but differing in meaning, e.g., "err," "air," and "heir." Puns of paronomasia are based on homophones. Homophonics are sentences that contain a pair of homophones, e.g., "He spilled flour all over the flower." Homophone cartoons are pictures illustrating the incorrect word from a homophonic pair, e.g., the drawing of an airplane to illustrate the word "plain."

A homonym is a word that is the same as another word in sound and spelling, but different in meaning, e.g., chase, "to pursue," and chase, "to ornament metal." It is the basis for puns of antanaclasis. Dmitri Borgmann, *Language on Vacation: An Olio of Orthographical Oddities,* uses homonymic transposals to designate letter transposals which also result in homonyms, e.g., brake and break. Borgmann suggests a form of word play based on homonyms: Write sensible sentences using the same homonym as many times in a row as possible, e.g., "That that that is the that that that that is meant to be is all that that that can be."

Borgmann also suggests a game based on homonyms. Homonyms are a source of all three types of pun. One player collects a group of homonyms and lists a brief definition for each. The object is for the other players to guess the homonyms.

Homonymbles is a combination of homonyms and Nymbles, and therefore deals with words that have the same spelling and pronunciation but different meanings, and with words that have the same pronunciation but different spelling.

A homograph is a word of the same written form as another word, but with a different origin and meaning.

A heteronym is a word that is spelled like another word but is different in sound and meaning, e.g., Polish, polish. This is another source for puns of antanaclasis.

Heterological words are those where the form of the word is different than the meaning of the word, e.g., long is actually a short word.

A zeugma is a pun of syllepsis where the word does not fit grammatically or idiomatically with one of the words it governs, e.g., "He *shot* his wife, and may Meghan too."

A few of the puzzles and games based on puns follow:

Baxterism is a form of punning where adjectives are attached to nouns to create humorous dual meanings, e.g., a sick prescription: a cure for a sickness, a bad idea, and a humorous idea.

I-can-give-you-a-sentence is the creation of sentences that have dual meanings as the result of puns of paronomasia:

The claws in the small print bothered him.
Jared was just wading for his ship to come in.
Angie wanted a Renaissance man with a lot of money, but Ryan was baroque.

Anguish languish is a term used by Howard Chace for elaborate puns of paronomasia. For purposes of humor, he would replace the words of familiar folk tales with other words similar in sound but unrelated in meaning.

Animal crackers is a term used by John G. Fuller for a group of punning games based on the characteristics of animals:

Fill in the blank with a word that has dual meanings:
As _____ as a fish (slippery: wet, shifty).

Appropriate names is another term used by Fuller for a form of punning. Here the object is to come up with a name for a person that puns on his profession:

Rusty Saw (carpenter)
Screwdriver Sue (barmaid)
Hotdog Hank (fast food cook)

In *jobbers,* the idea is to create a humorous name for a person in a specific occupation:

Captain Crunch: a football defensive tackle
Polly Tic: a United States senator

For additional word play based on puns, refer to Accidental Language, Autantonyms, Boner, Book Conversation, Burlesque, Catch, Chronograms, Coffee Pot, Confusing and Confounding Cats, Conundrum, Countdown Verses, Croakers, Cross-breed, Crossing Jokes, Daffy Definitions, Dear Departed, Double Entendre, Doubletones, Enigma, Euphemaken, Form-a-Word, Fractured Book-Reviews, Fractured Geography, Fractured Industry, Galaxy of Gals, Goldwynner, Improbable Opposites, Irish Bull, Joke, Jumbled Geography, Knockknock, Lampoon, Little Audrey, Little Willie, MADvertisements, Malapropism, Moron Joke, Nimblebreak, Nymble, Nymblebreak, Oxymoron, Paradox, Parody, Pasquinade, Riddle, Silly Similes, Sound Spelling, Split Words, Subject Matter, Thriftgram, Tom Swifties, Tonto, Vulture Up To? and What Is the Question?

BIBLIOGRAPHY

Bolton, W. F. *A Living Language: The History and Structure of English.* New York: Random House, 1982.
Bombaugh, C. C. *Gleanings for the Curious.* 1890. Reprint. *Oddities and Curiosities of Words and Literature,* ed. Martin Gardner. New York: Dover, 1961.
Borgmann, Dmitri A. *Beyond Language: Adventures in Word and Thought.* New York: Charles Scribner's Sons, 1967.
———. *Language on Vacation: An Olio of Orthographical Oddities.* New York: Charles Scribner's Sons, 1965.
Brandreth, Gyles. *The Joy of Lex: How to Have Fun with 860,341,500 Words.* New York: Quill, 1983.
———. *More Joy of Lex: An Amazing and Amusing Z to A and A to Z of Words.* New York: William Morrow and Co., 1982.
Corbett, Edward P.J. *Classical Rhetoric for the Modern Student.* 2d ed. New York: Oxford University Press, 1971.
Espy, Willard R. *An Almanac of Words at Play.* New York: Clarkson N. Potter, Inc., 1975.
———. *A Children's Almanac of Words at Play.* New York: Clarkson N. Potter, Inc., 1982.
———. *The Game of Words.* New York: Grosset & Dunlap, 1972.

———. *Have a Word on Me: A Celebration of Language*. New York: Simon & Schuster, 1981.

———. *Say It My Way*. New York: Doubleday, 1980.

Fogel, Stephen F. "Puns." In *Encyclopedia of Poetry and Poetics,* ed. Alex Preminger. Princeton: Princeton University Press, 1965.

Fuller, John G. *Games for Insomniacs; or, a Lifetime Supply of Insufferable Brain Twisters*. New York: Doubleday, 1966.

Hindman, Darwin A. *1800 Riddles, Enigmas and Conundrums*. New York: Dover, 1963.

King James Bible, 1611. Reprint. King James Version. Camden, N.J.: Thomas Nelson, Inc., 1970.

Koestler, Arthur. "Humor and Wit." In *Encyclopaedia Britannica: Macropaedia.* 1979.

Lederer, Richard. "Primer of Puns." *English Journal* 7 (October 1981): 32–36.

McKechnie, Jean L., et al., eds. *Webster's New Twentieth Century Dictionary of the English Language: Unabridged*. 2d ed. New York: World Publishing Co., 1971.

Moger, Art. *The Complete Pun Book*. Secaucus, N.J.: Castle, 1979.

Parlett, David. *Botticelli and Beyond: Over 100 of the World's Best Word Games*. New York: Pantheon Books, 1981.

Partridge, Eric. *Origins: A Short Etymological Dictionary of Modern English*. New York: Greenwich House, 1983.

Shakespeare, William. *Romeo and Juliet*. 1594. Reprint. *The Complete Signet Classic Shakespeare,* ed. Sylvan Barnet. New York: Signet, 1963.

Shipley, Joseph T. *Playing with Words*. Englewood Cliffs, N.J.: Prentice-Hall, 1960.

———. "Word and Letter Games." In *Encyclopaedia Britannica: Macropaedia*. 1979.

PUNCTUATION PUZZLES. See CHARADES.

PUT AND TAKE is word play involving Anagrams.

The object is to take two words (e.g., rings, gin) and remove one letter from the first and add it to the second to form two new words that are related in some sense (e.g., sings/gun can be changed to sing/sung).

For similar word play refer to Acrosticals, Add-on, Alfabits, Anablank, Anagame, Anagram, Cap Me, Category Puzzles, Circular Reversals, Crossword Puzzle, Doublets, Espygram, Flat, Jumbles, Last Word, Marsupials, Middleput, Missing Words, Name in Vain, Palindrome, Progressive Anagram, Quaternade, Reversible Anagram, Scaffold, Scramblegram, Word Knock-downs, and Word Ping-Pong.

BIBLIOGRAPHY

Shipley, Joseph T. *Playing with Words*. Englewood Cliffs, N.J.: Prentice-Hall, 1960.

PUZZLING SQUARES involves the solving of eight-letter words.

An eight-letter word is arranged in a square with one letter missing. The object is to solve the word:

```
p   u   z
g       z
n  __   l
```

Answer: i, puzzling.

For similar word play refer to Across-tic, Acrostic, Alphacross, Alphawords, Arrow of Letters, Black Squares, Crossword Puzzle, Flat, Forms, Last Word, Lynx, Magic Word Squares, Quizl, SCRABBLE, and Scramblegram.

BIBLIOGRAPHY

Adler, Irving, and Peggy Adler. *The Adler Book of Puzzles and Riddles, or Sam Loyd Up to Date*. New York: John Day Co., 1962.

Borgmann, Dmitri A. *Beyond Language: Adventures in Word and Thought*. New York: Charles Scribner's Sons, 1967.

Dudeney, Henry Ernest. *300 Best Word Puzzles*. New York: Charles Scribner's Sons, 1968.

Eckler, A. Ross. *Word Recreations: Games and Diversions from "Word Ways."* New York: Dover, 1979.

Espy, Willard R. *The Game of Words*. New York: Grosset & Dunlap, 1972.

Loyd, Samuel. *Sam Loyd's Cyclopedia of 5000 Puzzles, Tricks and Conundrums with Answers*. New York: Pinnacle Books, 1976.

QUADADE. See Quaternade.

QUATERNADE, also called quadade, is an Anagram puzzle.

The object is to form words from the fourth letters in succession of larger words, e.g., Vacation/Van or An if beginning with the fourth letter.

For similar word play refer to Acrosticals, Add-on, Alfabits, Anablank, Anagame, Anagram, Cap Me, Category Puzzles, Circular Reversals, Crossword Puzzle, Doublets, Espygram, Flat, Jumbles, Last Word, Marsupials, Middleput, Missing Words, Name in Vain, Palindrome, Progressive Anagram, Put and Take, Quinade, Reversible Anagram, Scaffold, Scramblegram, Word Knockdowns, and Word Ping-Pong.

BIBLIOGRAPHY

Borgmann, Dmitri A. *Language on Vacation: An Olio of Orthographical Oddities.* New York: Charles Scribner's Sons, 1965.

QUICK THINKING is a question and answer game.

The players make a list of random objects and, if they wish, a list of random questions. One player is chosen as the questioner. He takes two of the items from the list at random and, if a list of questions has been written up, a question; if no list of questions has been written up, he makes up his own.

He asks questions of the players in turn and requests that they include the two selected words in their answers. The answers must have some logical relationship to the question, or the players are eliminated.

This continues until all of the players except one have been eliminated. The remaining player wins and becomes the questioner for the next game.

For similar word play refer to Adverbs, Aesop's Mission, Alphabetical Adjectives, Charades, Initial Answers, and Password.

BIBLIOGRAPHY

Parlett, David. *Botticelli and Beyond: Over 100 of the World's Best Word Games.* New York: Pantheon Books, 1981.

QUINADE is an Anagram puzzle.

The object is to form words from the fifth letters in succession of larger words, e.g., Possible/Pi.

For similar word play refer to Acrosticals, Add-on, Alfabits, Anablank, Anagame, Anagram, Cap Me, Category Puzzles, Circular Reversals, Crossword Puzzle, Doublets, Espygram, Flat, Jumbles, Last Word, Marsupials, Middleput, Missing Words, Name in Vain, Palindrome, Progressive Anagram, Put and Take, Quaternade, Removers, Reversible Anagram, Scaffold, Scramblegram, Word Knock-downs, and Word Ping-Pong.

BIBLIOGRAPHY

Borgmann, Dmitri A. *Language on Vacation: An Olio of Orthographical Oddities.* New York: Charles Scribner's Sons, 1965.

QUIZL is a grid game.

A quizl is a sequence of letters that looks like it is going to form a word but does not. The object of the game is to trick the opposing player into believing that a five-letter word will be formed when it cannot.

Each player begins with two five by five grids (twenty-five total squares in each grid). In a column or a row (left to right or top to bottom) each player enters a word (all five letters must be different) in one of his grids. After each player has filled in his word, he fills in the rest of the grid with the remaining letters of the alphabet (using up all of the letters of the alphabet except one). No letter may be used more than once, and no other five-letter words may be formed.

Each player then attempts to guess his opponent's word before his own word is guessed. This is done in the following manner.

Each player in turn calls out a square, and his opponent indicates the letter in that square. The players begin filling in their empty grids with the letters they receive from their opponent's grid.

Eventually one player guesses his opponent's word. He then receives one point for every square not yet filled in. If a wrong guess is made, the player loses that turn. If a player entirely uncovers his opponent's word before guessing it, he loses.

David Parlett offers two possible variations. In the first, players call out letters instead of squares; in the second, anagrams are allowed.

For similar word play refer to Across-tic, Acrostic, Alphacross, Alphawords, Arrow of Letters, Black Squares, Crossword Puzzle, Flat, Forms, Last Word,

Lynx, Magic Word Squares, Puzzling Squares, Ragaman, SCRABBLE, and Scramblegram.

BIBLIOGRAPHY

Parlett, David. *Botticelli and Beyond: Over 100 of the World's Best Word Games.* New York: Pantheon Books, 1981.

QUIZ THAT MAN is a word guessing game.

One player offers clues to various words beginning with "man," and the other player or players attempt to guess the word:

What man is demanding?
(a mandate)

What man is a city in England?
(Manchester)

What man is a narcotic herb?
(mandrake)

For similar word play refer to Animalistics, Confusing and Confounding Cats, Cross-breed, Form-a-Word, Galaxy of Gals, Hidden Names, Hidden Words, Pun, Shifting, Spare the Prefix, and Vulture Up To?

BIBLIOGRAPHY

Morris, William, and Mary Morris. *The Word Game Book.* New York: Harper & Brothers, 1959.

R

RAGAMAN is a grid game.

The game is played on a grid with an odd number of squares (e.g., five by five or seven by seven).

The first player writes a vowel in the center square. Each player in turn writes any letter anywhere on the grid, provided it is adjacent to at least one other existing letter (horizontally, vertically, or diagonally).

Players score the combined length of any words they have formed (horizontally, vertically, and diagonally). No more than one word may be claimed in each direction. The words may be Anagrams.

For similar word play refer to Across-tic, Acrostic, Alphacross, Alphawords, Arrow of Letters, Black Squares, Crossword Puzzle, Flat, Forms, Last Word, Lynx, Magic Word Squares, Puzzling Squares, Quizl, SCRABBLE, and Scramblegram.

BIBLIOGRAPHY

Parlett, David. *Botticelli and Beyond: Over 100 of the World's Best Word Games*. New York: Pantheon Books, 1981.

Sharp, Richard. *Best Games People Play*. New York: Beckman Publ., n.d.

Sharp, Richard, and John Piggott. *The Book of Games*. New York: Galahad Books, 1977.

RAILROAD CARRIAGE GAME is a conversation game.

Two players are selected and given separate secret phrases. They are then placed as if they were sitting in a railway carriage, that is, face to face, and asked to have a conversation.

The object of the game is for one player to get his sentence into the logical continuation of the conversation before his opponent does: or, in a version offered by Gyles Brandreth, for one player to guess his opponent's phrase after the conversation is over (approximately five minutes).

The conversation should start with introductions and an established topic of discussion to avoid giving either player an advantage. Interruptions should not be allowed. The secret phrase need not be repeated exactly, as long as the key words and the meaning remain.

For similar word play refer to Inquisition.

BIBLIOGRAPHY

Brandreth, Gyles. *Indoor Games*. London: Hodder & Stoughton, Ltd., 1977.
Parlett, David. *Botticelli and Beyond: Over 100 of the World's Best Word Games*. New York: Pantheon Books, 1981.

RATE YOUR MIND PAL is a word version of the famous boss or fourteen/fifteen puzzle.

The original puzzle consisted of a shallow square tray or box that held fifteen square counters numbered one through fifteen and a square blank space in the lower right hand corner. The object was to slide the fifteen numbered counters (without lifting them from the box) about the tray until they were in the desired order.

In the original version created by Samuel Loyd about 1878, numbers one through thirteen were in serial order, but the final two numbers, fourteen and fifteen, were reversed. The object was to slide all of the numbered squares about the box until the numbers were in serial order.

1	2	3	4
5	6	7	8
9	10	11	12
13	15	14	

The puzzle was extremely popular in America and throughout Europe in the late 1870s, and numerous scholarly articles on it appeared in mathematical journals. Loyd offered $1,000 to anyone who could solve the puzzle. Thousands responded, but no one could offer adequate proof of a solution. The reason is simple: it cannot be solved. By 1879, two American mathematicians had shown that, because of what permutation mathematicians call "parity," only one-half of the 20 trillion possible permutations the pieces can assume are possible from any beginning position.

Briefly, the reasoning is as follows. No matter what path a counter takes to reach the lower right corner, it must pass through an even number of boxes. If all the numbers are in serial order, no number precedes any number smaller than itself. In any other arrangement one or more numbers will precede numbers smaller than themselves. Each time this happens, it is called an inversion. For example, in the sequence 7, 2, 3, 1, 8, number 7 precedes three numbers smaller than itself, 2 precedes one number smaller than itself, and 3 precedes one number smaller than itself, making a total of five inversions. If the total number of inversions is even, the puzzle can be solved. If the total number of inversions is odd, the puzzle cannot be solved.

Loyd's puzzle contained only one inversion and could not be solved. He probably realized this when he published his reward offer. No one doubted his mathematical genius. He published his first chess problem at the age of fourteen, was made problem editor of *Chess Monthly* at sixteen, and began writing a weekly chess page for *Scientific American Supplement* in 1877. By the time he died in 1911, he had established himself as America's undisputed puzzle king for over half a century.

The boss or fourteen/fifteen puzzle gained renewed popularity in the 1940s and can be bought in notion and toy stores today. A similar puzzle, the thirty-one puzzle, is also gaining popularity. In both cases, today's versions contain the correct parity for solution. Connections can also be made with Rubik's cube, which was wildly popular in the early 1980s, and its many offshoots.

The rate your mind pal puzzle is a variation of the boss puzzle where the words "rate, your, mind, pal" replace the fifteen numbers. Martin Gardner suggests mixing the letters in such a way that the second R replaces the first R in the puzzle. This usually fools the player into leaving the two Rs in the wrong places, in which case the puzzle is unsolvable.

R	A	T	E
Y	O	U	R
M	I	N	D
P	A	L	

BIBLIOGRAPHY

Adler, Irving, and Peggy Adler. *The Adler Book of Puzzles and Riddles, or Sam Loyd Up to Date.* New York: John Day Co., 1962.

Gardner, Martin. *The Scientific American Book of Mathematical Puzzles and Diversions.* New York: Simon & Schuster, 1956.

Loyd, Samuel. *Sam Loyd's Cyclopedia of 5000 Puzzles, Tricks and Conundrums with Answers.* New York: Pinnacle Books, 1976.

REBUS, also called letter words and wordles, is a representation of a word or phrase by symbols or pictures; it is a Riddle composed of symbols or pictures that suggest visually the sound of the words or syllables to be deciphered.

Ben Johnson ridicules the rebus in the following passage from *The Alchemist* (1610):

> I will have his name
> Formed in some mystic character, whose radii,
> Striking the senses of the passers-by,
> Shall, by a virtual influence, breed affections
> That may result upon the party owns it.
> As thus: He first shall have a bell—that's Abel;
> And by it standing one whose name is Dee,
> In a rug gown; there's D and rug—that's Drug;
> And right anenst him a dog snarling er —
> There's Drugger. ABEL DRUGGER, that's his sign,
> And here's now mystery and hieroglyphic.

Rudyard Kipling includes a description of how the alphabet was originally formed, "How the First Letter Was Written," in *Just So Stories* (1902), from a succession of rebuses.

The National Puzzlers' League includes the rebus and its various offshoots, including the rebus alternade (invented by Philip Cohen), among the standard Flats (see Flat).

Here are some examples of the rebus:

MT = Empty
NE1 = Anyone
URA2 × R = You are a two timer

$$\frac{Bills}{Money} = Zero \qquad \frac{Paid}{He} = He\ is\ underpaid$$

Roger Price calls a form of visual Pun a droodle (it is also called find the phrase). The game he develops out of droodles involves simply solving the visual puns:

An airplane with a wart.

Another form of Rebus is called letter-toons, cartoons where letters make fun of each other:

For similar word play refer to Alphabet Poetry, Animal Alphabet, Emblematic Poetry, Flat, Inversions, Looks Like Poetry, Palindrome, Pun, Riddle, Spine Poetry, Typitoons, and ZOO-LULU.

BIBLIOGRAPHY

Bombaugh, C. C. *Gleanings for the Curious.* 1890. Reprint. *Oddities and Curiosities of Words and Literature,* ed. Martin Gardner. New York: Dover, 1961.

Borgmann, Dmitri A. *Beyond Language: Adventures in Word and Thought.* New York: Charles Scribner's Sons, 1967.

Espy, Willard R. *A Children's Almanac of Words at Play.* New York: Clarkson N. Potter, Inc., 1982.

———. *The Game of Words.* New York: Grosset & Dunlap, 1972.

Gardner, Martin. *Perplexing Puzzles and Tantalizing Teasers*. New York: Simon & Schuster, 1969.
Johnson, Ben. *The Alchemist*. London, 1610.
Kipling, Rudyard. *Just So Stories*. 1902. Reprint. New York: Airmont Publishing Co., 1966.
Shipley, Joseph T. *Playing with Words*. Englewood Cliffs, N.J.: Prentice-Hall, 1960.

REBUS ALTERNADE. See FLAT.

REDUPLICATION. See DOUBLE-DACTYL; TAUTONYM.

REFLECTED WRITING, also called mirror writing, is a form of secret writing meant to be read by placing it next to a mirror.

Leonardo da Vinci used it for his notebooks. Henry Ernest Dudeney suggests an easy way to write in this manner. Take a pencil in each hand, place the points together on a sheet of paper, and write with one hand, willing the other hand to do the same.

For similar word play refer to Cipher, Cryptic Quotes, Cryptoglyphics, Cryptogram, Flat, Hidden Sentence Code, Musical Messages, Rebus, and Scramble Code.

BIBLIOGRAPHY

Dudeney, Henry Ernest. *300 Best Word Puzzles*. New York: Charles Scribner's Sons, 1968.

REMOVERS is a form of word play involving the sorting out of letters.

Two words are mixed together and a clue is given:

NTERWAKNRIOY
A form of transportation and the place it will take you.
Answer: Train, New York.

For similar word play refer to Acrosticals, Add-on, Alfabits, Anablank, Anagame, Anagram, Cap Me, Category Puzzles, Circular Reversals, Crossword Puzzle, Doublets, Espygram, Flat, Jumbles, Last Word, Marsupials, Middleput, Missing Words, Name in Vain, Palindrome, Progressive Anagram, Put and Take, Quaternade, Quinade, Reversible Anagram, Scaffold, Scramblegram, Word Knock-downs, and Word Ping-Pong.

BIBLIOGRAPHY

Hart, Harold H. *Grab a Pencil*. New York: Hart Publ. Co., 1958.
Shipley, Joseph T. *Playing with Words*. Englewood Cliffs, N.J.: Prentice-Hall, 1960.

RENGA, also called poem capping, is a Japanese game based on the Waka, a Japanese poem.

The waka does not rhyme, but consists of an upper clause (the *kami-ku*) of three lines of 5, 7, 5 syllables and a lower clause (the *shimo-ku*) of two lines of 7, 7 syllables. The first three lines generally suggest a thought or create an atmosphere; the last two lines express the idea:

Cold is the clear air,
Dew to the straight green grass clings,
Sky gray to blue turns;
Life begins anew each day,
Dark thoughts like morning dew pass.

The game can be played by two or more people. Each person writes either a *kami-ku* or a *shimo-ku*. The papers are then exchanged and the missing clause is supplied by the new holder of the paper.

For similar word play refer to Answer Verse, Cento, Clerihew, Bouts Rimés, Bouts Rimés Retournés, Constructapo, Homosyntaxism, and Pass It On.

BIBLIOGRAPHY
Shipley, Joseph T. *Playing with Words.* Englewood Cliffs, N.J.: Prentice-Hall, 1960.

REPEATED LETTER CHANGE. See FLAT.

REVERSAGRAM. See REVERSIBLE ANAGRAM.

REVERSAL. See FLAT.

REVERSIBLE ANAGRAM, also called semordnilap (Palindromes spelled backwards) and reversagram, is the forming of words by reversing other words.

The Elizabethan League of Darkness, including among its members Sir Walter Raleigh and Christopher Marlowe, suggested cynically that its acolytes spell God backwards.

In 1808, when he put an embargo on British goods, Thomas Jefferson was ridiculed by his opponents as O grab me (reversed, it spells embargo).

Lewis Carroll, *Sylvie and Bruno* (1889), points out that evil spells live backwards.

For similar word play refer to Acrosticals, Add-on, Alfabits, Anablank, Anagame, Anagram, Cap Me, Category Puzzles, Circular Reversals, Crossword Puzzle, Doublets, Espygram, Flat, Jumbles, Last Word, Marsupials, Middleput, Missing Words, Name in Vain, Palindrome, Progressive Anagram, Put and Take, Quaternade, Quinade, Scaffold, Scramblegram, Sotadic Palindrome, Word Knock-downs, and Word Ping-Pong.

BIBLIOGRAPHY
Bombaugh, C. C. *Gleanings for the Curious.* 1890. Reprint. *Oddities and Curiosities of Words and Literature,* ed. Martin Gardner. New York: Dover, 1961.

Borgmann, Dmitri A. *Beyond Language: Adventures in Word and Thought.* New York: Charles Scribner's Sons, 1967.
Espy, Willard R. *The Game of Words.* New York: Grosset & Dunlap, 1972.
Shipley, Joseph T. *Playing with Words.* Englewood Cliffs, N.J.: Prentice-Hall, 1960.

RHOPALIC is a sentence or passage in which each successive word has one more syllable (or letter) than the previous word (or letter); it is a series that grows gradually larger, e.g., I, in, tin, thin, thine, hinted, thinned, and so on; sometimes the rhopalic is reversed, growing steadily smaller.

According to C. C. Bombaugh, *Gleanings for the Curious,* the name was suggested by the shape of Hercules's club:

$$\overset{\smile}{P}\acute{o}\pi\alpha\lambda o\nu$$

Bombaugh offers the following examples:

Rem tibi confeci, doctissime, dulcisonoram.
Vectigalibus armamenta referre jubet Rex.

For similar word play refer to Möbius Strip and Progressive Anagram.

BIBLIOGRAPHY

Bombaugh, C. C. *Gleanings for the Curious.* 1890. Reprint. *Oddities and Curiosities of Words and Literature,* ed. Martin Gardner. New York: Dover, 1961.
Borgmann, Dmitri A. *Language on Vacation: An Olio of Orthographical Oddities.* New York: Charles Scribner's Sons, 1965.
Espy, Willard R. *An Almanac of Words at Play.* New York: Clarkson N. Potter, Inc., 1975.
Shipley, Joseph T. *Playing with Words.* Englewood Cliffs, N.J.: Prentice-Hall, 1960.

RHYME IN TIME. See CRAMBO.

RHYMING SLANG. See RHYMING SLANGUAGE.

RHYMING SLANGUAGE, also called rhyming slang, is a game based on Puns of paronomasia.

The idea is to substitute a rhyming word for the word in mind, e.g., "He's at the Shakey Car (for Bar)."

The game is to guess the real word a player has substituted a rhyme for. If a player guesses right, then he gives a rhyme to the next player. If a player guesses wrong, then he is out of the game.

Refer to Pun for other word play involving puns of paronomasia.

BIBLIOGRAPHY

Shipley, Joseph T. *Playing with Words.* Englewood Cliffs, N.J.: Prentice-Hall, 1960.

RHYMORIGINALS. See CRAMBO.

RIDDLE is a question stated to test one's ingenuity in discovering its meaning; it may be a puzzle in which the answer is blind, obscure, confusing, or misleading, and intended to be guessed.

Joseph T. Shipley, *Dictionary of Word Origins,* points out that "riddle" comes from *raedan* (Anglo-Saxon), which also meant to *read,* to make out the meaning.

According to Robert P. apRoberts, "Riddle" (*Encyclopedia of Poetry and Poetics*), riddles can be found in the Sanskrit *Rig Veda* (final version ca. 1000 B.C.), Al-Hariri's *Assemblies,* (A.D. 1054–1122), Firdausi's *Shah-Nameh* (tenth century), the poetic riddles of Symphosius (fifth century), and Aldehelm, *Epistola ad Acircium de Metris* (seventh century).

True riddles are those in which the answer is described in terms that suggest something else. The first half of the riddle is an attempt to mislead; the second half is closer to the truth. The following is a traditional Nursery Rhyme:

Little Nancy Etticoat,
With a white petticoat,
And a red nose;
She has no feet or hands,
The longer she stands,
The shorter she grows.
(Answer: a candle)

Archer Taylor, *The Literary Riddle Before 1600* and *English Riddles from Oral Tradition,* calls such riddles popular or folk riddles. Popular riddles are short nonesoteric riddles passed orally from generation to generation. Traditional Mother Goose rhymes are filled with them:

Humpty Dumpty sat on a wall,
Humpty Dumpty had a great fall;
All the king's horses and all the king's men
Could not put Humpty Dumpty together again.
(Answer: an egg)

As round as an apple, as deep as a cup,
And all the king's horses cannot fill it up.
(Answer: a well)

Old Mother Twitchett has but one eye,
And a long tail which she can let fly,
And everytime she goes over a gap,
She leaves a bit of her tail in a trap.
(Answer: needle and thread)

In contrast to the popular riddle, Taylor places the esoteric or literary riddle. A literary riddle generally consists of a long list of assertions and contradictions and an abstract theme. Here is an example from Jonathan Swift:

We are little airy creatures,
All of different voice and features;
One of us in ''glass'' is set,
One of us you'll find in ''jet,''
T'other you may see in ''tin,''
And the fourth a ''box'' within.
If the fifth you should pursue,
It can never fly from ''you.''
(Answer: the five vowels)

Riddles often appear in songs and may even be the basis of the entire song, as in this American version of an old Scottish ballad, ''I'll Give My Love an Apple'':

I'll give my love an apple without a core,
I'll give my love a dwelling without a door,
I'll give my love a palace where she might be
That she might unlock it without a key.

How can there be an apple without a core,
How can there be a dwelling without a door,
How can there be a palace where she might be
That she might unlock it without a key?

My head is an apple without a core,
My mind is a dwelling without a door,
My heart is a palace where she might be
That she might unlock it without a key.

I'll give my love a cherry without a stone,
I'll give my love a chicken without a bone,
I'll tell my love a story without any end,
I'll give my love a baby and no cryin'.

How can there be a cherry without a stone,
How can there be a chicken without a bone,
How can there be a story without any end,
How can there be a baby with no cryin'?

When the cherry is in blossom it has no stone,
When the chicken's in the egg it has no bone,
The story of I love you will never end,
When the baby's sleeping, there's no cryin'.

Riddles often appear as Conundrums, where the answer is based on a Pun:

How is a farmer like a seamstress?

(Answer: A farmer gathers what he <u>sows</u>; a seamstress <u>sews</u> what she gathers).

A conundrum is a form of sell (a riddle purposely intended to mislead):

What do you call a woman who has one leg shorter than the other?
(Answer: Aileen)

Riddles are an established form of battle in literature, e.g., the riddling contest between Bilbo and Gollum in J. R. R. Tolkien's *The Hobbit*.

Riddles also enter into the world of mathematics, e.g., "Write down four 9s that equal 100" (Answer: 99%).

Brian Sutton-Smith, "A Developmental Structural Account of Riddles," classifies riddles as follows:

1. Pre-riddles are questions in riddle form that actually take a simple, direct answer (often hard to distinguish from riddle parodies):

Why did the man eat supper?
(Answer: He was hungry.)

2. Implicit reclassifications (homonymic riddles) are riddles based on homonyms (a form of conundrum):

Why did the key eat bananas?
(Answer: Because it was a monkey.)

3. Riddle parodies are similar to pre-riddles, except that the idea of a satire on riddles is intended:

Why did the chicken cross the road?
(Answer: To get to the other side.)

4. Inverted relationships are riddles based on reversing standard patterns of behavior:

What did one dog say to the other?
(Answer: Should we take our humans for a walk?)

5. Explicit reclassifications (homonymic oppositional riddles) are riddles where a classification is established and then one of its critical attributes denied:

What has an eye but cannot see?
(Answer: A potato)

6. Classification on basis of noncritical attributes (Archer Taylor's popular riddles):

I'm white on the inside, yellow on the outside.
(Answer: A banana)

7. Multiple classification (in general, riddles that ask what is the difference between x and y). Brian Sutton-Smith calls these riddles conundrums:

How is a steer without any legs like a pound of hamburger?
(Answer: They are both ground beef.)

For similar word play refer to Catch, Conundrum, Enigma, Joke, Little Audrey, Little Willie, Moron Joke, and Pun.

BIBLIOGRAPHY

Adler, Irving, and Peggy Adler. *The Adler Book of Puzzles and Riddles, or Sam Loyd Up to Date.* New York: John Day Co., 1962.

Aldehelm. *Epistola ad Acircium de Metris* In *The Riddles of Aldehelm,* trans. James Hall Pitman. Yale Studies in English Ser. No. 67. Reprint. New York: Archon, 1970.

Roberts, Robert P. "Riddle." In *Encyclopedia of Poetry and Poetics,* eds. Alex Preminger, Frank J. Warnke, and O. B. Hardison, Jr. Princeton: Princeton University Press, 1965.

Bombaugh, C. C. *Gleanings for the Curious.* 1890. Reprint. *Oddities and Curiosities of Words and Literature,* ed. Martin Gardner. New York: Dover, 1961.

Eckler, A. Ross. *Word Recreations: Games and Diversions from "Word Ways."* New York: Dover, 1979.

Espy, Willard R. *An Almanac of Words at Play.* New York: Clarkson N. Potter, Inc., 1975.

———. *The Game of Words.* New York: Grosset & Dunlap, 1972.

———. *Have a Word on Me: A Celebration of Language.* New York: Simon & Schuster, 1981.

Gardner, Martin. *Perplexing Puzzles and Tantalizing Teasers.* New York: Simon & Schuster, 1969.

Koestler, Arthur. "Humor and Wit." In *Encyclopaedia Britannica: Macropaedia.* 1979.

Laubach, David C. *Introduction to Folklore.* Rochelle Park, N.J.: Hayden Book Co., 1980.

Loyd, Samuel. *Sam Loyd's Cyclopedia of 5000 Puzzles, Tricks and Conundrums with Answers.* New York: Pinnacle Books, 1976.

McKechnie, Jean L., et al. *Webster's New Twentieth Century Dictionary of the English Language: Unabridged.* 2d ed. New York: World Publishing Co., 1971.

Opie, Peter, and Iona Opie. *Children's Games in Street and Playground.* 1969. Reprint. New York: Oxford University Press, 1979.

———. *The Lore and Language of Schoolchildren.* 1959. Reprint. New York: Oxford University Press, 1980.

———. *The Oxford Dictionary of Nursery Rhymes.* 1951. Reprint. New York: Oxford University Press, 1983.

———. *The Oxford Nursery Rhyme Book.* 1955. Reprint. New York: Oxford University Press, 1984.

Shipley, Joseph T. *Dictionary of Word Origins.* New York: Philosophical Library, 1945.

———. *Playing with Words.* Englewood Cliffs, N.J.: Prentice-Hall, 1960.

———. "Word and Letter Games." In *Encyclopaedia Britannica: Macropaedia.* 1979.

Sanches, Mary, and Barbara Kirshenblatt-Gimblett. "Children's Traditional Speech Play and Child Language." In *Speech Play,* ed. Barbara Kirshenblatt-Gimblett. Philadelphia: University of Pennsylvania, 1976.

Sutton-Smith, Brian. "A Developmental Structural Account of Riddles." In *Speech Play,* ed. Barbara Kirshenblatt-Gimblett. Philadelphia: University of Pennsylvania, 1976.

———. *The Folkgames of Children.* Austin: University of Texas Press, 1972.

Taylor, Archer. *English Riddles from Oral Tradition.* Los Angeles: University of California Press, 1951.

———. *The Literary Riddle Before 1600.* Los Angeles: University of California Press, 1948.

ROUND is a term generally used to designate a song that runs back on itself, but it also refers to a form of word play where a story runs back on itself:

It was a stormy night. All of us sat around the fireplace. Our friend Jack entered and sat down by us and began a story. "It was a stormy night. Everyone was sitting around the fireplace. Bob entered and sat down and began a story. 'It was a stormy night . . .' " and so on.

For similar word play refer to Endless Tales.

BIBLIOGRAPHY

Shipley, Joseph T. *Playing with Words*. Englewood Cliffs, N.J.: Prentice-Hall, 1960.

S

SAUSAGES. See TEAPOT.

SCAFFOLD is a word search game.

The object is to list words that have a chosen three letters in order within them, e.g., a, t, l: b<u>attl</u>e. The player who can list the most in a given time limit is the winner.

For similar word play refer to Anagram, Flat, Marsupials, Middleput, Middletake and Shrdlu.

BIBLIOGRAPHY

Brandreth, Gyles. *The World's Best Indoor Games*. New York: Pantheon Books, 1981.

SCHOOLMARM'S QUIZ is a variation on Spelling Bee.

Players are given a list of words, some misspelled. The object is to mark each word right or wrong in a specified time limit.

Refer to Spelling Bee for similar word play.

BIBLIOGRAPHY

Morris, William, and Mary Morris. *The Word Game Book*. New York: Harper & Brothers, 1959.

SCOREWORDS. See CROSSWORD PUZZLE.

SCRABBLE is a crossword game copyrighted by Production and Marketing Company and marketed by J & M Spear in Britain and Selchow and Righter in the United States.

It was invented by Alfred Butts in the early 1930s and popularized by James Brunot in the early 1950s. Today it is second only to MONOPOLY in all-time sales of board games.

It is played on a fifteen by fifteen grid with a set of letter tiles (generally 100), each of which has a certain number value (e.g., B is worth three points). Certain squares on the board are worth more than others (e.g., the starred center square is worth a double word score).

The players each draw seven tiles from the stock of letter tiles, which are spread face down. The first player, using his rack of seven letters, begins by forming a word of at least two letters across the center square. He then adds up the number of points the letters in his word total, including any bonuses from squares indicating a bonus, and draws letter tiles from the stock to replace the number of tiles he used in his play. The next player then adds a word to the played word crossword fashion, scoring for the letters he uses plus any letters from the previous word included in the new word. The next player then adds a word to any of the letters on the board, once again crossword fashion, and scores in the same manner.

If more than one new word is created, the player scores for all of the words formed. Players may use a turn to exchange letter tiles in their rack for new ones from the stock. Play continues until all tiles have been played or until players cannot use any of their remaining letter tiles. If one player uses all of his letter tiles he receives the total value of all the unplayed tiles of the other players. The value of all unplayed letter tiles is deducted from the final score of the players they belong to.

For similar word play refer to Across-tic, Acrostic, Alphacross, Alphawords, Arrow of Letters, Black Squares, Flat, Forms, Last Word, Lynx, Magic Word Squares, Puzzling Squares, Quizl, Ragaman, and Scramble.

BIBLIOGRAPHY

Brandreth, Gyles. *The Joy of Lex: How to Have Fun with 860,341,500 Words.* New York: Quill, 1983.
_____. *More Joy of Lex: An Amazing and Amusing Z to A and A to Z of Words.* New York: William Morrow and Co., 1982.
Corbin, K. "More N-Tile Scrabble Records." *Word Ways: The Journal of Recreational Linguistics* 17, no. 1 (February 1984): 34–35.
Eckler, A. Ross. *Word Recreations: Games and Diversions from "Word Ways."* New York: Dover, 1979.
Frank, A. "Infinite Tile Scrabble." *Word Ways: The Journal of Recreational Linguistics* 17, no. 4 (November 1984): 216–217.
_____. "No Holds-Barred Scrabble." *Word Ways: The Journal of Recreational Linguistics* 17, no. 1 (February 1984): 37–38.
Sharp, Richard, and John Piggott. *The Book of Games.* New York: Galahad Books, 1977.

SCRABBLEGRAM is a trademark owned by Production and Marketing Company; it is a game variation on SCRABBLE.

William and Mary Morris describe it as follows:

1. The rules are the same as for SCRABBLE, except for the following:
2. A SCRABBLEGRAM grid is the same as a SCRABBLE board, except that it has four words included, as if four plays have already been made, and each player is given a separate copy of the grid.
3. Each player takes four turns, all at once (in fact, players may play simultaneously).
4. For each turn a player is given a separate rack of seven letters (a new rack for each of the four turns).
5. At the end of a turn the remaining letters must be crossed off.
6. All of the letters used in a turn must be played in a single line, vertical or horizontal, and form a complete word attached crossword fashion.
7. The scoring is done as in SCRABBLE, except that a player receives fifty points if he uses all seven letters in a turn.

Refer to SCRABBLE for the rules of SCRABBLE. For similar word play refer to Across-tic, Acrostic, Alphacross, Alphawords, Arrow of Letters, Black Squares, Flat, Forms, Last Word, Lynx, Magic Word Squares, Puzzling Squares, Quizl, Ragaman, and Scramble.

BIBLIOGRAPHY

Morris, William, and Mary Morris. *The Word Game Book*. New York: Harper & Brothers, 1959.

SCRAMBLE is a grid game.

Each player draws a grid of squares (ten by ten, or whatever is agreed upon). One player announces a theme (a word small enough to fit in the grid). Each player enters that word in his grid, beginning at the top left.

Then the players fill up their grids as fast as they can with other words relating to the first word, putting in black squares where necessary. The game ends when a player has filled up his grid and yells "stop." Other players are allowed to finish the word they are currently on.

Grids are passed and scored, one point for each letter of a correct word, a word that both fits the category and is correctly spelled.

It might be a good idea to establish a rule that the player who yells "stop" must have filled in at least 50 percent of his grid with words (as opposed to black squares).

In another version the players must fill up as much of their grid as they can Crossword Puzzle fashion in five minutes.

For similar word play refer to Across-tic, Acrostic, Alphacross, Alphawords, Arrow of Letters, Black Squares, Flat, Forms, Last Word, Lynx, Magic Word Squares, Puzzling Squares, Quizl, Ragaman, SCRABBLE, and SCRABBLE-GRAM.

BIBLIOGRAPHY

Brandreth, Gyles. *Indoor Games*. London: Hodder & Stoughton, Ltd., 1977.
_____. *More Joy of Lex: An Amazing and Amusing Z to A and A to Z of Words*. New
       York: William Morrow and Co., 1982.
Parlett, David. *Botticelli and Beyond: Over 100 of the World's Best Word Games*. New
       York: Pantheon Books, 1981.

SCRAMBLE CODE is a Code in which the order of the letters or words determines the code; for example, if the letters of the alphabet are used in reverse, ace would be spelled zxv.

For similar word play refer to Cipher, Code, and Scramblegram.

BIBLIOGRAPHY

Gaines, Helen Fouché. *Cryptanalysis: A Study of Ciphers and Their Solution*. New York:
       Dover, 1939.
Shipley, Joseph T. *Playing with Words*. Englewood Cliffs, N.J.: Prentice-Hall, 1960.

SCRAMBLEGRAM is an Anagram game where the letters of a word are mixed up and the object is to sort them out; it is sometimes called "pie" because to "pi type" is to mix together all the letters from a printing press before replacing them.

For similar word play refer to Acrosticals, Add-on, Alfabits, Anablank, Anagame, Cap Me, Category Puzzles, Circular Reversals, Crossword Puzzle, Doublets, Espygram, Flat, Jumbles, Last Word, Marsupials, Middleput, Missing Words, Name in Vain, Palindrome, Progressive Anagram, Put and Take, Quaternade, Quinade, Removers, Reversible Anagram, Scaffold, Word Knockdowns, and Word Ping-Pong.

BIBLIOGRAPHY

Shipley, Joseph T. *Playing with Words*. Englewood Cliffs, N.J.: Prentice-Hall, 1960.

SCRAMBLEKEY. See SLYGRAM.

SECRET MESSAGE SQUARES. See HIDDEN WORD SEARCH.

SELL. See RIDDLE.

SEMORDNILAP. See REVERSIBLE ANAGRAM.

SEND A WIRE, also called telegrams, is word play involving first letters.

A word of ten letters is chosen. Each player then attempts to write a ten-word telegram, the first letters of the words beginning with the letters of the key word in order:

The key word is "succession."
The telegram is: "See us carefully counting. Easy success soon is only noise."

Gyles Brandreth offers a variation. Each player in turn calls out a letter until some fifteen letters have been called out and listed in order. The players are then given five minutes to write telegrams, each word beginning with the letters listed in sequence.

For similar word play refer to Acromania, Across-tic, Acrostic, Acrosticals, Alphacross, Arrow of Letters, Black Squares, Combinations, Crossword Puzzle, Flat, Forms, Lynx, Magic Word Squares, Quaternade, Quinade, SCRABBLE, SCRABBLEGRAM, Scramble, Square Poem, and Triple Acrostic.

BIBLIOGRAPHY

Brandreth, Gyles. *The World's Best Indoor Games*. New York: Pantheon Books, 1981.
Morris, William, and Mary Morris. *The Word Game Book*. New York: Harper & Brothers, 1959.
Parlett, David. *Botticelli and Beyond: Over 100 of the World's Best Word Games*. New York: Pantheon Books, 1981.

SEQUENCES is word play involving letters in order.

The idea is to find words that have an established succession of letters, e.g., consecutive letters of the alphabet, as a and b are in sequence in "alphabet."

David Parlett sets up the following rules: Find as many words as possible that have two consecutive letters of the alphabet (as in alphabet), then as many as possible that have three consecutive letters of the alphabet (as in define), then as many as possible that have four consecutive letters of the alphabet (if any).

He also suggests a variation where the object is to list words that have only letters in a certain range of the alphabet, e.g., only words that have letters between h and m (as in him).

For similar word play refer to Acrostic, Alphabetical Adjectives, Alphabet Word Chain, A to Z Banquet, First Letters, Hypochondriac, I Gave My Love, I Love My Love, I Packed My Bag, I Went to Market, Nymphabet, Pangram, Shrdlu, and Travelling Alphabet.

BIBLIOGRAPHY

Borgmann, Dmitri A. *Beyond Language: Adventures in Word and Thought*. New York: Charles Scribner's Sons, 1967.
Parlett, David. *Botticelli and Beyond: Over 100 of the World's Best Word Games*. New York: Pantheon Books, 1981.

SHAFFE'S GAME is an oral form of Giotto.

One player thinks of a five-letter word. The other player attempts to find out what the word is by guessing other five-letter words and receiving responses as to how many letters of the guessed word are contained in the secret word. This is continued until the word is guessed.

For similar word play refer to Convergence, Giotto, and Uncrash.

BIBLIOGRAPHY

Parlett, David. *Botticelli and Beyond: Over 100 of the World's Best Word Games*. New York: Pantheon Books, 1981.

SHAGGY DOG STORY. See ENDLESS TALES.

SHAPE POETRY. See EMBLEMATIC POETRY.

SHIFTING is word play involving the forming of words from a common stem, e.g., cosmos, cosmetic.

For similar word play refer to Animalistics, Confusing and Confounding Cats, Cross-breed, Form-a-Word, Galaxy of Gals, Hidden Names, Hidden Words, Prefixes, Spare the Prefix, and Suffixes.

BIBLIOGRAPHY

Borgmann, Dmitri A. *Language on Vacation: An Olio of Orthographical Oddities.* New York: Charles Scribner's Sons, 1965.
Shipley, Joseph T. *Playing with Words.* Englewood Cliffs, N.J.: Prentice-Hall, 1960.

SHIFTY SENTENCES. See CHARADES.

SHORT STORY is word play involving three-letter words.

The object is to write as long a sentence as possible using words containing no more than three letters in a given amount of time (five to ten minutes).

For similar word play refer to Alphabent, Alphabet Word Chain, A to Z Banquet, First Letters, Hypochondriac, I Gave My Love, I Love My Love, I Packed My Bag, I Went to Market, Nymphabet, Pangram, Sequences, and Travelling Alphabet.

BIBLIOGRAPHY

Brandreth, Gyles. *Indoor Games.* London: Hodder & Stoughton, Ltd., 1977.
———. *The World's Best Indoor Games.* New York: Pantheon Books, 1981.

SHOUTING PROVERBS is a guessing game.

One player is sent out of the room. The other players choose a Proverb, and each takes one word from the proverb. When the player returns, the others each shout out the words assigned at the same time. The player attempts to guess the proverb.

For a discussion of proverbs and additional word play involving them, refer to Proverb. For additional word play involving guessing refer to Adverbs, Aesop's Mission, Password, and Quick Thinking.

BIBLIOGRAPHY

Parlett, David. *Botticelli and Beyond: Over 100 of the World's Best Word Games.* New York: Pantheon Books, 1981.

SHRDLU is a name for language games based on consecutive letters.

"Shrdlu" is the second half of a group of letters to be found by running a finger down the first and then the second left-hand vertical banks of a linotype to produce a temporary marking slug not meant to show up in the final printing; the entire group is "etaoin shrdlu."

As Dmitri Borgmann points out, etaoin is not meant to be confused with *Eothen,* the title of a book by Alexander W. Kinglake (1844), and the title of a chapter in William Thackeray's *Vanity Fair* (1847–1848).

John G. Fuller uses shrdlu as the title for a number of games. In the first the idea is to pick various combinations of letters and then attempt to find words containing them (e.g., th: too<u>th</u>, boo<u>th</u>, <u>th</u>en, <u>th</u>at, bro<u>th</u>er, mo<u>th</u>er, fa<u>th</u>er, and so on).

In the second the idea is to find words that contain four successive letters of the alphabet in order (e.g., im<u>pr</u>int, <u>fou</u>rth, va<u>rious</u>).

In the third the idea is to find words that contain five consecutive vowels (e.g., a<u>eriou</u>s).

In the fourth game the idea is to find words that contain five or more successive consonants (e.g., c<u>hemos</u>ynthesis).

In the fifth game the idea is to find words that contain double letters (e.g., le<u>tt</u>ers).

For similar word play refer to Scaffold, Sequences, and Shifting.

BIBLIOGRAPHY

Borgmann, Dmitri A. *Beyond Language: Adventures in Word and Thought.* New York: Charles Scribner's Sons, 1967.

Fuller, John G. *Games for Insomniacs; or, A Lifetime Supply of Insufferable Brain Twisters.* New York: Doubleday, 1966.

SIGHT RHYMES are a form of word play involving words that rhyme to the eye but not to the ear, e.g., tough/trough/through, and diet/Monet. Refer to Pun for a discussion of this and similar word play.

SILLY SIMILES is word play the object of which is to change one half of an overused simile to create a Pun; the more nonsensical the pun the better it is, e.g., "as right as rain" can be changed to "as right as mud."

For similar word play refer to Accidental Language, Back Slang, Boner, Burlesque, Cento, Constructapo, Conundrum, Fancy Fairy Tales, Hackneyed Images, Irish Bull, Malapropism, Möbius Strip, Number Associations, Parody, Perverb, Pun, Spoonerism, and Wellerism.

BIBLIOGRAPHY

Espy, Willard R. *A Children's Almanac of Words at Play.* New York: Clarkson N. Potter, Inc., 1982.

Parlett, David. *Botticelli and Beyond: Over 100 of the World's Best Word Games.* New York: Pantheon Books, 1981.

SINGLE-RHYMED ALPHABET is an alphabet spine with a common end rhyme.

This is one of the common forms of word play included in the nineteenth-century publication *Notes and Queries*. The object is to go through the alphabet, letter by letter, listing a subject that begins with each letter in turn, and having each line end with a common rhyme:

A was an <u>A</u>irplane to fly through the <u>sky</u>.
B was a <u>B</u>oy who liked to get <u>high</u>.
C was a <u>C</u>at who had a green <u>eye</u>.
And so on.

For similar word play refer to Acrostic, Alphabent, Alphabetical Adjectives, Alphabet Word Chain, A to Z Banquet, First Letters, Hypochondriac, I Gave My Love, I Love My Love, I Packed My Bag, I Went to Market, Nymphabet, Pangram, Sequences, Sliding Alphabet, and Travelling Alphabet.

BIBLIOGRAPHY

Espy, Willard R. *The Game of Words*. New York: Grosset & Dunlap, 1972.

SKIPPING RHYMES are verses to be said while skipping.
Peter and Iona Opie found the following skipping rhymes to be common among English school children.

Big Ben strikes one,
Big Ben strikes two,
Big Ben strikes three,
and so on.

London, Liverpool, Weekly Post,
I say number one, two, three.

I'm a knock-kneed chicken, I'm a bow-legged sparrow,
Missed my bus so I went by barrow.
I went to the café for my dinner and my tea,
Too many radishes—Hick! Pardon me.

For similar word play refer to Acting Out Rhymes, Ball Bouncing Rhymes, Charms, Counting Rhymes, Game Rhymes, Hand Clapping Rhymes, Incantations, Jump Rope Rhymes, Mnemonics, Nursery Rhymes, and Tongue Twister.

BIBLIOGRAPHY

Opie, Peter, and Iona Opie. *Children's Games in Street and Playground*. 1969. Reprint. New York: Oxford University Press, 1979.
————. *The Lore and Language of Schoolchildren*. 1959. Reprint. New York: Oxford University Press, 1980.
Shipley, Joseph T. *Playing with Words*. Englewood Cliffs, N.J.: Prentice-Hall, 1960.

SLIDING ALPHABET is an alphabet activity involving adjectives and nouns.

A letter of the alphabet is chosen. All of the nouns must begin with that letter. The object, then, is to write adjective-noun combinations, the adjective working its way through the alphabet, the noun beginning with the letter selected, e.g., apple pie, bad pig, cold pop, and so on.

For similar word play refer to Acrostic, Alphabent, Alphabetical Adjectives, Alphabet Word Chain, A to Z Banquet, First Letters, Hypochondriac, I Gave My Love, I Love My Love, I Packed My Bag, I went to Market, Nymphabet, Pangram, Sequences, Single-Rhymed Alphabet, and Travelling Alphabet.

BIBLIOGRAPHY

Brandreth, Gyles. *The World's Best Indoor Games.* New York: Pantheon Books, 1981.

Morris, William, and Mary Morris. *The Word Game Book.* New York: Harper & Brothers, 1959.

Parlett, David. *Botticelli and Beyond: Over 100 of the World's Best Word Games.* New York: Pantheon Books, 1981.

SLYGRAM, also called scramblekey, is the unscrambling of a scrambled passage of prose or poetry.

For similar word play refer to Cento, Constructapo, Homosyntaxism, Möbius Strip, Oulipo Algorithms, and Perverb.

BIBLIOGRAPHY

Shipley, Joseph T. *Playing with Words.* Englewood Cliffs, N.J.: Prentice-Hall, 1960.

SNOWBALL SENTENCES. See MOBIUS STRIP.

SOTADIC PALINDROME is a Reversible Anagram where the reversed words also present a moral injunction.

According to Dmitri Borgmann, Sotades of Maroneia, a Greek satirist of the third century B.C., who was prematurely killed when he satirized Ptolemy II Philadelphus, was the first to use palindromic sentences.

Perhaps the most famous sotadic palindrome is

Deliver no evil
Live on reviled.

Howard W. Bergerson quotes it, along with the following from Edwin Fitzpatrick, in his book *Palindromes and Anagrams:*

"Revolt, Capitano? No!
I tag it: 'Sacred Rose of Red.' "
"No! We talk lawsuit.
No petal, I presume, rips a dogma."
    "I deliver storied, sung, Astral Aid.
    O, profit on droll anger? Regnal Lord, not I!

For podial arts Agnus Dei rots.
Reviled I am, God.''
(Aspire, muser!
Pilate, Pontius, walk late—wonder! . . .)
''Foes order castigation!
On a tip act, Lover!''

For similar word play refer to Anagram, Charades, Flat, Phonetic Palindromes, and Reversible Anagram.

BIBLIOGRAPHY

Bergerson, Howard W. *Palindromes and Anagrams*. New York: Dover, 1973.
Borgmann, Dmitri A. *Language on Vacation: An Olio of Orthographical Oddities*. New York: Charles Scribner's Sons, 1965.

SOUND SPELLING is word play the object of which is to spell a sound in as many ways as possible.
Here is an example:

SH: ocean, pshaw, schist, she, sure, nation, mission, function, luscious, conscience, loquacious, nauseous.

In an attempt to overcome the obvious discrepancies between oral and written language, the International Phonetics Association came up with the International Phonetic Alphabet. Refer to Abbreviations for a discussion and examples.

Sound spelling is based on homophones (words that sound the same but are spelled differently), and homophones are the basis for Puns of paronomasia. Refer to Pun and Conundrum for discussions of homophones and puns of paronomasia.

BIBLIOGRAPHY

Myers, L. A., and Richard L. Hoffman. *The Roots of Modern English*. 2d ed. Boston: Little, Brown and Co., 1979.
Shipley, Joseph T. *Playing with Words*. Englewood Cliffs, N.J.: Prentice-Hall, 1960.

SOURCY is a game based on etymology.
A time limit is set, and players attempt to come up with as many words derived from a chosen language as they can in the set amount of time. For example, French is chosen. The following words had already entered the English language from French by 1300, and therefore would be acceptable: action, adventure, affection, age, cheer, city, flower, folly, labor, leopard, rage, rancor, reason, substance, sum, tavern, tempest, unity, and waste.

BIBLIOGRAPHY

Baugh, Albert C., and Thomas Cable. *A History of the English Language*. 3d ed. Englewood Cliffs, N.J.: Prentice-Hall, 1978.

Bolton, W. F. *A Living Language: The History and Structure of English.* New York: Random House, 1982.

Hunt, Cecil. *Word Origins: The Romance of Language.* 1949. Reprint. New York: Wisdom Library, 1962.

Myers, L. M., and Richard L. Hoffman. *The Roots of Modern English.* 2d ed. Boston: Little, Brown and Co., 1979.

Partridge, Eric. *Origins: A Short Etymological Dictionary of Modern English.* New York: Greenwich House, 1983.

Shipley, Joseph T. *Dictionary of Word Origins.* New York: Philosophical Library, 1945.

———. *Playing with Words.* Englewood Cliffs, N.J.: Prentice-Hall, 1960.

SPARE THE PREFIX is word play involving definitions and Prefixes.

The object is to remove prefixes from words and make up definitions for the remaining letters or words:

The prefix in is removed from the following, and made up definitions are added:

telligent: inform a man

censive: careless with money

duct: what Israel did when the pitcher threw a knock-down pitch

For similar word play refer to Animalistics, Confusing and Confounding Cats, Cross-breed, Form-a-Word, Galaxy of Gals, Hidden Names, Pun, Shifting, and Suffixes.

BIBLIOGRAPHY

Fuller, John G. *Games for Insomniacs; or, a Lifetime Supply of Insufferable Brain Twisters.* New York: Doubleday, 1966.

SPELLING BEE is a game involving the correct written forms of words.

The term "spelling bee" comes from a "bee," a gathering of people to help benefit one of the community, which in turn comes from the swarming social tendencies of bees.

Contestants in turn are asked to spell a word. If they misspell it, they are eliminated. The final contestant wins.

For similar word play refer to Schoolmarm's Quiz and Spelling Round.

BIBLIOGRAPHY

Brandreth, Gyles. *The World's Best Indoor Games.* New York: Pantheon Books, 1981.

Morris, William, and Mary Morris. *The Word Game Book.* New York: Harper & Brothers, 1959.

Parlett, David. *Botticelli and Beyond: Over 100 of the World's Best Word Games.* New York: Pantheon Books, 1981.

SPELLING ROUND is a variation on Spelling Bee.

In a spelling round each player in turn is asked to supply a subsequent letter to the same word, thus group spelling it. Whoever misses a letter drops out.

For similar word play refer to Schoolmarm's Quiz and Spelling Bee.

BIBLIOGRAPHY

Parlett, David. *Botticelli and Beyond: Over 100 of the World's Best Word Games.* New York: Pantheon Books, 1981.

SPELLS. See CHARMS.

SPHINX is a very long poem which is meant to be read without stopping for breath.

Sphinx literally means "strangler." Gilbert and Sullivan's "Nightmare Song of the Lord Chancellor" from *Iolanthe,* which ends with the Lord Chancellor falling on his seat exhausted, is a famous example:

When you're lying awake with a dismal headache, and
    repose is taboo'd by anxiety,
I conceive you may use any language you choose to in-
    dulge in, without impropriety;
For your brain is on fire—the bedclothes conspire of
    usual slumber to plunder you:
First your counterpane goes, and uncovers your toes, and
    your sheet slips demurely from under you;
Then the blanketing tickles—you feel like mixed pickles
    —so terribly sharp is the pricking,
And you're hot, and you're cross, and you tumble and
    toss till there's nothing 'twixt you and the ticking.
Then the bedclothes all creep to the ground in a heap,
    and you pick 'em up all in a tangle;
Next your pillow resigns and politely declines to remain
    at its usual angle!
Well, you get some repose in the form of a doze, with
    hot eye-balls and head ever aching,
But your slumbering teems with such horrible dreams
    that you'd very much better be waking;
For you dream you are crossing the Channel, and toss-
    ing about in a steamer from Harwich—
Which is something between a large bathing machine
    and a very small second-class carriage—
And you're giving a treat (penny ice and cold meat) to a
    party of friends and relations—
They're a ravenous horde—and they all came on board at
    Sloane Square and South Kensington Stations.
And bound on that journey you find your attorney (who
    started that morning from Devon);
He's a bit undersized, and you don't feel surprised when
    he tells you he's only eleven.

Well, you're driving like mad with this singular lad (by
   the by, the ship's now a four-wheeler),
And you're playing round games, and he calls you
   bad names when you tell him that "ties pay the dealer";
But this you can't stand, so you throw up your hand, and
   you find you're as cold as an icicle,
In your shirt and your socks (the black silk with gold
   clocks), crossing Salisbury Plain on a bicycle:
And he and the crew are on bicycles too—which they've
   somehow or other invested in—
And he's telling the tars all the particulars of a company
   he's interested in—
It's a scheme of devices, to get at low prices all goods
   from cough mixtures to cables
(Which tickled the sailors), by treating retailers as
   though they were all vegetables—
You get a good spadesman to plant a small tradesman
   (first take off his boots with a boot-tree),
And his legs will take root, and his fingers will shoot,
   and they'll blossom and bud like a fruit-tree—
From the greengrocer tree you get grapes and green pea,
   cauliflower, pineapple, and cranberries,
While the pastrycook plant cherry brandy will grant,
   apple puffs, and three-corners, and Banburys—
The shares are a penny, and ever so many are taken by
   Rothschild and Baring,
And just as a few are allotted to you, you awake with a
   shudder despairing—
You're a regular wreck, with a crick in your neck, and
   no wonder you snore, for your head's on the floor,
   and you've needles and pins from your soles to your
   shins, and your flesh is a-creep, for your left leg's
   asleep, and you've cramp in your toes, and a fly on
   your nose, and some fluff in your lung, and a fever-
   ish tongue, and a thirst that's intense, and a general
   sense that you haven't been sleeping in clover;
But the darkness has passed, and it's daylight at last, and
   the night has been long—ditto ditto my song—and
   thank goodness they're both of them over!

BIBLIOGRAPHY

Gilbert, Sir W. S., and Sir Arthur Sullivan. *Iolanthe*. 1882. Reprint. *The Complete Plays
   of Gilbert and Sullivan,* ed. Bennett A. Cerf and Donald S. Klopfer. New York:
   Modern Library, n.d.
Shipley, Joseph T. *Playing with Words*. Englewood Cliffs, N.J.: Prentice-Hall, 1960.

SPICY PROVERBS is word play combining spices and Proverbs.

The object is to replace an important word in a proverb with the name of a spice, e.g., "an oregano of virtue."

For similar word play refer to Charms, Incantations, Perverb, and Shouting Proverbs.

BIBLIOGRAPHY

Fuller, John G. *Games for Insomniacs; or, A Lifetime Supply of Insufferable Brain Twisters.* New York: Doubleday, 1966.

SPINE POETRY is verse where something (generally the alphabet or numbers) serves as a backbone for the verses; it may be a form of Acrostic.

"Solomon Grundy" is a well-known Nursery Rhyme that uses the days of the week as a spine:

Solomon Grundy,
Born on a Monday,
Christened on Tuesday,
Married on Wednesday,
Took ill on Thursday,
Worse on Friday,
Died on Saturday,
Buried on Sunday,
This is the end
Of Solomon Grundy.

For similar word play refer to Acromania, Across-tic, Acrostic, Acrosticals, Alliteration, Alphabent, Alphabetical Adjectives, Alphabet Pyramids, Alphabet Word Chain, Animal Alphabet, I Gave My Love, I Love My Love, I Packed My Bag, I Went to Market, Looks Like Poetry, and Single-Rhymed Alphabet.

BIBLIOGRAPHY

Espy, Willard R. *An Almanac of Words at Play.* New York: Clarkson N. Potter, Inc., 1975.
Gensler, Kinereth, and Nina Nyhart. *The Poetry Connection: An Anthology of Contemporary Poems with Ideas to Stimulate Children's Writing.* New York: Teachers & Writers, 1978.
Opie, Peter, and Iona Opie. *The Oxford Dictionary of Nursery Rhymes.* 1951. Reprint. New York: Oxford University Press, 1983.

SPLIT WORDS are Puns of paronomasia.

The idea is to separate words of two or more syllables into separate words on the basis of their sound, e.g., "Too sensible = Two cents a bull."

For a discussion of puns of paronomasia and additional word play based on them, refer to Pun.

BIBLIOGRAPHY

Borgmann, Dmitri A. *Beyond Language: Adventures in Word and Thought*. New York: Charles Scribner's Sons, 1967.

SPOONERISM is an unintentional transposition of sounds that creates an accidental new meaning.

The name is derived from Rev. W. A. Spooner (1844–1930), warden of New College, Oxford, who was constantly making such slips of the tongue.

Here is an example:

Let me sew you to your sheet instead of *Let me show you to your seat.*

The National Puzzlers' League uses spoonerism to designate one kind of Flat (see Flat).

For other similar word play refer to Accidental Language, Back Slang, Boner, Burlesque, Clerihew, Conundrum, Flat, Irish Bull, Malapropism, Oxymoron, Parody, Pun, and Wellerism.

BIBLIOGRAPHY

Brandreth, Gyles. *The Joy of Lex: How to Have Fun with 860,341,500 Words*. New York: Quill, 1983.
Eckler, A. Ross. *Word Recreations: Games and Diversions from "Word Ways."* New York: Dover, 1979.
Espy, Willard R. *An Almanac of Words at Play*. New York: Clarkson N. Potter, Inc., 1975.
_____. *A Children's Almanac of Words at Play*. New York: Clarkson N. Potter, Inc., 1982.
_____. *The Game of Words*. New York: Grosset & Dunlap, 1972.
Shipley, Joseph T. "Word and Letter Games." In *Encyclopaedia Britannica: Macropaedia*. 1976.

SQUARE POEM, also called word squares and word cubes, is a form of word play where the words of the first line are repeated down the left side of the poem:

EVEN
VANE
ENDS
NEST

The following example comes from Lewis Carroll:

I often wondered when I cursed,
Often feared where I would be—
Wondered where she'd yield her love,
When I yield so will she,
I would her will be pitied!
Cursed be love! She pitied me.

Henry Ernest Dudeney included the following in *The World's Best Word Puzzles* (1925):

The Abbey

'Twas spring. The abbey woods were decked with SECOND.
The abbot, with his FIFTH, no trouble reckoned;
But shared the meats and SEVENTH which every man
Who loves to feast he FIRST since time began.
Then comes a stealthy SIXTH across the wall,
Who FOURTHS the plate and jewels, cash and all,
And ere the abbot and the monks have dined,
He THIRDS, and leaves no trace or clue behind.

The word square key to the above poem:

PALATED
ANEMONE
LEVANTS
AMASSES
TONSURE
ENTERER
DESSERT

It is possible to carry this word play into three dimensions by constructing a cube, similar to Rubik's cube, where each corner letter combines with the others to spell three-dimensional words.

For similar word play refer to Acromania, Across-tic, Acrostic, Acrosticals, Alphacross, Arrow of Letters, Black Squares, Combinations, Crossword Puzzle, Flat, Forms, Lynx, Magic Word Squares, Pictorial Acrostic, SCRABBLE, SCRABBLEGRAM, Scramble, Send a Wire, and Triple Acrostic.

BIBLIOGRAPHY

Adler, Irving, and Peggy Adler. *The Adler Book of Puzzles and Riddles, or Sam Loyd Up to Date*. New York: John Day Co., 1962.
Borgmann, Dmitri A. *Beyond Language: Adventures in Word and Thought*. New York: Charles Scribner's Sons, 1967.
————. *Language on Vacation: An Olio of Orthographical Oddities*. New York: Charles Scribner's Sons, 1965.
Dudeney, Henry Ernest. *300 Best Word Puzzles*. New York: Charles Scribner's Sons, 1968.
Eckler, A. Ross. *Word Recreations: Games and Diversions from "Word Ways."* New York: Dover, 1979.
Espy, Willard R. *The Game of Words*. New York: Grosset & Dunlap, 1972.
Parlett, David. *Botticelli and Beyond: Over 100 of the World's Best Word Games*. New York: Pantheon Books, 1981.

STAIRWAY is a game based on Progressive Anagrams.

Players take turns adding to a word, creating ever longer Anagrams. The loser is the player who cannot come up with the next word:

Player One: do
Player Two: dog
Player One: good
Player Two: goody
Player One: cannot think of the next word and loses.

For similar word play refer to Acrosticals, Add-on, Alfabits, Anablank, Anagame, Anagram, Cap Me, Category Puzzles, Circular Reversals, Crossword Puzzle, Doublets, Espygram, Flat, Jumbles, Last Word, Marsupials, Middleput, Missing Words, Name in Vain, Palindrome, Progressive Anagram, Reversible Anagram, Scaffold, Scramblegram, Word Knock-downs, and Word Ping-Pong.

BIBLIOGRAPHY

Brandreth, Gyles. *Indoor Games.* London: Hodder & Stoughton, Ltd., 1977.
Parlett, David. *Botticelli and Beyond: Over 100 of the World's Best Word Games.* New York: Pantheon Books, 1981.

STEPLADDERS, also called word ladders and word stairs, is a form of Doublets.

The words always contain five letters. Two of the letters are given (the same two throughout the entire puzzle). Next to each word a definition is given.

A stepladder consists of a total of twenty-five words, five units or steps (in each step the two letters occur in the same position for each word) of five words each.

See example on following pages:

	1	2	3	4	5
1	T	H			
2	T	H			
3	T	H			
4	T	H			
5	T	H			
6		T	H		
7		T	H		
8		T	H		
9		T	H		
10		T	H		
11			T	H	
12			T	H	
13			T	H	
14			T	H	
15			T	H	
16				T	H
17				T	H
18				T	H
19				T	H
20				T	H
21	T				H
22	T				H
23	T				H
24	T				H
25	T				H

Definitions:	Answers:
1. next to forefinger	1. Thumb
2. to play a stringed instrument by plucking	2. Thrum
3. plural of that	3. Those
4. two plus one	4. Three
5. to employ one's mind	5. Think
6. a volatile, flammable liquid	6. Ether
7. the spirit of a culture	7. Ethos
8. an anti-knock fluid	8. Ethyl
9. additional or further	9. Other
10. a body of moral principles	10. Ethic
11. a South African statesman and general	11. Botha
12. a town in England	12. Hythe
13. declare, become known	13. Kithe
14. a machine for working wood and metal	14. Lathe
15. a city in East Germany	15. Gotha
16. truth, reality, fact	16. Sooth
17. a stall for sale of goods	17. Booth
18. opening meant for food	18. Mouth
19. value	19. Worth
20. sophisticated	20. Couth
21. strong and durable	21. Tough
22. used to bite	22. Tooth
23. a stick with a light at one end	23. Torch
24. the Old Testament	24. Torah
25. actual state or condition	25. Truth

For similar word play refer to Word Chains.

BIBLIOGRAPHY

Eckler, A. Ross. *Word Recreations: Games and Diversions from "Word Ways."* New York: Dover, 1979.
Hart, Harold H. *Grab a Pencil*. New York: Hart Publ. Co., 1958.

STEPPING STONES is a form of word play involving connections.

A player is given five subjects by the other players, e.g., art, cookies, cars, trees, houses. The player is then told to get from "art" to "house" by going through the other categories. The player is allowed nine steps to make the trip:

1. Andy Warhol painted soup cans. (art)

2. Some people eat soup and cookies together. (cookies)

3. Others eat cookies while they drive their cars. (cars)

4. Some people drive cars into trees. (trees)

5. Trees enhance the look of a house. (houses)

BIBLIOGRAPHY

Borgmann, Dmitri A. *Language on Vacation: An Olio of Orthographical Oddities.* New York: Charles Scribner's Sons, 1965.
Brandreth, Gyles. *The World's Best Indoor Games.* New York: Pantheon Books, 1981.
Parlett, David. *Botticelli and Beyond: Over 100 of the World's Best Word Games.* New York: Pantheon Books, 1981.

STINKY PINKY, also called hinky-pinky and prime-rhymes, is word play involving words that rhyme, have the same number of syllables, and fit a given definition.

The object is to find a rhyming adjective/noun couplet for another pair of words:

a big boat = a large barge
a fast hen = a quick chick
a Wagnerian opera = a long song
a slight indiscretion = a thin sin
a chicken purchaser = a fryer buyer

For similar word play refer to Double-Dactyl.

BIBLIOGRAPHY

Brandreth, Gyles. *The Joy of Lex: How to Have Fun with 860,341,500 Words.* New York: Quill, 1983.
Espy, Willard R. *A Children's Almanac of Words at Play.* New York: Clarkson N. Potter, Inc., 1982.
————. *The Game of Words.* New York: Grosset & Dunlap, 1972.

SUBER. See FLAT.

SUBJECT MATTER is a form of punning.

The object is to come up with a one-line Pun to go along with the title of a famous piece of literature:

The story of a famous comedian. (*Ham'et*)

For similar word play refer to Accidental Language, Autantonyms, Boner, Book Conversation, Burlesque, Catch, Chronograms, Coffee Pot, Confusing and Confounding Cats, Conundrum, Countdown Verses, Croakers, Cross-breed, Crossing Jokes, Daffy Definitions, Dear Departed, Double Entendre, Doubletones, Enigma, Form-a-Word, Fractured Book-Reviews, Fractured Geography, Fractured Industry, Galaxy of Gals, Goldwynner, Improbable Opposites, Irish Bull, Joke, Jumbled Geography, Knock-knock, Lampoon, Little Audrey, Little Willie, MADvertisements, Malapropism, Moron Joke, Nimblebreak, Nymble, Nymblebreak, Oxymoron, Paradox, Pasquinade, Riddle, Silly Similes, Sound Spelling, Thriftigram, Tom Swifties, Tonto, Vulture Up To?, and What Is the Question?

BIBLIOGRAPHY

Fuller, John G. *Games for Insomniacs; or, A Lifetime Supply of Insufferable Brain Twisters.* New York: Doubleday, 1968.

SUBSTITUTION CODE is a Code where the order of the letters in a message remains the same but each letter in the message is replaced by another letter, number, or symbol, e.g., the Morse code; Gregg's shorthand; the sign language of Gypsies; the drum languages of the African jungle; the peg pin code; the Masonic code based on a tic-tac-toe grid.

A central element of Edgar Allan Poe's "The Gold Bug" is the solving of a substitution code, where 5 = a, 8 = e, ? = u, ; = t, * = n, and so on.

Helen Fouché Gaines lists the following four types of substitution ciphers (codes):

1. The simple substitution, also called the monoalphabetic substitution, which employs only one cipher alphabet (as is the case in Poe's code).

2. The multiple-alphabet substitution, also called the double-key substitution, polyalphabetic substitution, and so on, which employs several different cipher alphabets according to some plan.

3. The polygram substitution, which provides a plan by which groups of letters are replaced with or integrated into other groups (as in a telephone cipher where the group ABC is represented by 2, DEF by 3, GHI by 4, JKL by 5, MNO by 6, PRS by 7, TUV by 8, and WXY by 9).

4. Fractional substitution, which breaks down the substitutes for single letters into further encipherment.

For similar word play refer to Cipher and Code.

BIBLIOGRAPHY

Borgmann, Dmitri A. *Language on Vacation: An Olio of Orthographical Oddities.* New York: Charles Scribner's Sons, 1965.

Eckler, A. Ross. *Word Recreations: Games and Diversions from "Word Ways."* New York: Dover, 1979.

Gaines, Helen Fouché. *Cryptanalysis: A Study of Ciphers and Their Solution.* New York: Dover, 1939.

Poe, Edgar Allan. "The Gold Bug." 1843. Reprint. *Eighteen Best Stories by Edgar Allan Poe,* ed. Vincent Price and Chandler Brossard. New York: Dell, 1984.

SUFFIXES is a game involving a word search.

The object of the game is to come up with as many words with the same suffix as possible. The player who finds the most is the winner. Generally, a time limit is established.

A suffix is a particle attached to the end of a word, often to indicate the part of speech the word assumes. Some words have more than one suffix. B. L. Ullman and Albert I. Suskin, *Latin for Americans,* include "functionalistically" as an example of a word with six suffixes.

Latin serves as an important source of English suffixes. Here are the more common Latin suffixes: alis, anus, aris, arium, arius, as, aticum, bilis (ble, able, ible), cia (ce), facio (fy), ia, icus (ic), idus (id), ilis, inus (ine), io (ion, sion), ium (y), ivus (ive), lus, men (min), mentum (ment), or, orium (ory), osus (ous), so, sura, tas (ty), to, tudo (tude), tura (ture), tus (tue), ura.

For similar word play refer to Animalistics, Confusing and Confounding Cats, Cross-breed, Form-a-Word, Galaxy of Gals, Hidden Names, Shifting, and Spare the Prefix.

BIBLIOGRAPHY

Parlett, David. *Botticelli and Beyond: Over 100 of the World's Best Word Games.* New York: Pantheon Books, 1981.

Ullman, B. L., and Albert I. Suskin. *Latin for Americans.* New York: Macmillan Co., 1965.

SUPER GHOST, SUPERGHOST. See GHOST AND SUPERGHOST.

SUSPENDED SENTENCES is a form of word play involving well-known phrases and sentences.

One player is designated the Quizzer. He chooses a short sentence from a book, preferably a well-known one, and announces the first letter of each of the words in the sentence.

The other players then create their own sentences, each sentence containing the initial letters of the words of the selected sentence in correct order.

The Quizzer collects all of the sentences, mixes them in with the original sentence, and reads them to the group. The object is for the other players to guess the original sentence.

A. Ross Eckler offers a variant where, instead of the initial letters of each word, the number of letters of each word is used.

For similar word play refer to Daffy Definitions and Dictionary Definitions Game.

BIBLIOGRAPHY

Parlett, David. *Botticelli and Beyond: Over 100 of the World's Best Word Games.* New York: Pantheon Books, 1981.

SWITCHBACK. See FLAT.

SYLLEPSIS. See PUN.

SYLLEPSIS CONUNDRUM. See CONUNDRUM.

SYNCOPATION. See Deletion under FLAT.

SYNOGRAM is word play based on Puns and Synonyms.

A category is established and a clue is given in the form of a synonym. The object is to guess the title that the clue is a synonym of:

Category: television shows
Clue: take it slowly
Answer: "One Day at a Time"

For similar word play refer to Antonym, Marsupials, Scaffold, Synonym, and Synonymbles.

BIBLIOGRAPHY

Borgmann, Dmitri A. *Beyond Language: Adventures in Word and Thought.* New York: Charles Scribner's Sons, 1965.
Dudeney, Henry Ernest. *300 Best Word Puzzles.* New York: Charles Scribner's Sons, 1968.
Shipley, Joseph T. *Playing with Words.* Englewood Cliffs, N.J.: Prentice-Hall, 1960.

SYNONYM is a word having the same or nearly the same meaning as another word.

Here are some synonyms for the word "evil": harmful, injurious, detrimental, hurtful, noxious, mischievous, ruinous, malefic, demolitionary, adverse, calamitous, toxic, wounding, crippling, bad, malicious, damaging, corrupt, vicious, insidious, treacherous, sapping, maleficent, malign, sinistrous, noisome, stunting, diabolic, brutal.

Dmitri Borgmann, *Language on Vacation: An Olio of Orthographical Oddities,* includes three forms of word play based on synonyms. The first he calls synonymic beheadments: beheadments in which both the original and the beheaded word have the same meaning, e.g., <u>crude</u> and <u>rude</u> can both mean <u>without culture</u>.

The second he calls synonymic reversals: reversals in which both the original and the reversed word have the same meaning, e.g., <u>ban</u> and <u>nab</u> can both mean to <u>stop</u>.

The third he calls synonymic transdeletions: deletions in which the removal of a letter and the rearrangement of the other letters produces words with the same meaning, e.g., <u>anger</u> and <u>rage</u> can both mean <u>a violent desire or passion</u>.

Synonyms can be combined with other forms of word play in the same manner to create slightly more sophisticated versions. Refer to Flat for types of word play that can be combined with synonyms. Refer to Antonym for similar word play.

BIBLIOGRAPHY

Borgmann, Dmitri A. *Beyond Language: Adventures in Word and Thought.* New York: Charles Scribner's Sons, 1967.
———. *Language on Vacation: An Olio of Orthographical Oddities.* New York: Charles Scribner's Sons, 1965.
Lewis, Norman, ed. *The New Roget's Thesaurus in Dictionary Form.* New York: G. P. Putnam's Sons, 1978.
McKechnie, Jean L., et al. *Webster's New Twentieth Century Dictionary of the English Language: Unabridged.* 2d ed. New York: World Publishing Co., 1971.

SYNONYMBLES is word play based on Synonyms.

Each player writes four synonyms for a chosen word. The papers are exchanged. Each player writes a sentence for each of the five synonyms.

For similar word play refer to Synonyms.

BIBLIOGRAPHY

Shipley, Joseph T. *Playing with Words.* Englewood Cliffs, N.J.: Prentice-Hall, 1960.

T

TABOO is a forbidden word game.

One player is chosen Questioner or Umpire. The Umpire writes a word on a sheet of paper. This is the taboo word.

The Umpire then asks each player in turn a question, attempting to get the player to say the taboo word in his response. Each time a player does not say the taboo word, the Umpire receives a minus point. Whoever says the taboo word becomes the Umpire for the next round. Whoever scores the fewest minus points at the end of the game is the winner.

For similar word play refer to Aesop's Mission, Botticelli, Charades, Initial Answers, Password, Quick Thinking, and Yes and No.

BIBLIOGRAPHY

Brandreth, Gyles. *Indoor Games*. London: Hodder & Stoughton, Ltd., 1977.
_____. *The World's Best Indoor Games*. New York: Pantheon Books, 1981.
Parlett, David. *Botticelli and Beyond: Over 100 of the World's Best Word Games*. New York: Pantheon Books, 1981.

TARGET. See WORD HUNT.

TARGETS. See WORD HUNT.

TAUTONYM, also called a reduplication, is a word with identical parts, e.g., "mama" and "papa."

Tautonyms are the basis for such word play as word squares (see Square Poem) and reversals (see Flat). They also often serve as either ABC Words or ACE Words. Refer to the above entries and to Double-Dactyl.

BIBLIOGRAPHY

Borgmann, Dmitri A. *Beyond Language: Adventures in Word and Thought.* New York: Charles Scribner's Sons, 1967.
————. *Language on Vacation: An Olio of Orthographical Oddities.* New York: Charles Scribner's Sons, 1965.

TEAPOT, also called bananas and sausages, is a word substitution game.

One player leaves the room, and the other players agree on a verb. The player who left the room then returns. His task is either to guess the hidden word or to make someone laugh.

He does this by asking questions and replacing the verb in his questions with the word "teapot." The players must answer as if the real word were used.

For similar word play refer to Aesop's Mission, Botticelli, Charades, Initial Answers, Password, Quick Thinking, and Taboo.

BIBLIOGRAPHY

Parlett, David. *Botticelli and Beyond: Over 100 of the World's Best Word Games.* New York: Pantheon Books, 1981.

TEETOTALER is a form of Beheading involving words beginning with the letter T.

The object is to find words beginning with T which form different words when the T is removed, e.g., tale/ale.

If played as a game, the players are given two lists. The first list contains clues to the word with the T. The second list contains clues to the word without the T. The players score one point for each word they come up with.

For similar word play refer to Beheading.

BIBLIOGRAPHY

Shipley, Joseph T. *Playing with Words.* Englewood Cliffs, N.J.: Prentice-Hall, 1960.

TELEGRAMS. See SEND A WIRE.

TELEPHONE is traditional word play involving close listening and careful repetition.

One person whispers something to the person next to him, who then whispers it to the person next to him, and so on. When the message has gone through all of the players, the final message is compared with the original message.

TELEPHONE WORDS are words that can be formed by dialing the telephone.

The word play may be limited in various ways, e.g., restricted to using only the odd numbers or the even numbers, or to using only enough letters to dial a standard telephone call.

For similar word play refer to Musical Messages.

BIBLIOGRAPHY

Borgmann, Dmitri A. *Language on Vacation: An Olio of Orthographical Oddities.* New York: Charles Scribner's Sons, 1967.

TELESTICH is the forming of an Acrostic by having the final letters of each line spell a word.

For example:

Beth
Tree
Fell
Plop

A more difficult form requires that the final letters spell the same word as the initial letters in reverse. For example:

T	hre	E
R	at	E
E	a	R
E	a	T

C. C. Bombaugh, *Gleanings for the Curious,* suggests that the initial letters spell one word and the final letters spell its Antonym. For example:

P	eruzz	I
R	etur	N
A	lgecira	S
I	guass	U
S	tendha	L
E	rec	T

For similar word play refer to Acrostic.

BIBLIOGRAPHY

Bombaugh, C. C. *Gleanings for the Curious.* 1890. Reprint. *Oddities and Curiosities of Words and Literature,* ed. Martin Gardner. New York: Dover, 1961.

TELL-A-TALL-TALE is a word play involving missing words.

A story is written with blanks for the missing words. Each new missing word is formed by changing just one letter of the previous missing word:

The _ _ _ _ boy played _ _ _ _ until _ _ _ _. Every day, his mother would _ _ _ _ from the _ _ _ _ to tell him to come and eat his _ _ _ _.

Missing Words: tall, ball, fall, call, mall, meal.

For similar word play refer to Chains, Echoes, Heads and Tails, Last and First, and Overlaps.

BIBLIOGRAPHY

Bombaugh, C. C. *Gleanings for the Curious.* 1890. Reprint. *Oddities and Curiosities of Words and Literature,* ed. Martin Gardner. New York: Dover, 1961.
Dudeney, Henry Ernest. *300 Best Word Puzzles.* New York: Charles Scribner's Sons, 1968.
Hart, Harold H. *Grab a Pencil.* New York: Hart Publ. Co., 1958.

TENNIS-ELBOW-FOOT GAME is word play involving quick responses.

Players sit in a circle. One player says a word. The next in turn must immediately respond with a word clearly related to the first word. The next player in turn must immediately come up with a word clearly related to the second word. If a player hesitates or comes up with an incorrect word he is out of the game.

Gyles Brandreth suggests a variation where rhyming connections are allowed.

For similar word play refer to Ad Lib and He Who Hesitates.

BIBLIOGRAPHY

Brandreth, Gyles. *Indoor Games.* London: Hodder & Stoughton, Ltd., 1977.
————. *The World's Best Indoor Games.* New York: Pantheon Books, 1981.
Parlett, David. *Botticelli and Beyond: Over 100 of the World's Best Word Games.* New York: Pantheon Books, 1981.

TERMINAL DELETION is also called terminal elision. See FLAT.

TERMINAL SWITCH. See METALLEGES.

THRIFTIGRAM is word play combining telegrams (see Send a Wire) and Puns.

A thriftigram is a telegram employing numerous words that are puns on other words:

Deer Fodder:
Centaur sun monknee. He is baroque.

Sin sear lee,
Sunknee

For similar word play refer to Pun.

BIBLIOGRAPHY

Gardner, Martin. *Perplexing Puzzles and Tantalizing Teasers.* New York: Simon & Schuster, 1969.

TIECLUES is a word puzzle involving the figuring out of a secret word.

The puzzle is set up as follows: One player chooses a word, mixes up its letters, and lists them down the left side of a sheet of paper. Then he writes a word next to each letter that begins with that letter and makes up a clue for each word (a Synonym, a definition, a description, and so on). Finally, he gives a clue for the entire word.

Here is an example:

Tomorrow is the secret word.
The letters of Tomorrow are mixed up, each given a word that begins with them, and listed as follows:

O: over
R: run
O: ox
W: word
R: raft
M: man
T: tall
O: oar

A clue is given for each of the listed words as follows:

above (four letters)
walk fast (three letters)
Paul Bunyan's friend (two letters)
speech (four letters)
flat boat (four letters)
male (three letters)
not short (four letters)
row (three letters)

A clue for the entire word is given: a time.

For similar word play refer to Acrostic and Crossword Puzzle.

BIBLIOGRAPHY
Shipley, Joseph T. *Playing with Words*. Englewood Cliffs, N.J.: Prentice-Hall, 1960.

TOM SWIFTIES are word play based on Adverbs.

In the Tom Swift and the Motor Boys Stratemeyer series popular in the 1920s, every time someone spoke, an adverb was used to describe how he spoke (e.g., Tom said very gravely, "My father is dead."). Ever since, people have been coming up with similar adverbial Puns.

For similar word play refer to Pun.

BIBLIOGRAPHY
Brandreth, Gyles. *The Joy of Lex: How to Have Fun with 860,341,500 Words*. New York: Quill, 1983.

Espy, Willard R. *An Almanac of Words at Play*. New York: Clarkson N. Potter, Inc.,
    1975.
———— . *A Children's Almanac of Words at Play*. New York: Clarkson N. Potter, Inc.,
    1982.
————. *The Game of Words*. New York: Grosset & Dunlap, 1972.
Fuller, John G. *Games for Insomniacs; or, A Lifetime Supply of Insufferable Brain
    Twisters*. New York: Doubleday, 1966.
Parlett, David. *Botticelli and Beyond: Over 100 of the World's Best Word Games*. New
    York: Pantheon Books, 1981.

TONGUE TANGLER. See TONGUE TWISTER.

TONGUE TWISTER, also called tongue tangler, is a string of words containing the same sound repeated rapidly.

The object is to repeat the passage quickly without stumbling over one's
tongue. Here are a few well-known examples:

She sells sea shells by the seashore.

Peter Piper picked a peck of pickled peppers.
Did Peter Piper pick a peck of pickled peppers?
If Peter Piper picked a peck of pickled peppers,
Where is the peck of pickled peppers Peter Piper picked?

Rubber baby buggy bumper.

For similar word play refer to Nursery Rhymes.

BIBLIOGRAPHY

Carpenter, Humphrey, and Mari Prichard. *The Oxford Companion to Children's Liter-
    ature*. New York: Oxford University Press, 1984.
Espy, Willard R. *An Almanac of Words at Play*. New York: Clarkson N. Potter, Inc.,
    1975.
————. *A Children's Almanac of Words at Play*. New York: Clarkson N. Potter, Inc.,
    1982.
————. *The Game of Words*. New York: Grosset & Dunlap, 1972.
————. *Have a Word on Me: A Celebration of Language*. New York: Simon & Schuster,
    1981.
Shipley, Joseph T. *Playing with Words*. Englewood Cliffs, N.J.: Prentice-Hall, 1960.

TONTO is a quick thinking game based on Puns.

According to David Parlett it was thought up by Pat McCormick and first
played at a National Puzzlers' League convention.

One player stands up and attempts to respond quickly to questions asked by the
other players. The answers must be the names of prominent people or historical
characters. If the player fails to respond, the questioner replaces him.

The answers are not meant to be correct in terms of historical fact, but are meant to be puns of paronomasia:

Question: Did the famous nineteenth-century painter stay to admire his Starry Night?
Answer: No—Van Gogh.

Refer to Pun for other word play based on puns. Refer to Ad Lib, He Who Hesitates, Railroad Carriage Game, and Tennis-Elbow-Foot Game for other word play based on quick thinking.

BIBLIOGRAPHY

Parlett, David. *Botticelli and Beyond: Over 100 of the World's Best Word Games.* New York: Pantheon Books, 1981.

TRAILERS is word play based on a series of overlapping words.
   A player states a two-word compound. Thereafter, each player in turn must come up with a compound based on the second part of the previous word plus a new second half, e.g., row<u>boat</u>, <u>boat</u>house, house <u>party</u>, <u>party</u> time, and so on.
   Refer to Trailing Cities for similar word play.

BIBLIOGRAPHY

Parlett, David. *Botticelli and Beyond: Over 100 of the World's Best Word Games.* New York: Pantheon Books, 1981.

TRAILING CITIES is word play involving the initial and final letters of cities.
   Each player in turn must name a city that begins with the same letter the previous city ended with, e.g., Minneapoli<u>s</u>, <u>S</u>an Dieg<u>o</u>, <u>O</u>range Grov<u>e</u>, <u>E</u>dinburg, and so on.
   Refer to Trailers for similar word play.

BIBLIOGRAPHY

Morris, William, and Mary Morris. *The Word Game Book.* New York: Harper & Brothers, 1959.

TRANSADDITIONS. See PROGRESSIVE ANAGRAM.

TRANSDELETION. See FLAT.

TRANSMUTATIONS. See DOUBLETS.

TRANSPOGRAM. See FLAT.

TRANSPOSAL is a form of Anagram.
   According to A. Ross Eckler, a transposal is the proper term for all anagrams

that do not transform one word into a word with the same meaning (e.g., eat/ate would be anagrams; team/tame would be transposals).

Eckler states that transposal word play did not really come into its own until the 1920s, when it began to appear in *The Enigma*. The first major book devoted to transposals, *The Nuttail Dictionary of Anagrams,* was put together by A. R. Ball and published by Frederick Warne & Co. in 1937.

For similar word play refer to Anagram and Flat.

BIBLIOGRAPHY

Eckler, A. Ross. *Word Recreations: Games and Diversions from "Word Ways."* New York: Dover, 1979.

TRANSPOSITION CODE, also called placement code, is a form of word play in which the spacing, placement, order, or position of the letters or words determines the message.

According to Helen Fouché Gaines, there are two general categories of transposition codes: regular and irregular.

The regular transposition code is based on a geometrical pattern (most often a square). Any game which provides a square pattern can serve as the key to the transposition code.

Magic Word Squares and knight's tours are two of the most popular. In a magic word square, the numbers are arranged so that, when added, the numbers of any row, column, or diagonal will have the same total. Since a square of twenty-five units is the closest to a twenty-six letter alphabet, a twenty-five unit square is often used:

1	20	16	23	5
15	7	12	9	22
24	18	13	8	2
4	17	14	19	11
21	3	10	6	25

All one need do is align the letters sequentially in standard reading fashion across the grid to have a transposition key: A = 1, B = 20, C = 16, D = 23, E = 5, F = 15, G = 7, H = 12, I = 9, J = 22, K = 24, L = 18, M = 13, N = 8, O = 2, P = 4, Q = 17, R = 14, S = 19, T = 11, U = 21, V = 3, W = 10, X = 6, Y = 25, and Z = 0.

In a knight's tour code, the movements of a knight in chess are employed to create the key. (See knight's-tour crypt under Extras.)

There are numerous other regular transposition codes (the nihilist transposition and the turning grille, and so on), but a detailed account of these is beyond the scope of this book.

Irregular transposition codes are all transposition codes that do not fit into some geometrical pattern. They are often deciphered by gathering statistical data on the frequency of each letter and matching the data to the following frequency-alphabet:

E T A O I N S R H D L U C M F W Y P G B V K J Q X Z

For similar word play refer to Cipher, Code, Extras, Flat, and Forms.

BIBLIOGRAPHY

Borgmann, Dmitri A. *Beyond Language: Adventures in Word and Thought.* New York: Charles Scribner's Sons, 1967.

————. *Language on Vacation: An Olio of Orthographical Oddities.* New York: Charles Scribner's Sons, 1965.

Collins, A. Frederick. *Fun with Figures.* New York: D. Appleton and Co., 1928.

Friend, J. Newton. *More Numbers: Fun and Facts.* New York: Charles Scribner's Sons, 1961.

Gaines, Helen Fouché. *Cryptanalysis: A Study of Ciphers and Their Solution.* New York: Dover, 1939.

Gardner, Martin. *Codes, Ciphers and Secret Writing.* New York: Simon & Schuster, 1972.

————. *Mathematical Carnival.* New York: Alfred A. Knopf, Inc., 1965.

Kraitchik, Maurice. *Mathematical Recreations.* 2d rev. ed. New York: Dover, 1953.

Simon, William. *Mathematical Magic.* New York: Charles Scribner's Sons, 1964.

TRAVELLER'S ALPHABET. See TRAVELLING ALPHABET.

TRAVELLING ALPHABET, also called traveller's alphabet, is a form of word play involving words beginning with successive letters of the alphabet.

The first player begins by saying: "I'm going on a journey to Amsterdam."

The other players ask, "What will you do there?"

He replies, "I shall always anger amazons."

This dialogue is repeated for each letter of the alphabet in turn.

For similar word play refer to Acrostic, Alphabent, Alphabetical Adjectives, Alphabet Word Chain, A to Z Banquet, First Letters, Hypochondriac, I Gave My

Love, I Love My Love, I Packed My Bag, I Went to Market, Nymphabet, Pangram, Sequences, Single-Rhymed Alphabet, and Sliding Alphabet.

BIBLIOGRAPHY

Brandreth, Gyles. *The World's Best Indoor Games*. New York: Pantheon Books, 1981.
Parlett, David. *Botticelli and Beyond: Over 100 of the World's Best Word Games*. New York: Pantheon Books, 1981.

TRIGRAMS is a form of word play involving words with three-letter combinations.

Each player in turn suggests a trigram (e.g., the), and the rest of the players attempt to list as many words as they can that contain that trigram (trigrams must appear within the words, not at either end):

Trigram = the
Possible responses: bother, brother, mother, father.

For similar word play refer to Anagram, Digrams, and Stepladders.

BIBLIOGRAPHY

Eckler, A. Ross. *Word Recreations: Games and Diversions from "Word Ways."* New York: Dover, 1979.
Parlett, David. *Botticelli and Beyond: Over 100 of the World's Best Word Games*. New York: Pantheon Books, 1981.

TRINADE. See Alternade under FLAT.

TRIPLE ACROSTIC is word play where tie words or spines are located at the beginning, middle, and end of each line:

Batman
Adagio
Nelson
Eterne
(bane, tale, none)

For similar word play and a discussion of acrostics, refer to Acrostic.

BIBLIOGRAPHY

Bombaugh, C. C. *Gleanings for the Curious*. 1890. Reprint. *Oddities and Curiosities of Words and Literature*, ed. Martin Gardner. New York: Dover, 1961.
Dudeney, Henry Ernest. *300 Best Word Puzzles*. New York: Charles Scribner's Sons, 1968.

TRUE RIDDLE. See RIDDLE.

TUCK THEM IN is word play involving word completions.

One player removes the first and final letters from a list of words. The other players attempt to guess the original words.

If the first and final letters of the words are identical (e.g., ki<u>ck</u>), the game is called twin ends.

BIBLIOGRAPHY

Shipley, Joseph T. *Playing with Words.* Englewood Cliffs, N.J.: Prentice-Hall, 1960.

TWENTY QUESTIONS, also called vegetable, mineral, animal, is a question and answer game.

Players ask the Quiz Master questions (twenty or whatever is agreed upon) to which he can only answer "yes" or "no." The object is to guess what the Quiz Master is thinking of.

For similar word play refer to Adverbs, Aesop's Mission, Botticelli, Charades, Initial Answers, Password, Quick Thinking, and Shouting Proverbs.

BIBLIOGRAPHY

Brandreth, Gyles. *Indoor Games.* London: Hodder & Stoughton, Ltd., 1977.
_____. *The World's Best Indoor Games.* New York: Pantheon Books, 1981.
Parlett, David. *Botticelli and Beyond: Over 100 of the World's Best Word Games.* New York: Pantheon Books, 1981.
Sharp, Richard, and John Piggott. *The Book of Games.* New York: Galahad Books, 1977.
Shipley, Joseph T. *Playing with Words.* Englewood Cliffs, N.J.: Prentice-Hall, 1960.

TWIN ENDS. See TUCK THEM IN.

TYPITOONS are word pictures created by hitting typewriter keys.

Here are a few examples:

```
$$$$$$  ////  ¢¢¢¢¢
        ////
        //

(opposite sides of the tracks)

&&&&&&&&
&&&&&&&&&&&&&&&&
&&&&&&&&&&&&&&&&&&&&&&&&&&

(and plus and plus and plus...:
the problem with lack of birth control)

x    x   xxxxx   xxxx
xx xx    x   x   x
x x x    xxxxx   xxxx
x   x    x   x   xxxx x

(Xmas: Christmas)
```

For similar word play refer to ABC Language, Flat, Rebus, and ZOO-LULU.

BIBLIOGRAPHY

Gardner, Martin. *Perplexing Puzzles and Tantalizing Teasers*. New York: Simon &
    Schuster, 1969.

U

ULTRAGHOST, also called license plate game and number plate game, is a game based on Ghost and Superghost.

David Parlett and Ajax (a pseudonym of one of the members of the National Puzzlers' League) created the game separately.

The object is to take three letters and come up with the shortest word possible including those three letters in sequence:

B,T,L
Bottle, Battle

Ajax titled his game license plate game, because it can easily be played by taking the first three letters of a license plate. Parlett adds the following restrictions:

1. To keep the letters random, each player (or three of the players) states one letter in rapid succession.
2. The player selected must come up with a word of at least four letters, otherwise as short as possible.
3. A time limit may be established.
4. If a player comes up with a word, he gets three points, unless someone else immediately comes up with a shorter word, in which case the player gets only one point instead of three. The player coming up with the shorter word does not get any points for it. If the length of the two words is the same, the best word is the one with the letters nearest the beginning of the alphabet. In this case the original player would score two points instead of three.
5. If a player cannot think of a word, he can either give up or challenge. If he gives up, he scores one point if no one else can come up with a word, but loses a point if someone

else comes up with a word. The same happens for a challenge, except the points are doubled.

6. Play continues until someone reaches an agreed upon score.

For similar word play refer to Ghost and Superghost.

BIBLIOGRAPHY

Parlett, David. *Botticelli and Beyond: Over 100 of the World's Best Word Games*. New York: Pantheon Books, 1981.

UNCRASH is a variation on crash (see Giotto).

A word is chosen (probably of three letters). Each player in turn writes a word. Each successive word must have no crashes (no letters used in the previous words or no letters in the same position as in the previous words):

Two
Not
Ate
Egg
Saw
Can: the A has been repeated here, and the player loses.

According to David Parlett, the game was developed by A. Ross Eckler and described in *Games and Puzzles* magazine.

For similar word play refer to Giotto, Last Word, and Up the Dictionary.

BIBLIOGRAPHY

Parlett, David. *Botticelli and Beyond: Over 100 of the World's Best Word Games*. New York: Pantheon Books, 1981.

UNIVOCALIC is writing containing only one vowel.

C. C. Bombaugh includes the following in *Gleanings for the Curious* (1890):

The Russo-Turkish War

Wars harm all ranks, all arts, all crafts appall:
At Mars' harsh blast, arch, rampart, altar, fall!
Ah! hard as adamant, a braggart Czar
Arms vassal swarms, and fans a fatal war!
Rampart at that bad call, a Vandal band
Harass, and harm, and ransack Wallach-land.
A Tartar phalanx Balkan's scarp hath past,
And Allah's standard falls, alas! at last.

The Fall of Eve

Eve, Eden's Empress, needs defended be;
The Serpent greets her when she seeks the tree.

Serene, she sees the speckled tempter creep;
Gentle he seems,—perversest schemer deep,—
Yet endless pretexts ever frest prefers,
Perverts her senses, revels when she errs,
Sneers when she weeps, regrets, repents she fell;
Then, deep revenged, reseeks the nether hell!

The Approach of Evening

Idling, I sit in this mild twilight dim,
Whilst birds, in wild, swift vigils, circling skim.
Light winds in sighing sink, till, rising bright,
Night's Virgin Pilgrim swims in vivid light!

For similar word play refer to Isogram, Letter-adds, Lost Letter Puzzles, and Pangram.

BIBLIOGRAPHY

Bombaugh, C. C. *Gleanings for the Curious.* 1890. Reprint. *Oddities and Curiosities of Words and Literature,* ed. Martin Gardner. New York: Dover, 1961.
Espy, Willard R. *An Almanac of Words at Play.* New York: Clarkson N. Potter, Inc., 1975.
————. *The Game of Words.* New York: Grosset & Dunlap, 1972.

UP THE DICTIONARY, also called Last Word, is word play involving words with one letter in common.

According to David Parlett, the game was invented by Dave Silverman and first published under the title "Last Word" in *Word Ways.*

Players agree on the length of the words to be used, say five letters. The first player chooses a five-letter word beginning with A, say "Alpha." Then each player in turn must come up with a five-letter word that comes later in the dictionary than the previous word and contains at least one crash (letter in the same position) with the previous word:

Alpha
Blame
Drake
Truck
Wreck
Yield
Zimbi
Zombi (the player who comes up with this word wins, because none of the other players can find another word)

The game can be varied by starting at other points in the alphabet and considering the alphabet to be a continuous circle (e.g., A follows Z).

For similar word play refer to Giotto, Last Word, and Uncrash.

BIBLIOGRAPHY

Eckler, A. Ross. *Word Recreations: Games and Diversions from "Word Ways."* New York: Dover, 1979.

Parlett, David. *Botticelli and Beyond: Over 100 of the World's Best Word Games.* New York: Pantheon Books, 1981.

V

VEGETABLE, MINERAL, ANIMAL. See TWENTY QUESTIONS.

VERBAL SPROUTS. See ARROW OF LETTERS.

VOCABULARYCLEPT POETRY. See CONSTRUCTAPO.

VOWELS is a form of word play that involves finding words that use the same vowel at least twice.

A vowel is chosen. The players then list as many words as they can in ten minutes that conform to the following rules:

1. Each word must be at least five letters long.
2. Each word must contain only the vowel listed and must contain it at least twice.
3. Proper names, foreign words, and hyphenated words are not allowed.

E is the vowel chosen:
letter, beets, steep, tepee, meets, weeks, seeks, trefle, seeker, keckle, tenrec.

BIBLIOGRAPHY

Brandreth, Gyles. *The World's Best Indoor Games.* New York: Pantheon Books, 1981.

VULTURE UP TO? is word play based on Puns.

According to Willard R. Espy, *The Game of Words,* it is his name for a game that *Time* magazine introduced to its readers in 1970.

The idea is to provide a given name or surname for an animal that results in some familiar word or phrase when combined with the animal name:

Ardice
Cow Ardice
Cowardice.

For similar word play refer to Animalistics, Cross-breed, Form-a-Word, Galaxy of Gals, Hidden Names, Hidden Words, Pun, Shifting, and Spare the Prefix.

BIBLIOGRAPHY

Espy, Willard R. *The Game of Words*. New York: Grosset & Dunlap, 1971.
Parlett, David. *Botticelli and Beyond: Over 100 of the World's Best Word Games*. New York: Pantheon Books, 1981.

WAKA. See RENGA.

WELLERISM is an accidentally humorous comparison.

The Wellerism gets its name from Sam Weller, Mr. Pickwick's personal attendant in Charles Dickens's *The Pickwick Papers* (1839), a character who was continually uttering absurd but amusing comparisons.

Some examples from *The Pickwick Papers* are:

"There's nothing so refrishin' as sleep, sir, as the servent-girl said afore she drank the egg-cupful o' laudanum."

"If you walley my precious life don't upset me, as the gen'l'm'n said to the driver when they was carryin' him to Tyburn."

"Now, gen'l'm'n, 'fall,' as the English said to the French when they fixed bagginets."

"Why, I think he's the wictom of connubiality, as Ble Beard's domestic chaplain said, with a tear of pity, ven he buried him."

Though such amusing comparisons are called Wellerisms, they actually pre-date *The Pickwick Papers*. Simon Spatterdash, a character in Samuel Beazley's comedy, *The Boarding House; or Five Hours at Brighton* (1811), was constantly uttering Wellerisms. Here are two examples:

"Sharp work for the eyes, as the devil said when the broad-wheeled waggon went over his nose."

"I'm all over in a perspiration, as the mutton chop said to the gridiron."

Refer to Boner, Goldwynner, Irish Bull, Malapropism, Paradox, Pun, and Spoonerism for similar word play.

BIBLIOGRAPHY

Dickens, Charles. *The Posthumous Papers of The Pickwick Club.* ed. Boz. March 1836–
    October 1837. Reprint. *The Pickwick Papers.* Garden City, N.Y.: Dodd Mead &
    Co., 1944.
Shipley, Joseph T. *Playing with Words.* Englewood Cliffs, N.J.: Prentice-Hall, 1960.
————. "Word and Letter Games." In *Encyclopaedia Britannica: Macropaedia,* 1979.

WHAT DOES IT MEAN? is word play that requires examples of words rather than definitions.

Players in turn choose words that other players are required to use in a sentence:

What does "annoyance" mean?
Answer: Go away; you're bothering me.

The game is more challenging if played in reverse—the example given and the players required to come up with the word.

BIBLIOGRAPHY

Shipley, Joseph T. *Playing with Words.* Englewood Cliffs, N.J.: Prentice-Hall, 1960.

WHAT DO THEY STAND FOR? is word play involving initials.

The object is to figure out what important or well-known initials stand for:

What does V.I.P. stand for?
Very Important Person.

For similar word play refer to Name That Gov't Agency.

BIBLIOGRAPHY

Morris, William, and Mary Morris. *The Word Game Book.* New York: Harper & Broth-
    ers, 1959.

WHAT IS THE QUESTION? is also called find the question.

The answer is given, and the object is to come up with the question:

Answer: Chicken Teriyaki
Question: Who was the last surviving Japanese kamikaze pilot?

For similar word play refer to Conundrum and Pun.

BIBLIOGRAPHY

Shipley, Joseph T. *Playing with Words.* Englewood Cliffs, N.J.: Prentice-Hall, 1960.

WHAT NONSENSE. See AD LIB.

WHO AM I? See BOTTICELLI.

WILD CRASH. See GIOTTO.

WORD ADVERTISEMENTS. See ADVERTISING WORDS.

WORD ALCHEMY. See DOUBLETS.

WORD ASSOCIATIONS is a form of word play based on quick responses.

Players form a circle. The first player says whatever comes to his mind. The second player immediately responds with the first word that comes to his mind. Play continues in this manner, eliminating anyone who hesitates. The final remaining player wins.

For similar word play refer to Ad Lib and Monosyllables.

BIBLIOGRAPHY

Brandreth, Gyles. *The World's Best Indoor Games.* New York: Pantheon Books, 1981.

WORD BOWLING. See WORD KNOCK-DOWNS.

WORD BUILDER. See WORD HUNT.

WORD CHAINS is a general term for word play involving linking words together in one manner or another. Refer to Alphabent, Alphabet Poetry, Alphabet Word Chain, Heads and Tails, Stepladders, and Word Rings.

BIBLIOGRAPHY

Dudeney, Henry Ernest. *300 Best Word Puzzles.* New York: Charles Scribner's Sons, 1968.
Morris, William, and Mary Morris. *The Word Game Book.* New York: Harper & Brothers, 1959.

WORD DELETION. See FLAT.

WORD HUNT, also called key words, targets, word builder, word makers, word targets, and words-within-words, is an Anagram game.

The object is to find as many words within a given word as possible. Gyles Brandreth calls this form of word play word builder and suggests the following rules:

1. Each word must contain at least four letters.
2. Proper nouns are not allowed.
3. Foreign words, abbreviations, and plurals are not allowed.

4. Letters may not be used in any word any more times than they appear in the original word.

In targets, nine letters are given on a three by three grid, and a target score is established (e.g., twenty is poor, twenty-five is average, thirty is excellent). Furthermore, in target, every word must include the letter in the center of the grid.

In word targets, words are formed as if they were spokes on a wheel, each word ending with the letter in the hub:

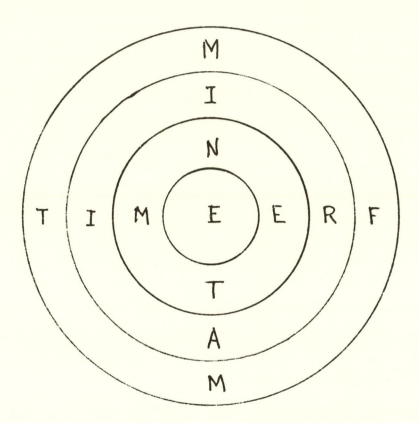

For similar word play refer to Acrosticals, Add-on, Alfabits, Anablank, Ana-game, Anagram, Cap Me, Category Puzzles, Circular Reversals, Crossword Puzzle, Doublets, Espygram, Flat, Jumbles, Last Word, Marsupials, Mid-dleput, Missing Words, Name in Vain, Palindrome, Progressive Anagram, Put and Take, Quaternade, Quinade, Removers, Reversible Anagram, Scaffold, Scramblegram, Word Knock-downs, and Word Ping-Pong.

BIBLIOGRAPHY

Brandreth, Gyles. *Indoor Games*. London: Hodder & Stoughton, Ltd., 1977.
———. *The World's Best Indoor Games*. New York: Pantheon Books, 1981.
Morris, William, and Mary Morris. *The Word Game Book*. New York: Harper & Brothers, 1959.
Parlett, David. *Botticelli and Beyond: Over 100 of the World's Best Word Games*. New York: Pantheon Books, 1981.

WORD INTERLOCK. See FLAT.

WORD KNOCK-DOWNS, also called knock-downs and word bowling, is a form of Progressive Anagrams in reverse.

The object is to start with a word and remove letters one at a time, each time spelling a word, until only one letter is left.

Martin Gardner includes a form of word knock-downs in *Perplexing Puzzles and Tantalizing Teasers* that he calls word bowling. A ten-letter word is written down, one letter for each pin (if the word has fewer letters, fewer pins are used). The object is to knock down one pin at a time, always leaving a word.

For similar word play refer to Acrosticals, Add-on, Alfabits, Anablank, Anagame, Anagram, Cap Me, Category Puzzles, Circular Reversals, Crossword Puzzle, Doublets, Espygram, Flat, Jumbles, Last Word, Marsupials, Middleput, Missing Words, Name in Vain, Palindrome, Progressive Anagram, Put and Take, Quaternade, Quinade, Removers, Reversible Anagram, Scaffold, Scramblegram, Word Hunt, and Word Ping-Pong.

BIBLIOGRAPHY

Gardner, Martin. *Perplexing Puzzles and Tantalizing Teasers*. New York: Simon & Schuster, 1969.

WORD LADDERS. See DOUBLETS; STEPLADDERS.

WORDLES. See REBUS.

WORD MAKERS. See WORD HUNT.

WORDNUMS. See NUMWORDS.

WORD PING-PONG is an Anagram game based on the scoring of ping-pong.

According to David Parlett, word ping-pong was created by P. Perkins and first published in *Games and Puzzles* magazine.

Each player in turn serves for five points, until someone reaches twenty-one points and wins. A player must win by at least two points or the game goes into overtime (service alternating) until someone is two points ahead.

One player serves by writing down a word of four letters. The other player must write down another word differing from the first by only one letter. The server may change only the first or second letter; the receiver may change only the third or fourth letter. The served word must be capable of being changed on the third or fourth letter at least once; if not, the receiver gets the point.

The same word may appear only once in a rally, the same word service only once in a game. Neither player may use the same letter in the same position more than three times in a rally. A player scores a point when the opponent cannot think of a new word.

Doubles may be played by alternating each time. Three or more may also play. If so, each player writes a four-letter word in turn that differs from the previous word by one letter. No player may change either of the two letters introduced by the two previous players. No letter may appear more than five times in any single position. When a player cannot play he scores a penalty point. When no one can continue the serve passes.

For similar word play refer to Acrosticals, Add-on, Alfabits, Anablank, Anagame, Anagram, Cap Me, Category Puzzles, Circular Reversals, Crossword Puzzle, Doublets, Espygram, Flat, Jumbles, Last Word, Marsupials, Middleput, Missing Words, Name in Vain, Palindrome, Progressive Anagram, Put and Take, Quaternade, Quinade, Removers, Reversible Anagram, Scaffold, Scramblegram, Word Hunt, and Word Knock-downs.

BIBLIOGRAPHY

Eckler, A. Ross. *Word Recreations: Games and Diversions from "Word Ways."* New York: Dover, 1979.
Parlett, David. *Botticelli and Beyond: Over 100 of the World's Best Word Games.* New York: Pantheon Books, 1981.

WORDPOWER. See GIOTTO.

WORD PYRAMIDS. See PROGRESSIVE ANAGRAM.

WORD RINGS is a form of Word Chains that circles back on itself.

The object is to use the same two letters in each word, the final two letters of the first word becoming the first two letters of each succeeding word; the first word must reappear after the third word, completing a ring:

into, tooth, thin, into

For similar word play refer to Alphabet Word Chain, Alphabent, Alphabet Poetry, Heads and Tails, and Stepladders.

BIBLIOGRAPHY

Dudeney, Henry Ernest. *300 Best Word Puzzles.* New York: Charles Scribner's Sons, 1968.

Morris, William, and Mary Morris. *The Word Game Book*. New York: Harper & Brothers, 1959.

WORD SCRAMBLES is a form of word play involving the unscrambling of words that fit into a chosen category:

Category:		Sports
ABASBLLE	=	BASEBALL
SITENN	=	TENNIS
LFOG	=	GOLF

Refer to Scramblegram for similar word play.

BIBLIOGRAPHY

Morris, William, and Mary Morris. *The Word Game Book*. New York: Harper & Brothers, 1959.

WORD SEARCH. See HIDDEN WORD SEARCH.

WORDSQUARES. See CROSSWORD PUZZLE.

WORD SQUARES AND WORD CUBES. See SQUARE POEM.

WORD STAIRS. See DOUBLETS; STEPLADDERS.

WORD STARS involves arranging words in the shape of stars.
Ten letters are so placed that they visually form a star and each of the five lines of four letters forms a word:

The words: then, that, teem, meat, teen.

For similar word play refer to Forms and Square Poem.

BIBLIOGRAPHY

Dudeney, Henry Ernest. *300 Best Word Puzzles*. New York: Charles Scribner's Sons, 1968.

WORDS-WITHIN-WORDS. See WORD HUNT.

WORDSWORTH. See CROSSWORD PUZZLE.

WORD TARGETS. See WORD HUNT.

WRAITHS. See GHOST AND SUPERGHOST.

WRITTEN CHARADES. See CHARADES.

Y

YES AND NO, also called yessir/nossir, is a dialogue game that requires fast thinking.

Each player is given five match sticks. The players then carry on a dialogue. The object is for each player to get the other player to say either "yes" or "no." Each time a player says "yes" or "no" he must give a match to the other player. The winner is the player who ends up with all of the matches.

In yessir/nossir, one player attempts to get another player to say either "yes" or "no" by asking him rapid-fire questions to which he must respond quickly.

For other quick thinking games refer to Aesop's Mission, Botticelli, Charades, Initial Answers, Password, Quick Thinking, and Taboo.

BIBLIOGRAPHY

Brandreth, Gyles. *Indoor Games*. London: Hodder & Stoughton, Ltd., 1977.
_____. *The World's Best Indoor Games*. New York: Pantheon Books, 1981.
Parlett, David. *Botticelli and Beyond: Over 100 of the World's Best Word Games*. New York: Pantheon Books, 1981.

YESSIR/NOSSIR. See YES AND NO.

Z

ZEUGMA. See PUN.

ZOO-LULU is a form of Rebus combining drawing and writing.

The term was thought up by Max Brandel and used for the ZOO-LULUs he creates for *Mad* magazine.

Here is one of mine:

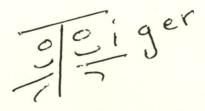

For similar word play refer to Emblematic Poetry, Rebus, and Typitoons.

BIBLIOGRAPHY

Gardner, Martin. *Perplexing Puzzles and Tantalizing Teasers*. New York: Simon & Schuster, 1969.

BIBLIOGRAPHY

The Enigma is the most important monthly publication for serious language play. It is published by the National Puzzlers' League and (as of September 1985) can be obtained by sending $10.00 to David A. Rosen, 15 Hecla Street, Buffalo, N.Y. 14216. *Word Ways: The Journal of Recreational Linguistics,* is the other important continuous publication for serious language play. It is published quarterly (February, May, August, and November) and can be obtained by sending $12.00 to A. Ross Eckler, Spring Valley Road, Morristown, N.J. 07960. *Games* is an important popular magazine for language play. It can be obtained by sending $15.97 to *Games,* 515 Madison Ave., New York, N.Y. 10022.

The following bibliography contains those books that have important collections of language puzzles and games. Since each entry in this dictionary has its own bibliography, the following lists only those books that discuss a number of forms of language play.

Abrahams, Roger D. *Jump-Rope Rhymes: A Dictionary.* Austin: University of Texas, 1969.

Abrahams, Roger D., and Lois Rankin. *Counting-Out Rhymes: A Dictionary.* Austin: University of Texas, 1980.

Adler, Irving, and Peggy Adler. *The Adler Book of Puzzles and Riddles, or Sam Loyd Up to Date.* New York: John Day Co., 1962.

Bergerson, Howard W. *Palindromes and Anagrams.* New York: Dover, 1973.

Bombaugh, C. C. *Gleanings for the Curious.* 1890. Reprint. *Oddities and Curiosities of Words and Literature,* ed. Martin Gardner. New York: Dover, 1961.

Borgmann, Dmitri A. *Beyond Language: Adventures in Word and Thought.* New York: Charles Scribner's Sons, 1967.

————. *Language on Vacation: An Olio of Orthographical Oddities.* New York: Charles Scribner's Sons, 1965.

Brandreth, Gyles. *Indoor Games.* London: Hodder & Stoughton, Ltd., 1977.

————. *The Joy of Lex: How to Have Fun with 860,341,500 Words.* New York: Quill, 1981.

————. *More Joy of Lex: An Amazing and Amusing Z to A and A to Z of Words*. New York: William Morrow and Co., 1982.

————. *The World's Best Indoor Games*. New York: Pantheon Books, 1981.

Brooke, Maxey. *150 Puzzles in Crypt-Arithmetic*. 2d ed., rev. New York: Dover, 1969.

Dudeney, Henry Ernest. *300 Best Word Puzzles*. New York: Charles Scribner's Sons, 1968.

Eckler, A. Ross. *Word Recreations: Games and Diversions from "Word Ways."* New York: Dover, 1979.

Espy, Willard R. *An Almanac of Words at Play*. New York: Clarkson N. Potter, Inc., 1975.

————. *A Children's Almanac of Words at Play*. New York: Clarkson N. Potter, Inc., 1982.

————. *The Game of Words*. New York: Grosset & Dunlap, 1971.

————. *Have a Word on Me: A Celebration of Language*. New York: Simon & Schuster, 1981.

————. *O Thou Improper, Thou Uncommon Noun*. New York: Clarkson N. Potter, Inc., 1978.

————. *Say It My Way: How to Avoid Certain Pitfalls of Spoken English Together with a Decidedly Informal History of How Our Language Rose (or Fell)*. New York: Doubleday, 1980.

Fixx, James. *Games for the Super-intelligent*. New York: Doubleday, 1972.

————. *Solve It! A Perplexing Profusion of Puzzles*. New York: Doubleday, 1978.

Fuller, John G. *Games for Insomniacs; or, A Lifetime Supply of Insufferable Brain Twisters*. New York: Doubleday, 1966.

Gaines, Helen Fouché. *Cryptanalysis: A Study of Ciphers and Their Solution*. New York: Dover, 1939.

Gardner, Martin. *Martin Gardner's Sixth Book of Mathematical Games from "Scientific American."* 1963. Reprint. San Francisco: W. H. Freeman and Co., 1971.

————. *Perplexing Puzzles and Tantalizing Teasers*. New York: Simon & Schuster, 1969.

————. *The Scientific American Book of Mathematical Puzzles and Diversions*. New York: Simon & Schuster, 1956.

————. *Wheels, Life and Other Mathematical Amusements*. New York: W. H. Freeman and Co., 1983.

Hart, Harold H. *Grab a Pencil*. New York: Hart Publ. Co., 1958.

Hindman, Darwin A. *1800 Riddles, Enigmas and Conundrums*. New York: Dover, 1963.

Laubach, David C. *Introduction to Folklore*. Rochelle Park, N.J.: Hayden Book Co., 1980.

Loyd, Samuel. *Sam Loyd's Cyclopedia of 5000 Puzzles, Tricks and Conundrums with Answers*. New York: Pinnacle Books, 1976.

Morris, William, and Mary Morris. *The Word Game Book*. New York: Harper & Brothers, 1959.

Opie, Peter, and Iona Opie. *Children's Games in Street and Playground*. 1969. Reprint. New York: Oxford University Press, 1979.

————. *The Lore and Language of Schoolchildren*. 1959. Reprint. New York: Oxford University Press, 1980.

————. *The Oxford Dictionary of Nursery Rhymes*. 1955. Reprint. New York: Oxford University Press, 1984.

———. *The Oxford Nursery Rhyme Book*. 1955. Reprint. New York: Oxford University Press, 1984.

Parlett, David. *Botticelli and Beyond: Over 100 of the World's Best Word Games*. New York: Pantheon Books, 1981.

Phillips, Hubert. *My Best Puzzles in Logic and Reasoning*. New York: Dover, 1960.

Sharp, Richard, and John Piggott. *The Book of Games*. New York: Galahad Books, 1977.

Shipley, Joseph T. *Playing with Words*. Englewood Cliffs, N.J.: Prentice-Hall, 1960.

Sutton-Smith, Brian. *The Folkgames of Children*. Austin: University of Texas Press, 1972.

The following serve as important reference sources for analyzing and playing word puzzles and games. Some of the references below might have been put in the previous bibliography or the other way around (the books by Peter and Iona Opie, for example), and a somewhat arbitrary decision had to be made based on whether the book was more concerned with how to play the games and puzzles or with other matters that happen to be of importance to that play. The unabridged second edition of *Webster's New Twentieth Century Dictionary of the English Language*, for example, is indispensable for playing the various flats; yet in and of itself it is unconcerned with flats.

Baugh, Albert C., and Thomas Cable. *A History of the English Language*. 3d ed. Englewood Cliffs, N.J.: Prentice-Hall, 1978.

Bolton, W. F. *A Living Language: The History and Structure of English*. New York: Random House, 1982.

Byrne, Josefa Heifetz. *Mrs. Byrne's Dictionary of Unusual, Obscure, and Preposterous Words*, ed. Robert Byrne. New York: Washington Square Press, 1974.

Cirlot, J. E. *A Dictionary of Symbols*. Trans. Jack Sage. London: Routledge & Kegan Paul, 1976.

Corbett, Edward P.J. *Classical Rhetoric for the Modern Student*. 2d ed. New York: Oxford University Press, 1971.

Daiches, David; Malcolm Bradbury; and Eric Mottram. *The Avenel Companion to English and American Literature*. New York: Avenel Books, 1981.

Davies, Peter. *Roots: Family Histories of Familiar Words*. New York: McGraw-Hill, 1981.

Frazer, Sir James. *The Golden Bough*. 1890. Reprint. *The New Golden Bough (A New Abridgement of the Classic Work)*, ed. Dr. Theodore H. Gaster. New York: S. G. Phillips, Inc., 1968.

Head, R. *A Classical Dictionary of the Vulgar Tongue*. 2d ed., 1788. Reprint. *1811 Dictionary of the Vulgar Tongue: A Dictionary of Bucksih Slang, University Wit, and Pickpocket Eloquence*. London: Bibliophile Books, 1984.

Hill, Robert H. *A Dictionary of Difficult Words*. New York: New American Library, 1975.

Holman, C. Hugh. *A Handbook to Literature*. 4th ed. Indianapolis: Bobbs-Merrill Educational Publishing, 1980.

Humez, Alexander, and Nicholas Humez. *Alpha to Omega: The Life and Times of the Greek Alphabet*. Boston: David R. Godine, 1985.

Hunt, Cecil. *Word Origins: The Romance of Language*. New York: Philosophical Library, 1962.

Leland, Charles Godfrey. *Gypsy Sorcery and Fortune Telling*. New York: University Books, 1963.

Lewis, Norman, ed. *The New Roget's Thesaurus of the English Language in Dictionary Form*. Lib. ed. New York: G. P. Putnam's Sons, 1978.

Liles, Bruce L. *A Basic Grammar of Modern English*. Englewood Cliffs, N.J.: Prentice-Hall, 1979.

McKechnie, Jean L., et al. *Webster's New Twentieth Century Dictionary of the English Language: Unabridged*. 2d ed. New York: World Publishing Co., 1971.

Mager, N. H., and S. K. Mager. *The Morrow Book of New Words: 8500 Terms Not Yet in Standard Dictionaries*. New York: William Morrow and Co., 1982.

Moger, Art. *The Complete Pun Book*. New York: Castle, 1979.

Moore, Thurston. *The Original Word Game Dictionary*. New York: Stein and Day, 1984.

Morris, William, and Mary Morris. *Dictionary of Contemporary Usage*. New York: Harper & Row, 1985.

Myers, L. M., and Richard L. Hoffman. *Companion to "The Roots of Modern English."* Boston: Little, Brown and Co., 1979.

———. *The Roots of Modern English*. 2d ed. Boston: Little, Brown and Co., 1979.

Partridge, Eric. *Origins: A Short Etymological Dictionary of Modern English*. New York: Greenwich House, 1983.

Preminger, Alex; Frank J. Warnke, and O. B. Hardison, Jr. eds. *Encyclopedia of Poetry and Poetics*. Princeton: Princeton University Press, 1965.

Shipley, Joseph T. *Dictionary of Word Origins*. New York: Philosophical Library, 1945.

Spears, Richard A. *Slang and Euphemism: A Dictionary of Oaths, Curses, Insults, Sexual Slang and Metaphor, Racial Slurs, Drug Talk, Homosexual Lingo, and Related Matters*. Middle Village, N.Y.: Jonathan David Publishers, Inc., 1981.

Stein, Jess, ed. *The Random House Dictionary of the English Language: The Unabridged Edition*. New York: Random House, 1983.

Train, John. *Remarkable Words with Astonishing Origins*. New York: Clarkson N. Potter, Inc., 1980.

Urdang, Lawrence. *The Basic Book of Synonyms and Antonyms*. New York: New American Library, 1978.

There is also an important article by Joseph T. Shipley, "Word and Letter Games," in *Encyclopaedia Britannica: Macropaedia*, 1979.

Thurston Moore includes a list of *commercial* word games, most of which are offshoots of the word play discussed in this book. Refer to Thurston Moore, *The Original Word Game Dictionary*, for manufacturers' names and brief discussion of those games.

Dmitri A. Borgmann, *Beyond Language: Adventures in Word and Thought,* includes an extensive, yet very tentative bibliography of books he considers of interest to "those who pursue language recreationally." It is a valuable bibliography, if for no other reason than that, as he states, "no work resembling it is known to exist." He is also quick to point out that it must be both subjective and incomplete. The same statements apply to the bibliographies included in this book.

INDEX

Page numbers in *italics* refer to main entries in the dictionary.

About the Author

HARRY EDWIN EISS is an Assistant Professor in the Department of Arts and Languages at Northern Montana College, Havre, Montana. He has contributed to *Our Twentieth Century's Greatest Religious Poems, Rainbows, Dreams, and Butterfly Wings, Instructor,* and *World Treasury of Great Poems.*